Parent and Child Relations

John M. Carlevale, Sr.
Department of Human Services
Community College of Rhode Island
Warwick, Rhode Island 02886

Consortium Publishing
640 Weaver Hill Road
West Greenwich, Rhode Island 02817
Telephone: (401) 397-9838

Published and bound in the United States of America by

Consortium Publishing

640 Weaver Hill Road
West Greenwich, Rhode Island 02817
Telephone: (401) 397-9838

Reproduced by photo-offset directly from the author's typed manuscript.

Cover Photo Sources: Irene Clark (top left), George Aiken (top right), Amelia Martinelli (bottom left), Richard and Susanne Archambault (bottom right).

ISBN 0-940139-23-5

Table of Contents

Dedication

This book is dedicated to many important people in my personal and professional life.

First and foremost, this book is dedicated to my mother, Amelia L. Martinelli, who raised three children as a single parent. As a wife and mother she has survived divorce, first her own and later a son's, poverty, the accidental death of a son, the significant health loss in a daughter, the death of her second husband and more. I have always been amazed at how she has managed so well with so little. And throughout she has been kind, forgiving, helpful, supportive, hopeful or optimistic and always available.

Second, I dedicate this book to my two children, Veronica and John, so different in so many ways, so alike in some, and so unique, who individually and collectively have added the most important dimension - parenthood - to my life and living. Above all, each in her and his unique way has helped me become more fully human. In fact, it was the anticipated birth of my daughter that was the impetus for me to enroll in a child development course. That single event changed the thrust and direction of my professional development and brought me in contact with some significant others.

Third, I dedicate this book to the many parents, children, and families I have worked with as a family practitioner and educator. Their life stories and particular situations have educated me throughout my professional career. Their individual and collective life experiences represent a large measure of the content of this book.

Acknowledgements

In the life of each person there are many non-related people who influence one's growth and development personally and professionally. I have had a substantial complement of such people myself. A few deserve special acknowledgement herein.

First, there is George Fitzelle of the Department of Child Development and Family Relations, University of Rhode Island. Over the years George has been my instructor, my mentor, my colleague and my friend. It was he who encouraged me to pursue graduate study in child development and family relations. At his retirement party, many spoke of their personal relationship with George. What was so interesting is that each person felt that what George had given to each of them was uniquely their own but in fact was common to all. What is so special about George is that he made everyone feel uniquely special.

Second, there are Russell Smart and Mollie Smart also of the University of Rhode Island. Their book, *Children: Development and Relationships* [1] is known world-wide by many child development professionals. It is for me, as it is for many, a desk reference. Russell was my major professor and adviser during my graduate studies and I am indebted to him and also to Mollie for their individual and collective guidance, insight and scholarship.

Third, I must acknowledge Robert W. Chamberlain of the Department of Pediatrics, University of Kentucky Medical Center for his comprehensive (and for me, seminal) work in the area of child rearing philosophy and practices and their effects upon children's development and behavior. My initial introduction to his works [2,3,4] confirmed for me many observations I had made and insights I had begun to develop. His work has become so much a part of my knowledge base and thinking that I often do not know where his input ends and my own begins.

Fourth, I must acknowledge my colleague and friend, Richard Archambault of the Department of Human Services, Community College of Rhode Island, who I met through George Fitzelle. Richard was instrumental in encouraging me to join the faculty at CCRI. Over the years, he has challenged, supported and innervated me in many ways. But most importantly he introduced me to and placed me in colleagueship with Georgia Bradley Houle.

Fifth, Georgia Bradley Houle has been my colleague, personal and professional mentor, and dear friend. She has provided encouragement, support, guidance, education and training, and above all friendship. She prodded me to write my first book. She encouraged me to write my second book. She expected me to write this book.

I thank and acknowledge you all.

Preface

In my view, the parent and child relationship is the most important of interpersonal relationships. Parent and child interaction influences the growth, development and behavior of both parent and child. Richard Gardner concludes that "most psychological disturbances that therapists deal with are, in part, the result of difficulties in the parent - child love relationship." [5] I substantially agree with this conclusion. Furthermore, I believe that most psychological health can be substantially attributed to healthy and wholesome parent and child interaction. Of course, there are many other factors and conditions that affect individual growth, development and behavior. We must know what these are and how they influence parent and child interaction in particular.

This book is an attempt to place this most important of interpersonal relationships in perspective vis-a-vis the more salient factors and conditions that affect it so significantly. The framework of this book is basically a *developmental* and *interactional* perspective. [6] That is, there is a recognized dynamic interaction between the child, parent and other important factors and conditions. Each person vis-a-vis his or her developmental status interacts dynamically with the other person and other important variables. Each influences the growth, development and behavior of the other. This dynamic interaction takes place within a context that parent and child share and that may or may not be unique to them.

This book is intended for human service professionals and parents in practice and/or training. This book attempts to provide to the reader a framework and knowledge base for better understanding the parent and child relationship, especially in terms of those aspects or features of the relationship that are most crucial to its establishment, development and maintenance. There are certain concepts and interactional phenomena that are important to be aware of if better understanding is to be realized. Therefore, this book shall identify describe, and illustrate how these concepts and phenomena influence parent and child interaction and the development of the relationship itself.

The concepts and interactional phenomena identified and described in this book are those which I have learned as a family practitioner and educator to be most crucial. All the important topics, concepts, phenomena, etc. are not covered herein. What is included are those which I believe are most influential to the development of the parent and child relationship and that are most essential to our understanding of it. This understanding is necessary if we as human service professionals and/or parents are to take effective action in promoting human growth and development. Our effectiveness as professionals and as parents is largely a function of what we know, what we can do and who we are as people. In essence this book is an effort to add to the reader's knowledge base and skill repertoire and promote insight concerning the reader's personal development thereby increasing the reader's effectiveness as a human service professional or parent.

Furthermore, the perspective taken in this book maintains that the parent and child relationship is a *reciprocal* one. Who the parent is as a person, what the parent knows and is able to do as a parent has great influence on parental effectiveness and relationship development. Likewise, who the child is as a person and what the child knows and is able to do also have a profound influence on parental effectiveness and the development of the parent and child relationship. Parents exert a significant influence on the growth, development and behavior of their children. Children also exert a significant influence on parental growth, development and behavior. Their relationship is one of *mutual influence*. The parent and child relationship is reciprocal as are all love relationships.

A brief comment about nomenclature and usage: Throughout this book I have tried to consistently use the words "parent" and "child" generically without reference to gender. However, in using pronouns, I have tried to avoid the awkward use of "he and/or she" and "him and/or her" by simply using "she" or "her" in place of the noun "parent" and "he" or "him" in place of the noun "child", knowing fully well that parents and children come in both genders. I have employed this approach for simplicity, consistency, and to minimize confusion and improve readability.

I anticipate that a substantial majority of those who read this book shall be female. With this fact in mind, I ask that my female readers make a conscious and determined effort to share this book with at least one male. I sincerely believe that males must also educate themselves for parenthood. I hope my female readers agree and shall share this book with the males in their life. Thank you.

This book is not a final product. It represents where I am presently in my thinking and experience. Therefore, I extend an open invitation to the reader to correspond with me through the publisher, if you have any comments, concerns, suggestions, criticism, etc. you wish to share with me. You do not need to like what is contained herein to correspond. However, if you do like a particular aspect or treatment, please let me "hear" from you, as I need to know what is helpful as well as what is not helpful. I shall thank you in advance for your time, effort and thoughtfulness should you decide to share your views with me.

Warmest regards,

John M. Carlevale
June 1991

---

[1]Mollie S. Smart and Russell C. Smart, *Children: Development and Relationships* (New York: Macmillan Publishing Co., Inc., 1977)

[2]Robert W. Chamberlin, "A Study of an Interview Method for Identifying Family Authority Patterns," *Genetic Psychology Monographs*, 1967, p 129-148.

[3]Robert W. Chamberlin, "Approaches to Child Rearing: Their Identification and Classification," *Clinical Pediatrics*, 1965, 4, p 150-159.

[4]Robert W. Chamberlin, "Approaches to Child Rearing II: Their Effects on Child Behavior," *Clinical Pediatrics*, 1966, 5, p 688-669.

[5]Richard A. Gardner, *Understanding Children* (New York: Jason Aronson, Inc., 1973), p 61.

[6]F. Ivan Nye and Felix M. Berardo, Editors, *Emerging Conceptual Frameworks In Family Analysis* (New York: The Macmillan Company, 1966).

Chapter 1

Kinds of Parent and Child Relationships

There are many different kinds of parent and child relationships. Distinctions can be made qualitatively in terms of good vs. bad, desirable vs. undesirable, loving vs. hostile, etc. These qualitative distinctions are important to make because they often mean the difference between relationships that are satisfying or dissatisfying, effective or ineffective, growth enhancing or growth stifling, etc. Such qualitative differences shall be addressed subsequently in this volume.

However, in this section, a distinction will be made on the basis of kind as it pertains to a broad classification that may be applied irrespective of such exclusionary qualitative features as mentioned above. There are different classes or sorts which can be identified without having to distinguish them as being good or bad, effective or ineffective, etc. In fact, good and bad, effective and ineffective, etc. may be found within the same classification or sort. Consequently, after these different classifications are made and described, subsequent chapters shall look at those qualitative features that distinguish relationships as being good or bad, satisfying or dissatisfying, etc. within a given classification.

An analogy may be helpful to clarify this perspective at this time. There are different kinds or types of automobiles: Ford, Chevrolet, Plymouth, Cadillac, BMW, Mercedes Benz, Rolls Royce. These can be distinguished from one another. Some are more common than others. Some are more desired than others. Some are regarded as having greater quality, reliability, longevity, etc. Although each has its distinguishing features, and variations in perceived quality and actual quality, all have common elements that make them automobiles and members of the same classification. An exceptionally good or bad one can be found within each make or type.

So is the case with the parent and child relationship. There are many different types that can be distinguished from one another. Some are perceived as being qualitatively better than others; yet, they all have common attributes that make them members of the same classification. This chapter shall identify and describe eleven different kinds of parent and child relationships. Later chapters shall address the qualitative common features referred to initially and that separate the good from the not so good.

Among the different types that shall be identified and describe herein, which one or more best describes your relationship with your parents? If you are a parent also, which one or more best describes your relationship with your child or children? Be mindful of these questions as each is identified and described.

BIOLOGICAL PARENT AND CHILD RELATIONSHIP

The biological parent and child relationship is defined by the biological connection between the parent and child. The parent begets the child. The child is of the parent's body. There is a "blood" relationship. More accurately, the parent has participated in the natural creation of another human being by contributing his sperm or her egg. Each biological parent contributes half of the child's total genetic makeup. The child has obtained all his genetic material from his biological parents. The parent and child share or have in common a degree of genetic material. It is this shared or common genetic material that accounts for some of the similarity we observe in appearance, health, temperament, etc. among parents and their biological children.

This is a natural process that has been taking place since the emergence of mankind. Hence this relationship is also referred to as the "natural" parent and child relationship. Therefore, we find that the terms "biological" and "natural" are often used interchangeably.

Becoming a Biological Parent

What does it take to establish a biological parent and child relationship? The minimum requirement on the part of the female is physiological reproductive maturity. Generally speaking, she must be able to produce a viable egg, be able to conceive, carry to term and deliver the unborn child successfully. The minimum requirement on the part of the male is also physiological reproductive maturity. Generally speaking, he must be able to produce

viable sperm and impregnate a female. Almost all healthy men and women are able to meet these prerequisites or requirements. Becoming a parent is relatively easy. However, being a parent is not.

It must also be acknowledged however that given the current state of knowledge and skill in the area of reproductive biology, it is no longer a requisite for the female to conceive, carry to term and deliver and unborn child. A female may just have to produce a viable egg. Modern technology then can help her become a biological parent without having to fulfill the remaining general prerequisites identified. Likewise, the male does not need to impregnate but simply supply a viable sperm and assistance forthcoming in the form of artificial insemination enables him to become a biological parent.

So all in all, that is what it takes to become a biological parent. Nothing more, nothing less is required. There are far more requisites in obtaining a driver's license or a credit card. Likewise, the requirements my friend Fred had to meet before he was issued a vendor's license to sell hot dogs at a roadside stand were much more substantial and demanding and stringent that those for biological parenthood.

When I obtained my driver's license, society was reasonably assured that I could drive an automobile and was cognizant of the rules of the road and good driving. When I was issued my first credit card, the creditor was reasonably assured that I had the ability to pay my indebtedness. When people purchased hot dogs at Fred's hot dog cart, they did it with the assumption that the food was being handled in accordance with Health Department standards. What assurance did our children have that we could parent them reasonably well?

ADOPTIVE PARENT AND CHILD RELATIONSHIP

The adoptive parent and child relationship is defined not on the basis of biological connectedness but rather on the basis of law or legal connectedness. There is no biological connection between the adoptive parent and child. The connection is established initially by law and the legal process. The Family Court System establishes the relationship and gives it legal sanction. Once that sanction is given, the adult and child are joined together as parent and child with the same legal status as the biological parent and child relationship. The Family Court System , however, cannot give or establish biological connectedness. Nevertheless, the eyes of the court, society, and people in general see the adoptive parent and child relationship as being the same as the biological parent and child relationship, at least under the law.

Some facts concerning adoption: Two million families in America are waiting to adopt a child. Twenty-five percent of the adoptions involving preadolescent and adolescent children fail. ("A Closer Look," NBC , April 4, 1991) The adoption of younger children is more successful. The greatest incidence of success is with the youngest children.

Becoming an Adoptive Parent

What does it take to establish an adoptive parent and child relationship? The process of creating an adoptive parent and child relationship is significantly more involved than in establishing a biological relationship. It involves many steps and procedures that are not even remotely considered by most who become biological parents. Furthermore, it involves people other than the parents who play a crucial role in the process and its eventual outcome. What follows immediately describes this process in general terms.

Prior Deliberation

Even before the process of becoming an adoptive parent is initiated, the prospective adoptive parent typically engages in a substantial amount of deliberation about becoming a parent in general and an adoptive parent in particular. Such prior deliberation is typically uncommon for the first time biological parent. For the biological parent the process is natural and taken for granted. For the prospective adoptive parent, the natural process may not have been fruitful and, therefore, can no longer be taken for granted. Or there may be moral, altruistic, religious, and other considerations that motivate the prospective adoptive parent to seek this alternative to establishing a parent and child relationship.

Third Party Involvement

Once the decision has been made by the prospective adoptive parent to pursue this alternative, this decision ushers in the involvement of other professional people, or what is referred to as "third party involvement." The prospective adoptive parent must initiate contact with an adoption agency and make application to adopt a child.

The application process: The application process typically involves a social worker, who specializes in adoption. However, attorneys and other professional persons may also be involved in the application process. When a social case worker is involved, the application making begins a sometimes lengthy process which is referred to in the child placement profession as the "Family Study." The application to adopt is taken and an initial assessment is made by the social case worker. This initial assessment is a rough screening to determine if the prospective adoptive parent generally meets agency requirements and therefore qualifies to continued to the next phase of the process. Adoption agency standards vary and prospective parents may qualify in one agency and be disqualified in another. Those who qualify will be made ready for the Family Study process.

The family study process: The Family Study is the agency's way of learning about the prospective adoptive parent through a series of meetings and interviews. The social case worker and other agency representatives will collect data and develop impressions about the prospective adoptive parent. These shall form the basis for an evaluation of suitability or acceptability to determine the probability for success in parenting. The family study process is the agency's procedure for estimating the prospective adoptive parent's potential to parent reasonably well. Once the assessment is concluded with the impression that the prospective adoptive parent is acceptable to the agency, involvement with the agency continues but with a different focus. An unfavorable assessment would result in the agency discontinuing its relationship with the prospective adoptive parent or terminating the adoption process at this time.

Finding, matching, and placing children: Third party involvement continues but the focus of this involvement changes. When the adoption agency has determined to its satisfaction that the prospective adoptive parent has potential to parent successfully, the agency will then begin the process of finding a child that is a good match for the prospective adoptive parent and placing the child with the adult. Much time may pass and more than one child may be seriously considered during this phase of the adoption process. At some point a child and an adult are brought together under agency supervision.

The child may be placed with the prospective adoptive parent for varying durations of time so they may get to know each other at a reasonable pace in reasonable circumstances. At some point the child may actually be placed with the prospective adoptive parent for an extended period of time to determine if they can live together successfully. When consensus is reached on the part of child, prospective adoptive parent, and agency, a decision is made by the adoption agency to place the child for adoption. This decision initiates the involvement of the Family Court System or the next phase of the adoption process.

Family Court and Legal Sanction

When the decision has been made to place the child for adoption, the adoption agency must petition the Family Court or present its plans for the child to the Family Court for its approval or legal sanction. If the plans for the child are acceptable, Family Court grants the adoption pending a final hearing on the matter. This decree begins the "grace period" during which time the adoption agency continues its active supervision of the child within the context of the placement. Family Court officially oversees the adoption from this point until such time as the adoption is finalized or

terminated.

There is some variation as to the duration of this "grace period" but it typically lasts one year. The adoption agency continues to maintain its supervision while providing support and encouragement to the adoptive parent and child while at the same time continuing to assess the appropriateness of the placement and the probability for success of the relationship. The adoptive parent assumes parental responsibility for the care and supervision of the child while the agency maintains its titular guardianship of the child along with the court.

Eventually the anniversary date approaches and a final hearing is held by Family Court. The adoption agency submits its placement report to the Family Court and its recommendations to finalize or discontinue the adoption. If all parties concur, the adoption is made final and guardianship is granted to the adoptive parent. Family Court thereby has given its full legal sanction to this parent and child relationship. All rights, privileges, and responsibilities which accrue to the biological parent now become those of the adoptive parent.

Under the law, there is no difference once the adoption is finalized. The biological parent's rights and claims to the child were previously terminated and the finalization of the child's adoption confirms that once again. Family Court and adoption agency supervision and guardianship are terminated with the final decree. The case, in effect, is closed. The adoptive parent and child relationship has been established with the final decree.

Permanence

This relationship is permanent under the law as the biological parent and child relationship is considered permanent under the law. This notion of permanence is important to how our culture views the parent and child relationship. It also serves as a distinguishing feature. You will notice that other kinds of parent and child relationships do not possess this feature even though they may be given legal sanction.

FOSTER PARENT AND CHILD RELATIONSHIP

The foster parent and child relationship is one that is designed to provide temporary parenting to another person's child. The child's parent, for whatever reason, is unable to provide parental care and supervision. The child's need for parenting continues nonetheless. In such cases the child may be placed in the care of a foster parent for a temporary period of time by a child placement or child protection agency which has guardianship of the child. In the state of Rhode Island, the agency which has guardianship is the Department for Children and Their Families (DCF). It or its designee (a child placement agency) may place the child in foster care and supervise the placement.

Becoming a Foster Parent

How does one become a foster parent? You will note that the process is very similar to what has been described as applicable to the process of becoming an adoptive parent. However, there are some important distinguishing features. Please note them.

Prior deliberation

Adults who are interested in providing foster care, typically engage in much forethought and inquiry before coming to the decision to become foster parents. There are many factors to consider. Of prime importance is the notion of receiving a child for care, providing that care and eventually having the child removed from your care. If the adult believes he or she can manage the psychological stress of the process of coming together, connecting, then later separating reasonably well and believes that such stress is counterbalanced or even outweighed by the satisfaction of being able to provide care to a child in need, then the adult elects to become a foster parent.

Third party involvement

The decision to become a foster parent necessitates that the prospective foster parent shall make an application to a foster placement agency to become a foster parent. The making of an application initiates the third party involvement of the child placement agency. The application process for prospective foster parents is for all intent and purposes the same as that for prospective adoptive parents. These two processes are often managed by the same agency and people. Therefore the procedures and criteria are often highly similar and sometimes identical.

The family study process: The prospective foster parent must undergo a similar (and in some instances identical) family study experience as does the prospective adoptive parent. The procedures and purposes are the same. The criteria are often the same. In short, the child placement agency wishes to determine or assess the prospective foster parent's potential to parent well and to cooperate with the child placement agency in the provision of foster care services.

When a favorable determination is made, the foster parent becomes an important resource to the child placement agency in providing care and protection to a child in need of care. In a sense, the child placement agency and the foster parent become partners in parenting. If the agency makes a favorable determination regarding the prospective foster parent's application, their relationship or partnership continues. If it does not, their relationship is terminated.

Finding, matching and placing children: When the prospective foster parent is found to meet agency requirements and expectations, the agency then begins its efforts to find children who seem appropriate for placement in the foster home. When placements are made, they are made with the understanding that the placement is temporary. The ultimate goal of the child placement agency is to return the foster child to the care of his or her parent or find an adoptive home for the child or some other appropriate but more permanent placement. The time a child spends in a foster home varies considerably. For some it is a matter of days. For others the placement may extend over a period of years. Nevertheless, the placement in theory is temporary; in practice, it may appear to be otherwise for some children.

Legal Sanction

The child placement agency places the child with foster parent consensus; but, may remove the child without it. The foster parent provides parental care and supervision. The placement agency exercises guardianship and assumes responsibility for the child in lieu of the child's parent. The placement agency provides support and guidance to the foster parent and child while simultaneously planning for the child's return to the parent or to an adoptive home or to another alternative. The foster placement agency provides these services with legal sanction under the state's child protection law and under the aegis of the Family Court System. The foster parent has no legal rights or claim to the foster child, despite the strong attachments that often develop between foster parent and foster child.

Whatever privileges the foster parent may enjoy or whatever responsibilities the foster parent may assume are accrued by the foster parent by association with the child placement agency. Some foster parents continue their association with the placement agency for many years and provide parental care and supervision to many children. Some foster parents even become adoptive parents when that very special match and set of circumstances and opportunity take place and conditions permit. It should also be noted in this connection that not only is there legal sanction of the foster parent and child relationship but also widespread societal sanction for this needed form of parenting. In most states, foster parents receive a stipend to reimburse the foster parent for part of the cost of providing care and supervision to the child.

COMMON-LAW ADOPTIVE PARENT AND CHILD RELATIONSHIP

The common-law adoptive parent and child relationship is similar to the adoptive parent and child relation in that the adult assumes the care and supervision with the intent of permanence and provides care and supervision to the child as though the child were his or her own. However, it is distinguished from the adoptive parent and child relationship in that there is no third party involvement and no legal sanction. There may or may not be a formal agreement

between parent and the common-law adoptive parent. If there is an agreement, it typically would be informal and verbal.

There may or may not be a biological connection between the common-law adoptive parent and the child or the child's parent. Sometimes adult relatives assume responsibility for the child; sometimes non-relatives do. But it is done without third party involvement and without legal sanction. That is, there is no child placement agency involved. There is no Family Court involvement either.

Becoming a Common-law Adoptive Parent

How do such relationships come about? One possible scenario is offered here to illustrate and answer this question.

Mr. and Mrs. Jones have been happily married for several years and have two young children from their union. They have worked very diligently to create a good home environment and they enjoy the good relationships their care has created. Notwithstanding a few minor problems, life is good for the Jones family.

Circumstances change drastically when Mrs. Jones is killed in an automobile accident. The children and Mr. Jones are distraught. The family situation deteriorates rapidly as Mr. Jones is unable to cope with the loss of his wife and the severe impact that loss has had upon his children. Severe depression ensues, followed by excessive drinking, job absences, impatience with the children, and more depression. A bitter, vicious cycle of downward spiralling behavior engulfs him.

These conditions continue to worsen significantly. Despite a very understanding employer, Mr. Jones' poor work performance and frequent absences eventually result in the loss of his job, which further intensifies the problem. Mr. Jones is jobless and without financial resources. He is unable to recover from these losses and eventually the bank forecloses the mortgage on the Jones' home. This leaves the family homeless.

It is at this point that Mr. Jones' sister offers to look after the children if he is willing

6

to admit himself into a residential treatment program for help. With reluctance he does so; but improvement is not forthcoming. Mr. Jones eventually decides that he needs to make a completely new start. He approaches his sister with his plans to leave the state and start over. It is at this time that he asks his sister to assume full and permanent responsibility for his children. Despite her argument that the children still love and need him, his plans remain unchanged.

There seems to be an impasse. But eventually Mr. Jones' sister agrees to care for his children on a permanent basis. In so doing, she becomes the common-law adoptive parent to her brother's children. This is accomplished without third party involvement of a child placement agency, or attorney, and without the legal sanction of Family Court. Hence no formal and legal document nor any legal sanction of this arrangement exists. This is one way an adult might become a common-law adoptive parent.

Such arrangements are made with surprising frequency. They are of rather common occurrence. Although this example depicted a certain set of circumstances, there are many different situations that precipitate such decisions on the part of the parent and result in the establishment of a common-law adoptive parent and child relationship. This example depicted a relative who became a common-law adoptive parent. But non-related persons are frequently involved. Sometimes the parent has a long-standing relationship with the common-law adoptive parent. Sometimes these relationships are of short term. Sometimes the parent has no direct involvement with the adult who may be known directly or indirectly to a friend or a relative of the parent. People who work in the child welfare field are destined to make acquaintance with such arrangements as I have many times in my past experience in the child welfare field.

COMMON-LAW FOSTER PARENT AND CHILD RELATIONSHIP

The common-law foster parent and child relationship is like the common-law adoptive parent and child relationship in that there is no third party involvement and no legal sanction of the relationship and the arrangements that are made on behalf of the child. It is distinguished from the common-law adoptive parent and child relationship in that it is temporary rather than permanent in intent. This temporariness makes it like the foster parent and child relationship which in theory is always temporary, which implies that a future permanent arrangement is part of the plans for the child.

The example of the Jones' family would have fallen into the category of common-law foster parent and child relationship had Mr. Jones indicated to his sister that her care and supervision of his children would be temporary and would continue until such time that his personal circumstances permitted him to resume full and permanent responsibility for his children. Such an arrangement would have been non-permanent or temporary. It would have been his intention and the understanding of all involved that the children would be returned to his care and supervision at a future time. It is this temporary feature that makes the relation that is established a common-law foster parent and child relationship rather than a common-law adoptive parent and child relationship. It is this temporary feature that also distinguishes the foster parent and child relationship from the adoptive parent and child relationship.

STEP-PARENT AND CHILD RELATIONSHIP

The step-parent and child relationship is established when one is married to another who has a child. Thirteen hundred step-families are established each day. Unfortunately, 60% will end in divorce. One in five children under six years of age lives in step-families. The step-parent may or may not assume responsibility for the care and supervision of the child. The parent of the child may or may not desire the step-parent to assume such responsibility. The child may or may not accept parenting from the step-parent.

The step-parent and child relationship is the result of one adult marrying another adult who just happens to be a parent. There is no third party involvement of a child placement agency and no legal sanction of the Family Court. The step-parent and child relationship results from the marital union of two adults. The step-parent does not have any legal responsibility for or rights pertaining to the child, even though the step-parent may behave as though this were so or assumes this were so. Some step-parents assume such responsibility in word and deed and some do not.

Some step-parents assume this responsibility to such a degree that they may eventually adopt the step-child, which in effect terminates the step-parent and child relationship and establishes the adoptive parent and child relationship. When the adoptive parent and child relationship evolves out of a step-parent and child relationship, the adoptive parent accrues all the legal rights and responsibilities that this relationship has. But possibly more importantly, it communicates a very powerful psychological message to the child. Namely, that the step-parent wants to be a parent to the child to the extent that this is possible even though there is no biological connectedness. The step-parent wants to show full commitment to the child as parent. The step-parent wishes to demonstrate that parenthood is by choice not simply the result of marriage to the child's parent.

Of course, it must be stated that notwithstanding this intent, adoption is possible only if the child is free to be adopted. That is, the child's parent or parents must consent and one parent shall have to give up his or her rights to the child. This is not always achievable, despite the good intentions of the step-parent.

COMMON-LAW STEP-PARENT AND CHILD RELATIONSHIP

This classification is to be credited to my students for its articulation and name. The common-law step-parent and child relationship incorporates the situation commonly referred to as "living together" and the adult known as the "live in." When two adults live together in conjugal fashion but are not legally married, their relationship is often described as a "common-law marriage" or marital relationship. Hence the derivation of this classification. When an adult with a child resides with another adult in conjugal fashion, the non-parent is the common-law step-parent. This situation occurs with considerable frequency in contemporary American culture and deserves a special classification to depict and acknowledge it.

This category does not include adults who live together and share in parenting but do not live together in the conjugal sense. An example of this situation might be two adult friends or siblings who reside together and share in the parenting of a child or one another's children. This arrangement is commonly referred to as "co-parenting." It is not a common-law step-parent and child relationship.

BLOCK PARENT AND CHILD RELATIONSHIP

There are adults toward whom neighborhood children gravitate. These are people who genuinely like children and enjoy having them around. They may or may not have children of their own. For those who have children, their children must learn to share their parent with other non-related children. Their homes and yards are often the place where many neighborhood children gather to play or simply mark the passage of time. These adults are usually very nurturing people. Children recognize this and often seek their counsel, guidance, support, encouragement and nurturing. In practice, neighborhood children seek and receive parenting from them, hence the terms "neighborhood parent" or "block parent."

You may recall such a person in your neighborhood. As a child, I remember such people. Possibly your parent fits this category. In fact, my mother was one of these special people - kind, caring and often available. A large contingent of neighborhood children could be found in my yard. We could dig holes in the yard, build forts, and do other things in our yard that some parents would not permit in their yard. I recall neighborhood children ringing the doorbell to our home. And when I would answer, I would be greeted with "Hi. Is your mother home?" In a short time I realized that not all the children who came to my home were coming to see me, or my sister, or my brother. In fact, some were coming to pay my mother a visit. To this day I still meet peers who are far more interested in my mother's status and welfare than in my own.

The relationship established between block parents and neighborhood children is sometimes long-standing. Some children refer to the block parent as an aunt or uncle, a grandmother or a grandfather, or a second mother or second father. Some of these relationships continue into adulthood and throughout. On occasion I find a childhood playmate at my mother's home when I am making a visit. I know that they did not stop by my mother's home on the remote chance that I might stop by.

Also there are adults in the community who, although they were less directly involved with the neighborhood children than the block parent, nevertheless, looked after the welfare of the children and offered commiseration, guidance, and even protection and/or sanctuary when needed. They sometimes fed children, provided clothing, an occasional gift or lunch money. These were people who valued children and were concerned for their general welfare. A spirit of caring prevailed among them and the community knew who they were and valued them.

Block Parent Programs, Child Watch Programs

Such an era seems to have passed as such people seem to be in short supply. Fewer and fewer of these genuinely caring people are identifiable in the community today. In an effort to recreate the community attitude prevalent in former times and to reestablish neighborhoods as being safe for children, some communities have created formal "block parent" programs or "child watch" programs. Typically adults must complete an application through some community social service agency which sponsors the program. Criminal clearance is often required. Here is another example of third party involvement.

When an applicant meets the requirements, he or she is given an identifying marker to place on or near the home. This marker signifies that an approved block parent resides therein. This communicates to neighborhood children that the adult therein shall provide

assistance if needed and can be regarded as a person who can be trusted. The block parent may provide a place for a child to stay until a parent or older sibling arrives home to assume responsibility for the child's care and supervision. The block parent may provide an after school snack or a toilet facility to use as needed. Likewise, commiseration, guidance, and even protection and/or sanctuary may be offered.

DONOR PARENT AND CHILD RELATIONSHIP

There are in excess of one million people living in the United States of America whose biological parent is a donor parent. A donor parent is one who donates a sperm or egg and that gamete is used in the fertilization process to create another human being. Almost all donor parents donate their gametes anonymously. It is often their intent to remain unknown. Anonymity is often a precondition of donation. Almost all donor parents are unknown to the children derived from their contribution and likewise the children are unknown to the donor parents.

Most gamete donations are made through hospital fertility clinics or genetic clinics, which are often affiliated with medical schools. Potential donors are often recruited from the medical school student population as they typically represent a desirable gene pool. Policy and procedures are designed to insure privacy, confidentiality, and anonymity.

Anonymity, Confidentiality and Privacy Challenged

In recent years many donor children who are the creative result of a donor parent's gamete have attempted to challenge this anonymity and right to privacy and the shroud of confidentiality. The reasons behind this challenge have their origin in typically one or both of the following situations. Since a substantial portion of donor children are of child bearing age themselves and actively considering having children of their own, there is a desire to find out more about their genetic profile or background.

9

Concerns generally focus on the following: Might there be particular genetically transmitted problems, errors of metabolism, or disease that are part of their genetic background that may influence their decision to have or not have children? Therefore, the donor child often believes that he or she has the right to know and should be given access to such information before child bearing decisions are made. In other instances, donor children have parented a child who has been born with a particular condition that is or may be genetically transmitted. The parent of this child believes he or she has the right to know and should be given access to such information that will help determine if the parent's genetic background may be associated with the problem first and foremost. Secondly, a decision to have or not have subsequent children may be influenced by what is ascertained about the genetic background.

Was the child's condition directly associated with the gene pool? If so, what is the probability of reoccurrence. Was the condition simply a matter of chance and not directly related to the child's genetic background? These are reasonable questions for any parent or prospective parent to ask. However, when the person asking such questions is a donor child, matters become extremely complicated and frustrating.

This right to know, desire to know, and access to information is similar to that which is experienced by adoptive children. Adoptive children in recent years have generally been given access to such information when they reach adulthood. In contrast, donor children have met with great resistance and have been, for the most part, unsuccessful in gaining access to information concerning their genetic background. This is true generally, even when the donor child expresses no desire to know who the donor parent is but rather expresses wanting access only to information pertaining to genetic background. The majority of those who want such information fall into this category.

This challenge has generated much legal controversy and has shed much light on the power of medical schools and hospital administrators to resist what seems to many to be a reasonable request. Resistance, non-compliance, obstruction and destruction of records have taken place even in the face of court orders to make such information available to donor children.

SURROGATE PARENT AND CHILD RELATIONSHIP

Surrogate parenting has gained great media attention recently through such highly publicized cases as the Baby M custody battle and the Canadian baby abandonment case. Because of such publicity, most Americans are aware that the surrogate parent is a female who carries an unborn child in her womb through the gestation period, delivers the baby, and then gives the newborn to another adult (the recipient parent) to be parented. The surrogate parent and the recipient parent may have entered into an agreement and there are many variations along this theme that call into question many legal and sociological questions when one or both of the adults involved fail to follow through on the agreement. It is the failed agreement that gains media attention. We rarely hear of the many successes of this kind of arrangement. But there are many indeed.

Many Adults Involved

There are numerous variations in the nature of the adult's relationship to the child and other adults involved in this agreement. The adults involved include the surrogate parent, the recipient parent, the biological parent, and other adults such as physicians, attorneys, relatives, friends, etc.

The Surrogate Parent

The surrogate parent may or may not have a genetic connection to the child. Sometimes the surrogate parent contributes her egg and in fact is the biological parent of the child. In such cases, she may legally retain or surrender that relationship. Surrendering her rights to the child requires Family Court action. Sometimes the surrogate parent has no genetic connection to the child. The fertilized egg she receives in her womb is from another female, who is the biological parent of the child. The biological parent in this case may legally retain or surrender that relationship.

10

The surrogate parent's relationship with the recipient parent and others varies. The surrogate parent and the recipient parent may or may not be related to one another. You may recall media coverage of a sister serving as a surrogate parent for her sister or brother. In some instances, the surrogate parent donated her egg, in other instances the egg or sperm came from the sister or brother. In other instances the egg or sperm came from a non-related person.

Such relationships may be complicated by the fertilization method employed. Although artificial insemination and/or external (in vitro) fertilization are most common, fertilization of the egg may be performed through copulation by the surrogate parent and male parent, who may or may not be related or known to one another.

The Recipient Parent

Although recipient parents commonly come in pairs, single males and females are also found among the recipient parent population. Some recipient parents choose to parent the child within the context of a marital or couple relationship. Others choose to parent singularly.

As stated previously, the recipient parent may or may not be genetically related to the child. In couple situations, one or both of the recipient parents may contribute a gamete. When both contribute, both are genetically related to the child; both are the child's biological parents. When one is genetically related and the other is not, the former is the biological parent and the latter has no biological relationship to the child at all. The non-biological parent may choose to adopt the child after taking possession of the child. Of course this would require legal action of the Family Court system and a surrendering of parental rights on the part of one of the biological parents.

When neither recipient parent is genetically related to the child, one or both may desire to adopt the child. As in all adoption cases, the child must be freed for adoption by having both biological parents give up their rights to the child. This procedure is performed under the aegis of the Family Court System. Such procedures may become complicated if one or both of the biological parents are either inaccessible, anonymous, or have a change of mind or intent.

As indicated, the recipient parent may not be related to or known to the surrogate parent. When the surrogate parent and recipient parent are not genetically related, the biological parents may or may not be known to either one or both. In instances when the surrogate parent and the recipient parent are not the biological parent, we have adults who are the biological parent of the child but presumably have no desire or intention to parent the child.

Other Adults Involved

Adults other than the surrogate parent, recipient parent and the biological parent are involved. There are legal personnel who are part of the scenario. These usually include one or more attorneys, the Family Court judge, and possibly other legal and para-legal personnel. As a point of interest, there have been instances when one or more of the legal personalities have been related or otherwise previously known to the surrogate parent or recipient parent or both.

Of course there are medical personnel involved. The physician who performs the fertilization and implantation procedure is one. The obstetrician/gynecologist that monitors the pregnancy and helps the surrogate parent deliver is another. The pediatrician that cares for the child after birth is another key person among the medical personnel involved. All have their own views, pro and con, concerning the surrogate parenting arrangement. Sometimes these views are expressed and are counterproductive to the arrangements that have been entered into by the surrogate parent and recipient parent.

Likewise, relatives, friends, acquaintances, media personnel, etc. may be involved. They have their views which when expressed may be supportive or non-supportive to the arrangement.

Surrogate Parenting: Success or Failure?

If you feel a little bewildered, it is understandable. Surrogate parenting arrangements have the legal, medical, child welfare, and legislative communities bewildered also. The complexities and the many unexpected outcomes of these arrangements have created a legal quagmire for attorneys and the Family Court system. Much frustration has been experienced by legislators and others who either wish to facilitate or impede surrogate parenting arrangements. Child welfare professionals have often been forced to intercede on behalf of the child. The dreams and plans for pleasant outcomes have sometimes been transformed into nightmares and unfinished, unkept agreements for surrogate parents and recipient parents. The child has become the pawn and innocent victim of adult and system failures.

A case which illustrates such failures is a Canadian case. A surrogate parent gave birth to a child who was born with serious and significant birth defects of the magnitude that he would require extensive medical care and supervision for the remainder of his life. The recipient parents refused to take possession of the child. It was their contention that their agreement implied a "perfect" child. The surrogate parent refused to accept the child. Her contention was that the agreement required her to give the child to the recipient and she was adhering to that agreement. The child was left without an adult to accept and care for him. The Canadian child protection agency had to step in and take possession of the child, who is now a ward of the state.

RELATIVE SUCCESS OF THE DIFFERENT RELATIONSHIPS

As you review these different kinds of parent and child relationships, various thoughts may have emerged about the probability for success or for problem occurrence within certain relationships. Certainly your own personal experience with these different kinds of relationships may have helped you formulate certain impressions about such matters. Actual concrete data about success rate, problem occurrence, etc. is difficult to come by. It is

even difficult to determine what percentage of the total parenting population is represented by each category identified so far. However, we do know that the majority of intact parent and child relationship are biological.

So when making comparisons about success or failure or problem occurrence, it is essential to factor out the differences in the actual numerical or relative percentile size of each category. Comparative research into these areas is sorely lacking as is reliable data. Such research and data would be very beneficial to our general understanding of such matters. If anyone is looking for a research topic, I would suggest that this area be seriously considered. In view of the paucity of research and data in this area, my comments will be highly impressionistic. Nevertheless, they are supported by not only my own personal and professional experience but also by the experience of other professionals working in the child welfare, child development, and related fields.

Child Abuse and Neglect

Biological Relationships

It seems that biological parents are more prone to abuse and neglect their children. The number of reported cases is staggering and is rising each year. The number of unreported cases is open for speculation. Societal awareness of this problem has increased substantially and this awareness, in part, has contributed to the significant rise in recent years in the incidence of reports of suspected cases of child abuse and/or neglect. A substantial portion of these reported cases are confirmed by investigations made by the child protection agency.

There are innumerable factors that cause and precipitate child abuse and/or neglect. We know that biological parents are significantly younger when parenting is begun. They may simply not be mature enough or ready to assume the stresses associated with parenting, especially at a younger age. The younger biological parent is more likely to have less income, live in less suitable housing, or be less well educated, etc. These factors and more are part of an interactive system of conditions that influence one another and contribute to the problem under consideration. These are offered not to excuse. Child abuse and neglect are inexcusable! These contributing factors are offered to promote our understanding of the problem and guide our actions as citizens and professionals as we attempt to intervene and/or prevent such problems from happening.

Adoptive Relationships

Of the relationships that are characterized by regular interaction, the adoptive parent seems to be the least prone to abuse and neglect the child. In fact, the incidence of this occurence is quite small. In comparison, the adoptive parent typically begins parenting later in his or her development and is not only older but also more mature. The adoptive parent is more likely to have greater income, live in more suitable housing, be better educated, etc. The adoptive parent characteristically has engaged in considerable forethought about being a parent and parenting. The adoption process strengthens and also requires this deliberation.

Step-parent Relationships

The incidence of abuse and/or neglect within the step-parent and child relationship is less than it is among the biological parent and child relationship but significantly more than among the adoptive parent and child relationship. This is of no surprise, for many of us have images of Cinderella's step-mother and Hansel and Gretel's step-mother, when we consider this category.

Other Relationships

The incidence of abuse and/or neglect within the foster parent and child relationship and the block parent and child relationship is relatively low. It occurs and we are often made aware of this by the media as the media points out the failings of our society's child protection systems. However, child abuse and neglect is not characteristic of these types. A substantially large portion of foster and block parents do an admirable job of parenting. The rather good rate of success in these categories is due in part to the fact that these parents are usually screened well and monitored by a child placement agency or another community

service or human service representative. When cases of abuse or neglect occur, they are usually of short duration and are terminated very quickly by the supervising agency. Of course this does not negate some of the "horror stories" that we have heard happening in foster care placements both locally and nationally.

Child abuse or neglect is virtually non-existent among the donor parent and child relationship and the surrogate parent and child relationship. Donor parents do not have interactive contact with the donor child. The duration of contact between the surrogate parent and child is minimal. Children are typically surrendered to the recipient parent shortly after birth and long before the stresses of parenting are experienced.

Problem Occurrence

There are many problems that emerge during the parenting period. Most are common problems that are generally short-lived or resolved in a short period of time. Such problems are considered by some as not problems at all but merely the intermittent challenges of raising children. Certainly there are problems that are more extreme but also less common. These are typically of longer duration and not easily reconciled. It is the latter type that I have in mind for the following discussion, excluding the problem of child abuse and/or neglect that has been previously discussed.

Foster Relationships

The foster parent and child relationship seems to be problem prone. This is typically because the child brings to this relationship pre-existing problems from another parenting context. The child is placed in foster care because his life circumstances have necessitated intervention of a child welfare agency. The child may be a victim of abuse and/or neglect. He may have suffered the loss of one or both parents due to accident, illness, abandonment, etc. The child's parent may, for any number of reasons, be unable to provide adequate care and supervision. The child may have special needs which require special care and supervision, which the parent is not able to adequately meet, satisfy, or provide.

13

These problems, concerns, needs, etc. are not left behind. They accompany the child and are brought into the foster parent and child relationship and the foster parent must cope with, manage, and attempt to resolve these. The ongoing support and encouragement of the child placement agency is often required to maintain the placement and help the foster parent and foster child live successfully together. This is typically a very demanding relationship. The problems are often severe. Adequate agency support and encouragement is not always forthcoming, expedient or appropriate. And there never seems to be an adequate supply of good foster homes to call upon when children are in need.

Step-parent Relationships

The step-parent and child relationship seems to be another type that is moderately prone to problems. The source of these problems are usually different than the problems that characterize the foster parent and child relationship. Dr. Benjamin Spock has written about this relationship frequently because he has been a step-parent for more than twenty-five years. In his writings and in a personal conversation with me, he characterizes this relationship as the most demanding that he has experienced. He continues to point out that there are regularly recurring problems and a considerable amount of testing of the relationship. This creates stress for the step-parent, the step-child, the biological parent and siblings, and others closely affiliated with the family.

A problem of attitude: What accounts for these problems? Certainly the underlying causes are many and varied. However, a substantial influence seems to be the psychological posture or attitude assumed by those involved. It is common for the child to take the position that since the step-parent is not the "real" parent, the step-parent has no jurisdiction over the child. The step-child may proclaim: "He can't tell me what to do." "She has no business meddling into my affairs." Such a position is less likely to be found among very young children but they too can display a similar attitude toward the step-parent.

The biological parent may communicate the attitude to the step-parent and child that the step-parent is to mind his or her own business, when it comes to matters involving the child. The biological parent in essence reserves the parenting for himself or herself and excludes the step-parent from having any significant input. This minimizes the step-parent and child's opportunities to develop a meaningful parent and child relationship. Likewise, the non-custodial biological parent may communicate a similar "hands off" message to the step-parent, the custodial biological parent, and the child.

The step-parent may assume a position of non-involvement with the step-child. The idea underlying this position may be that the child is not my child and I should mind my own business and steer clear of any significant child rearing involvement. Such an attitude minimizes the opportunities for building a meaningful relationship. The child may receive a message of detachment and disinterest and thus avoid or minimize contact with the step-parent.

Or in contrast, the step-parent may be extremely intrusive or demanding or bossy. Such qualities not only create problems but also alienate the child from the step-parent. Such negative involvement would minimize their chances for developing a positive parent and child relationship.

Others may also have a crucial role in creating a counterproductive attitude in those directly involved in the step-parent and child relationship. Grandparents, siblings, other relatives and friends may communicate messages that contribute to a poor attitude in the child, biological parent, or step-parent. The messages to the child may be: Don't let the step-parent tell you what to do; ignore him; pay no attention to her; listen to just your real parent. The biological parent may be told by others not to let the step-parent interfere; the step-parent has no right to tell the child what to do; tell the step-parent to stay out of your child's business. The step-parent may be told directly by any number of different people to steer clear; this is not you child, so mind your own business; don't get involved; don't put yourself in the middle.

These and similar messages help create a particular psychological posture or attitude that characterizes the step-parent and child relationship all too often. However there are many step-parent and child relationships that are characterized by much more positive attitudes and as a result they enjoy a much more positive experience and relationship. There are step-parent and child relationships that are successful and rewarding for all involved. And there are people who are involved directly and indirectly who possess a positive attitude and behave in ways that support the development of a good step-parent and child relationship. In large measure it is a matter of attitude. Having the right attitude is productive. Having the wrong attitude is counterproductive.

ESTABLISHING THE PSYCHOLOGICAL PARENT AND CHILD RELATIONSHIP:

A PREREQUISITE FOR SUCCESS

In the preceding sections the relative probability for success or failure of the different parent and child relationships was discussed. It was also noted that some kinds of parent and child relationships are more prone to having problems than others because of the special nature of these relationships and the circumstances that are commonly associated. Notwithstanding these considerations, each of these various kinds of parent and child relationships have the potential for success. Success in parenting depends on many factors. Some of these will be the focus of the chapters that follow.

However, one of the prime or most important of these is the establishment and maintaining of a psychological parent and child relationship. The extent to which any of the ten previously identified relationships are successful will largely be influenced by the quality of the psychological parent and child relationship that is established and maintained.

The extent to which the biological parent and child relationship is successful is dependant upon the quality of the psychological parent and child relationship that is established within that context. If the adoptive parent and child relationship is to be successful, a psychological parent and child relationship must be established and maintained within that context. Foster placement professionals are mindful that the foster parent and foster child must be able to make a psychological connection and maintain it if the placement is to succeed.

The establishment of a psychological parent and child relationship is of primary importance to the success of any parent and child relationship. Once established it must be maintained. It must be maintained at a particular level of quality for it is the quality of the psychological parent and child relationship that forms the foundation for successful parenting.

Being a biological parent or having a biological parent and child relationship does not give the parent, child or the relation an edge or an assurance of success. The same can be said of the other types. Assurances are difficult to come by, especially regarding interpersonal relationships. However, the psychological parent and child relationship forms the foundation for the parent and child relationship irrespective of kind. It serves as the substructure upon which the relationship is built and provides a connectedness and strength that helps make success probable. The next chapter shall describe in more detail this very special and most important parent and child relationship - the psychological parent and child relationship.

References

1. "A Closer Look", NBC News, April 4, 1991.

2. Goldstein, J., Freud, A., and Solnit, A. *Beyond The Best Interest Of The Child*, (New York: The Free Press, 1973).

Resources

1. Children's Defense Fund, 122 C Street, N.W., Washington, D.C. 20001, Telephone: 202-628-8787.

2. Child Welfare League of America, Inc., 440 First Street, N.W., Suite 310, Washington, D.C. 20001-2085. Telephone: 202-638-2952.

3. Massachusetts Adoption Resource Exchange, 867 Boylston Street, Boston, Massachusetts 02116. Telephone: 800-882-1176

4. National Committee for the Prevention of Child Abuse, 332 South Michigan Avenue, Suite 1600, Chicago, Illinois 60604-4357. Telephone: 312-663-3520.

5. Step-Families Association of America, 602 East Joppa Road, Baltimore, Maryland 21204, Telephone: 301-823-7570.

Activities

1. Among the different types of parent and child relationships described in this chapter, which one or more best describes your relationship with your parents?

2. Among the different types of parent and child relationships described in this chapter, which one or more best describes your relationship with your child or children?

Chapter 2

The Psychological Parent and Child Relationship

As stated in the preceding chapter, the establishment of the psychological parent and child relationship is of primary importance to the success of any kind of parent and child relationship. Once established it must be maintained. It must be maintained at a particular level of quality; for it is the <u>quality</u> of the psychological parent and child relationship that forms the foundation for success - a successful relationship and successful parenting. This chapter shall examine how the psychological parent and child relationship is established or how the <u>psychological connection</u> is established between parent and child. It shall also identify what factors support and maintain it over time. Other attributes of this relationship shall also be identified and discussed.

ESTABLISHING
THE PSYCHOLOGICAL PARENT AND CHILD RELATIONSHIP

The establishment of the psychological parent and child relationship and its maintenance is a major feature of quality parent and child relationships. The psychological parent and child relationship is in itself an attribute that sets it apart or distinguishes it from other relationships of lesser quality where psychological connectedness has not been either established or properly maintained. It is a feature that establishes the relationship as being a quality one. It is not only an essential attribute but also of primary and major importance.

Interaction Is Required

The establishment of this unique relationship requires the interaction of both parent and child. This interaction is contingent upon the response and responsiveness of each. The psychological parent and child relationship is the consequence of day to day interaction, ongoing care and supervision provided to the child by the parent, the sharing of both positive and negative experiences, and a desire on the part of the parent to parent the child and the child's favorable responses to being parented.

The Type of Interaction Is Crucial

Positive or constructive interaction is essential to the formation and continuation of the psychological parent and child relationship. The quality of these interactions will influence the quality of the psychological parent and child relationship. If the child is handled gently with care and love, he develops feelings of safety. Might these early feelings be the origins of a gentle, caring and loving person? Yes, I think so! In contrast, a child who is handled roughly with poor care and indifference will develop a very different feeling tone or sense of what it feels like to be cared for and loved. Might these feelings be the origin of sadomasochism? Yes, I think so!

The parent who is able to manage the child well, meet his needs and generally experience the satisfactions of successful parenting will feel competent as a parent. In contrast, the parent who is not able to manage the child well, is unable to meet his needs with ease, and generally does not experience satisfaction but rather dissatisfaction in parenting will feel incompetent as a parent. Such experiences and feelings will shape how the parent and the child view the parent and child relationship.

Quality of Interaction Varies

Hence we can see as a consequence of what the parent and child bring to and experience within the context of this relationship that there will be obvious variations in the quality of their interaction and their relationship. The quality of this relationship is a very important dimension. The word "quality" has a variety of meanings when it is used to describe the parent and child relationship. In this connection, quality may refer to a particular property inherent in the relationship that sets it apart as being good or desirable. Yet, we must realize that when the word quality is used here and elsewhere it may refer to a feature that may be negative or undesirable. For example, a relationship of poor quality.

Quality Defined

In the context of the psychological parent and child relationship quality often refers to a particular feature that distinguishes it as being good or desirable. A particular relationship may be regarded as a quality relationship because it possesses an attribute (irrespective of degree) that another relationship may lack entirely.

On the other hand, it is not always the case that a relationship simply possesses or lacks an attribute. Various relationships may have common attributes; yet, not all possess these attributes to the same degree. Therefore, there will exist varying gradations of the same attribute. Hence, one relationship may be regarded as being of greater quality than another because it possesses more of a particular attribute.

In assessing the quality of the relationship, distinctions are made on the basis of certain attributes and these particular attributes are viewed as essential or of major importance. Therefore, if these attributes are lacking then the relationship is not regarded as a quality relationship. If these attributes are present then the relationship is regarded as a quality relationship. Hence the possession of certain attributes may distinguish a relationship as being a quality one. However, quality is used most often to refer to a degree of excellence or superiority of a relationship that sets it apart from others of lesser quality or sets it apart a being a quality relationship.

Individual Perception

The matter of individual perception plays strongly in how the psychological parent and child relationship is viewed. Recall the saying "One man's junk is another man's treasure." Likewise, one man's pain is another man's pleasure. One man's satisfaction is another man's dissatisfaction. And so it goes. The point is that perceptions about a given relationship can vary greatly among those involved. And these variations in perception shall influence how the participants think, feel and interact with each other. Of course, there may exist substantial consensus about the quality of the relationship shared and this consensus shall exert an influence on the thoughts, feelings and behavior of those involved.

Perception of the quality of the relationship and its various distinguishing characteristics is of crucial importance. As Carl Rogers discovered in his research in the counseling profession, the client's perception of the counselor is as crucial as the counselor's knowledge, skill and personal characteristics. If the client perceives the counselor to be in possession of certain essential qualities, then the helping process proceeds in a constructive manner. If the client perceives the counselor as lacking these, then the counselor's effectiveness is minimized or even negated.

Likewise, the parent and child must have a positive perception of their relationship, one another and themselves respectively. Each must perceive that the relationship has or is characterized by certain important, positive features. Each must perceive in the other certain qualities that are regarded as attributes. Each must perceive the self as having certain qualities that contribute positively to the relationship.

There also must be a high degree of concurrence in these perceptions. The parent who perceives herself to be loving and caring will enjoy a more favorable relationship if the child likewise perceives the parent as loving and caring. If the child does not perceive the parent as such, the quality of interaction will be significantly affected. Similarly, if the child perceives himself as helpful and is regarded as so by the parent, then their interaction will be significantly different than if the parent perceived the child as a pest, who is always in the way and makes more work for the parent.

Consensus is important. If both parent and child believe they share a good relationship, their interactions will reflect this favorable view. However, if one views the relationship as good and the other has a negative view of the relationship, then their differences in perception will have a negative impact on their interactions.

Quality and Quantity

The quality of the relationship is crucial and influences the perception that the parent and child develop regarding their relationship. However, quality cannot be viewed separate and apart from frequency of interaction. That it, the amount or quantity or frequency of interaction is also important. Occasional high quality interactions are of limited value in strengthening and maintaining the psychological parent and child relationship. Good interactions must occur with sufficient regularity. As one book title suggested, once is not enough. Quality alone is simply not enough! For the parent and child to receive the potentially good benefit of high quality interaction, these interactions must be experienced on a regular and ongoing basis.

Psychological Connectedness

The important attribute of psychological connectedness is one of those features that distinguishes the psychological parent and child relationship from other kinds of parent and child relationships. The psychological parent and child relationship is first and foremost characterized by a degree of psychological connectedness that exists between the parent and the child. This psychological connectedness is the result of ongoing interaction. The quality of this relationship is the result of the quality and frequency of these interactions. Therefore, the many and varied characteristics that describe the psychological parent and child relationship are measures of the quality and extent of this psychological connectedness.

Psychological connectedness is the basis for the psychological parent and child relationship. Once the psychological parent and child relationship is established, it forms the foundation for a quality relationship. Furthermore, this feature must be built upon, strengthened and maintained well, if this relationship is to be a relationship characterized as a quality one. Other features will be added to the psychological parent and child relationship that will either enhance or diminish the quality of the relationship. Consequently, the psychological parent and child relationship will exhibit varying gradations of quality and the degree of quality of this relationship will have a major impact upon the growth and development of both the parent and the child.

A parent who is extremely harsh or rigid in her discipline of the child may suffer a loss of quality even though all other interactions are very positive and constructive. The child may experience considerable positive interactions in all other areas but the harshness of the parent's disciplinary approach may overshadow these positive interactions and create in the child a negative perception of the parent. In contrast, another child may be able to overlook or forgive this harshness of discipline because of the positive strength of all other interactions. Therefore, he does not develop an overriding negative view of the parent. Rather, the child is able to put the relationship within a perspective that enables the child to emerge with a positive attitude about the relationship and the parent. Gradation in the quality of the relationship will exist not only as a result of characteristics present and absent, but also as a result of how these characteristics are perceived by the parent, the child, and others closely affiliated.

The Establishment of Psychological Connectedness

The psychological parent and child relationship is the consequence of day to day, ongoing interactions. These interactions contribute to the formation and continuation of the psychological parent and child relationship. When these interactions are positive and constructive, they have a beneficial impact. When interaction is less positive and less constructive, they have a less beneficial effect. These interactions, positive and negative, productive and counterproductive, influence the perceptions each develops of the self and one another within the context of the relationship. Hence, the psychological parent and child relationship is influenced by the unique psychological posture assumed by the parent and the child as a consequence of their unique interactions with each other over time.

As a consequence of this day to day, ongoing interaction with one another, the parent and the child come to regard the other in a certain and very special way. The child

comes to regard the parent as a very special adult who shall behave in very special ways toward the child. The child comes to expect certain behaviors that he may not expect from other adults or at best secondarily from other adults. These expected behaviors include but are not limited to love, care, nurturing, protection, support, encouragement, and guidance. The child comes to regard this special adult as "parent" and this has very special meaning in all cultures.

Likewise, the parent comes to regard the child as a very special person with whom the parent will have very special interactions. The parent expects to behave in certain ways toward the child that are not expected of other adults closely or remotely affiliated with the child. These special behaviors include but are not limited to love, care, nurturing, protection, support, encouragement, and guidance. In optimum situations, the parent and the child have similar expectations of each other.

Additionally, the parent comes to expect that the child will behave in very special ways toward the parent. These behaviors include but are not limited to love, care, respect, loyalty or devotion, and trust. These are rather common expectations that parents have of their children throughout most cultures.

The Psychological Parent

The person who consistently functions within the parental role and gives to the child that which promotes the child's growth and development will come to be regarded as the "psychological parent." These "parenting" behaviors will play a substantial part in establishing the psychological parent and child relationship and maintaining it over time. Regardless of the adult's relationship with the child, the adult who engages in these parenting behaviors begins to be regarded as the "parent" or more precisely as the "psychological parent" by the child and possibly others. Likewise, the person who engages in these parenting behaviors also begins to perceive himself or herself as the psychological parent.

I recall the instructions given to a close friend of mine by the adoption agency concerning what she should tell her adopted daughter about her adoption. The advice was to inform the child that she was adopted and to refer to her biological mother as "the lady whose body she came out of" and to refer to herself as mother by stating emphatically and definitively, "I am your mother!" The idea here is that the person who parents you is your psychological parent. The person who begets you may or may not become your psychological parent. The point here is that people <u>become</u> psychological parents. They become it the hard way; they earn it. It is not a relationship that is bestowed by another or accrued by status.

Likewise, the child who responds to these parenting behaviors in ways that are consistent with reasonable expectations for the child (given his developmental level) will help to strengthen or reinforce the psychological parent and child relationship. Hence both may contribute positively or negatively to its establishment and maintenance over time.

Hierarchy of Psychological Parenthood

The adult who is primarily responsible for parenting and plays a substantial role in caring for and promoting the child's growth and development shall come to be regarded as the *primary* psychological parent;. Others who also play a substantial role in parenting the child may come to enjoy *secondary* or *tertiary* status as a psychological parent.

In American culture, the mother often has primary responsibility for parenting and often acquires primary psychological parent status. The father often has secondary responsibility for parenting and thereby acquires secondary psychological parent status. This primary and secondary status is not characteristic of all psychological parent and child relationships nor of all cultures. An adult other than the mother or father may have primary parenting responsibility. In some instances a non-adult may have primary parenting responsibility as in the case of an older sibling or baby-sitter.

Depending on the culture and/or circumstances, the father, grandmother, grandfather, aunt, uncle, sibling, another relative or friend may acquire primary psychological parent status. In some instances, a professional person such as a professional child care provider, day care or nursery school teacher, nanny, foster parent, group home worker, etc. may come to be regarded by the child and others as the primary psychological parent.

PSYCHOLOGICAL PARENT CONCEPT APPLIED

The application of the concept of the psychological parent has other significant uses. It is the main concept in Solnit, Freud and Weinbaum's book, *Beyond The Best Interest Of The Child*, which addresses the application of this concept within the child welfare services profession. In cases of child care custody decisions, the idea of which adult is most capable of parenting the child is of concern. These concerns are also part of child placement decision such as foster care, adoption, and emergency care.

To make proper placement of children in such cases, the adults ability to parent the child well and establish a psychological connection with the child is most important. And of course, the adult's ability in this regard will greatly influence the child's ability to make a similar connection to the adult. The potential success of these kinds of placements will be influenced by the potential of the people involved to establish and maintain a psychological parent and child relationship. Hence, the notion of the psychological parent plays an important role not only in child custody decisions but also in child placement decisions.

A Short History of Child Custody

Schickendanz, Schickendanz and Forsyth provide a short history of child custody concerns and decisions which underscore the importance of the psychological parent and child relationship and its application in this area of decision making involving children. I believe you will find it interesting and informative.

> Prior to 1900 it was the father rather than the mother who customarily received custody of children following the dissolution of a marriage. This practice was based on views about the disposition of family property, not on attitudes about parental competence. Children were

considered property and went to their father along with other family possessions.

At the turn of the century, however, psychological literature began to stress the special fitness of the mother for the parenting role. This led to the *"tender years doctrine"* in law, which held that the mother should receive custody of the children unless she was proven unfit. As a result of this doctrine few fathers were awarded custody of their children during the first three-quarters of this century.

Recently, however, the *"tender years"* doctrine has been changing. Current research on attachment indicates that the biological relationship of a parent and a child is less important than the quality of the adult's interaction with the child. An important consideration in awarding custody is which adult is the child's "psychological parent" - which parent the child has the best relationship with. Fathers are currently being awarded custody more often than they were in the past.

Changing views about sex roles have also encouraged more fathers to seek custody and have influenced the attitudes of judges and society as a whole. It is no longer assumed that fathers are less capable than mothers.

A remaining obstacle to the equal consideration of fathers and mothers for custody is the difference between the incomes of men and women. Because men's incomes are still substantially higher than women's (*America's Children*, 1976; Pearce, 1979), it is usually considered more practical economically for the mother to take custody so that child care responsibilities do not jeopardize the father's job performance. We are unlikely to see true equality in child custody until men and women receive comparable salaries and participate equally in the labor force. (p 527)

MAJOR CHARACTERISTICS OF THE PSYCHOLOGICAL PARENT AND CHILD RELATIONSHIP

If they are to be viable, the psychological parent and child relationship is an essential feature of all parent and child relationship types. Adoption, foster care, etc. are viable to the extent to which psychological connectedness is established. This connectedness forms the foundation or primary matrix to which other characteristics are added and integrated. Some of these essential features or major characteristics of the psychological parent and child relationship shall be identified and described in the remaining sections of this chapter.

Furthermore, herein and and throughout the remainder of this text, I will be speaking primarily of the psychological parent and child relationship. I will specify other types or make distinctions between types only when such distinctions are necessary.

It must be remembered that the psychological parent and child relationship is the result of special interactions between parent and child. These special interactions help establish the psychological parent and child relationship and maintain it over time. Please note that many of these features also characterize other interpersonal relationships. What distinguishes the parent and child relationship from other interpersonal relationships is the amount, intensity or degree of integration of these features into the relationship. The psychological parent and child relationship characteristically possesses these to a far greater extent than is typically characteristic of other important interpersonal relationships. A closer look will be taken at some of these special characteristics and interactional features of the psychological parent and child relationship.

Every person, thing or situation has certain characteristics or attributes that distinguish it or set it apart or help identify it appropriately. Likewise, the parent and child relationship has certain features that distinguish it or set it apart from other relationships or help identify its unique and special aspects. Some of these features are common to other important interpersonal relationships, while other aspects are unique to it. When commonality exists, the significant difference is often one of degree, not kind. The special features identified below are what are considered by many as the major characteristics of the parent and child relationship that distinguish it from other relationships if not necessarily in kind but certainly in degree.

Psychological Connectedness

In order to mininize repetition, suffice it to say that the psychological parent and child relationship is first and foremost characterized by the psychological connectedness that exists between the parent and the child. As explained earlier, this psychological connectedness is the result of ongoing interaction. The quality of the relationship is a result of the quality and frequency of these interactions. Therefore, the following characteristics are measures of the quality and extent of this connectedness or features of the parent and child interactional milieu.

Bonding and Attachment

The strength of the bond and the nature of the attachment that results from parent and child interaction is noteworthy. Parent and child attachment is usually greater or at least equivalent to other significant interpersonal relationships.

As parent and child interact with one another in favorable ways, a psychological bond is established. Continued favorable interaction strengthens that bond and creates a sense of attachment. In simple terms, attachment is the desire to be in contact with or in close proximity to another person or thing. Parents and children who are positively and strongly bonded want to be with one another. Their attachment keeps them in contact or in close proximity to one another. This is especially so when children are young.

The need to be in contact with or in close proximity to one another qualitatively changes as child and parent grow in their relationship and along personal dimensions. When the bond is strong and attachment is healthy, parents and children continue to seek and enjoy one another's presence through the duration of their relationship. The strength of this attachment behavior will ebb and flow as the relationship, the parent and the child grow and develop and change. Separation anxiety and separation discomfort will likewise ebb and flow and change in intensity as parent and child accommodate and adjust to the many circumstances that necessitate their separation as life proceeds. Nevertheless, few relationships will show the same strength of bonding and degree of attachment as the parent and child relationship, especially if it is a high quality relationship.

Although positive interaction is essential to the development of healthy connections between parent and child, relationships that experience a high degree in negative interaction still develop feelings of connectedness and attachment. Some relationships develop within the context of a great deal of maladaptive or psychopathological behavior. Such individuals are connected to one another, but their bond and attachment may be highly maladaptive or pathological. The bond may be weak or it may be strong but it exists nonetheless. This is why children who have been removed from parental care because of abuse or neglect still suffer the trauma of separation and want to know when they will go home to their parents. Indeed this is a confounding predicament for child welfare professionals.

The strength of the bond and degree of attachment is illustrated through the use of certain dilemmas I have posed to my students who are happily married or have a special relationship with another adult and also have children of their own. One such dilemma is the burning house dilemma. How would you respond, if faced with the following predicament?

The Burning House Dilemma

You arrive home late one evening to find your house on fire. Your spouse or special person and child are in the home and have been overcome by fumes and are unconscious and therefore are unable to escape. The fire is raging. You will be able to enter the house in time to save one but not both. Which one will you chose to save?

This is a difficult choice to make indeed! It is a heart wrenching one to be sure! You do not have time to rationalize or weigh the pros and cons. You must act and you must act quickly. Whom will you save?

Some people make this choice quickly. Others agonize over it. Some even become angry with me for posing such a question. This is the most difficult of dilemmas. What is your choice? How will you act? Make your choice before you read further.

It has been my experience that in over 90% of the cases, the parent chooses to save the child. In real life comparable situations (a burning house, a sinking boat, an automobile accident, etc.), parents choose to save their child first in almost all instances. Spouse, friend, and others take a second position to the child. Such dilemmas, real or imagined, support the notion that the strength of the bond and degree of attachment for parent and child is usually greater or at least equivalent to other significant interpersonal relationships.

After having restated the latter point, it must be pointed out that there is also a qualitative and quantitative difference between the strength of the bond and the degree of attachment that the parent experiences as compared to what the child experiences. The parent is connected to the child differently. The child is connected to the parent differently. These connections are qualitatively and quantitatively different. The degree of difference will vary and be influenced by each person's individual place in his own respective life cycle. Nevertheless, the parent is connected to the child differently (qualitatively) than the child is connected to the parent. Furthermore, the degree or extent (quantitative) of their connectedness is also different.

Burning House Delemma Revisited

To illustrate this difference, consider the burning house dilemma once again. However, this time your parent and your child are the two occupants and you must choose one to save. Which one will you choose? Your parent or your child?

Make your choice before you read further.

When posed with this variation, most parents will choose to save their child. This suggests that parents may be more strongly connected to their children than they are to their parents. Individuals who do not have children of their own are inclined to choose significantly differently. Why do you suppose? Might it be a matter of ego investment? Do parents have greater vested interest in their child than in their parents? I believe so. But, this may not be an easy pill for parents to swallow.

By similar comparison, take the case of the three-year-old attending nursery school for the first time. He may want to stay with and cling to the parent more than the parent wants him to do so. However, in contrast some parents would have mixed feelings if the child were to separate easily and quickly from the parent and join the other three-year-olds in play. Some parents might wonder if the child loves them.

So are the differences in the strength of the bond and the degree of attachment for the child and parent respectively. They differ depending on where each is in his or her respective life cycles and the nature of their relationship with one another. They can never be equal;

therefore, we must accept and understand these differences. This is the same as realizing that we do not love everyone equally or the same. We love each person differently. We too must also accept and understand this difference. It is the inevitable outcome of the unique type of interaction we have with each person. Viva la difference!

Contingency of Responsiveness

The behavior of the parent or the child is contingent or dependent upon the behavior of the other. The responses or responsiveness of the child is influenced by what the parent does or does not do. Likewise, the responses or responsiveness of the parent is contingent upon the way the child responds to parental care giving, etc.

The degree and/or quality of responsiveness is also contingent upon the behavior or responses of the other. A parent who provides gentle care and handles the child with skill and confidence will typically elicit a good response from the child. A parent who handles the child roughly and provides care in a clumsy unskilled manner may find that the child responds with stiffness and anxiousness.

However, this is not a one way street. The response behaviors do not originate solely with the parent. The infant for example may have a heightened sensitivity to touch and respond in an atypical manner. Normal care and handling may cause discomfort in the child and he may respond to normal handling in an adverse way. The child's atypical response may then cause a variety of thoughts and feelings that may cause the parent to behave in a guarded fashion. Such guardedness on the part of the parent may cause further anxiety and discomfort in the child. Hence, the response pattern that evolves from this interaction is cyclical and may propel interaction in a less desirable direction.

Reciprocity of the Relationship and Interaction

As suggested in the previous paragraph, parent and child interaction moves back and forth between them. This interaction is like a two way street; there is movement in both directions, simultaneously. There is give and take on the part of both. One smiles; the other feels joy and satisfaction. One responds negatively; the other experiences the impact in a negative fashion. The effects they have on one another are reciprocal. The parent and child relationship is reciprocal.

All love relationships are reciprocal. We satisfy and we are satisfied within the context of our love relationships. If interaction is unilateral, that is, if we give but do not receive something in return, then we "fall out of love." When we do not receive from a relationship what we need to grow and develop positively, we stagnate. The relationship is stagnant. Relationships that continue without reciprocity are not love relationships. Call them infatuations, idolizations, indentured servitude. Call them what you may, but do not call them love relationships. A loving relationship must be reciprocal for us to have loving thoughts and feelings.

Mutual Adaptation and Mutual Regulation

The parent and child engage in a process of mutual adaptation and regulation. If the infant is permitted to determine its own intake, the parent adapts to the child's need and routine and the parent permits the infant to decide when and how much it will consume. The parent is learning to adapt to the child's needs and rhythms. The child's needs and rhythms regulate or establish the parameters for parental behavior. In order to be responsive to the infant's needs, the parent learns to put some of his or her desires in second place or temporarily on hold.

Likewise, there may be times when the parent may not be able to or not want to respond immediately to the infant's requirements and so the infant must adapt to those circumstances and wait. The infant is being regulated by the parent and is learning to adapt to a situation that requires new behaviors on the part of the infant. The infant is learning to wait and manage his own behaviors as he makes this adjustment or adaptation to parental behavior. In this fashion, the infant is developing coping skills. As he sucks on a teething ring or babbles to himself while waiting for the response he desires, he learns to entertain himself constructively; he learns to depend on himself for management of the situation.

Priority

The parent is the child's first teacher. We must remember this and respect this. The parent's influence is first and foremost and consequently will influence the child's development in all areas, especially early development. By the time the child begins school, the parent's influence on relationship development, language, interests, object orientation, task orientation, career choice, demeanor, and much much more is well established.

Recall the concept of reciprocity. For the parent, this is usually the first relationship where someone is totally dependent upon the parent and that person (the child) has a profound influence on the parent. The parent, realizing the seriousness and importance of this responsibility, may make changes in attitude and behavior. The parent may say to himself or herself, "I am a parent now. My child is dependent on me. I have to begin behaving like a parent."

Pervasiveness of Influence

Parents potentially influence almost every aspect of the child's development in significant and in subtle ways. This influence occurs first within the context of the family unit but soon expands and reaches outside of the home environment. Parents potentially influence the child's use of media (T.V., books, magazines, records, etc.), his social relationships, his exposure to social, cultural, and religious institutions, professional and vocational options, and generally very much of the child's total experience.

The child in turns exerts a similar influence. The child will significantly alter the parent's personal development, life and living. The child has an equally pervasive influence on the parent. Our children will influence where we choose to live, our living arrangements, personal and marital satisfaction, feelings of success and competence, and much much more.

27

Duration of the Relationship

Parent and child interaction usually extends from birth of the child, through maturity, to death of one, and beyond. The parent and child relationship is typically one of the longest lasting interpersonal relationships, often outlasting the spousal relationship. The marital relationship may be terminated by divorce or death, but the relationship with the child remains.

For some, parent and child interaction begins even before birth. For women especially, the relationship may have its start during pregnancy as the female is significantly influenced and changed by the physical and psychological changes of pregnancy. Women can be found patting or stroking their abdomens during pregnancy and engaging in conversations with their unborn child.

Fathers can and should be involved during this period and not excluded. When included, fathers can also be found patting or stoking the abdomens of their pregnant mates and engaging in similar conversations with their unborn child. The father's participation in child birth classes may be of significant importance. Data from research investigations show the positive impact such participation has on not only the father's connection to the child at birth but also on his connection to his spouse. These behaviors and involvements significantly influence the bonding process and affect the degree and quality of attachment at birth.

For some, relationships begin before conception takes place. Prospective parents plan their pregnancy, and imagine what parenthood and their child will be like. They may decide on a name and begin to renovate a room so it will be ready for the child's arrival. Many plans, big and small are made. Many dreams are transformed into reality in due time. Relationships are being established. Yes, before conception.

Early childhood experiences are a factor for some parents, especially for females. Our young children engage in play where they take on the role of parent. It is during these play situations that they in part learn to be nurturing, provide care and supervision, and take on the parental perspective. In effect, they are learning to parent. It is especially important for early childhood professionals and parents to be mindful of this phenomenon, for we can guide children in their play and help them learn to be nurturing, caring, and a host of other important qualities essential for good parenting.

The parent and child relationship may continue beyond the death of one. Individuals who have a deceased parent may continue to be influenced, positively or negatively, by the relationship they shared. We sometimes consult our deceased parent, who when alive was a guiding force. We wonder what advice might have been given. We imagine the response and sometimes act upon it. Likewise, we curse a deceased parent, who was often critical, especially of our mistakes. We can hear the criticism. We feel its negative influence upon us. Even in death, our parent may make us feel small and incompetent.

Similar occurences take place between parents and their deceased children. We miss them. We wonder what they would be like now. We imagine what they would have accomplished. We speculate about the joy or frustration they would have brought to our lives. The joy makes us feel good inside. The anticipated frustration may make us feel guilty for having such a notion. The influence continues after death.

Continuity or Continuousness

The parent and child relationship is usually not interrupted particularly during early childhood, except for brief separations. Extended separations are of concern to child care professionals because of the possible negative effects of separation from the parent and the ensuing deprivation of parental care and nurturing.

Early childhood programs must accommodate and adapt to this factor. We must recognize and validate that these are normal feelings for the child and parent. We must make provisions for parent and child to become comfortable with their eventual separation from one another. We accomplish this not by excluding parents or mandating separation but by allowing parent and child to become comfortable with the new arrangements. This may mean that some parents will spend some time in the classroom

28

or close by within the building, so that both may learn to cope with their separation from one another at a comfortable pace with ample time allotted for each to acquire the coping skills and confidence needed.

Hospitalization of child or parent present special problems and concerns. When the child is hospitalized, "rooming-in" arrangements are made and these have beneficial results on both parent and child. When the parent is hospitalized, visiting hours are modified to accommodate the family, especially the young child. All feel better when they can visit for extended periods of time at their convenience and see for themselves that all are managing adequately. Hospitals that genuinely care about the status of their patients will make such provisions, because they not only have benefit for the patient but also for the hospital's personnel and services.

The continuity or continuousness of the parent and child relationship helps establish feelings of comfort, safety, predictability, and more. This continuity provides us with our anchor, our frame of reference, our knowing where we belong, to whom we belong and who belongs to us. This continuity influences and guides our interactions with one another over time. We come to rely on the other to behave in certain ways toward us and so we measure our own behavior accordingly.

Time and Energy Intensive

The total amount of time and energy expended by the parent during parent and child interaction, particularly individualized interaction, is usually greater than it is with other adults the child typically interacts. Similarly the parent's expenditure of time and energy is usually greater with the child than it is with other non-related children and adults with whom the parent interacts. The point is that children require and consume large amounts of parental time and energy.

Occasionally, one parent may not have a realistic appreciation of the time and energy demanded of the other parent, especially when parenting the very young child. The other parent may feel "short-changed" or deprived or jealous of the time and energy given to the child. This understanding must be worked on

and worked through. A helpful strategy is to promote a greater amount of sharing of parental responsibilities. This helps one parent appreciate more concretely the demands of parenting. This gives the other parent some respite from parenting. All benefit from shared parenting.

Diversity of Interaction

The parent shares more different and extensive situations with the child than do other adults. Our relationships with our children typically involve greater variety of interaction than our relationship with other adults. We do more and different things with our children than we do with others. We share more and different experiences.

Parents diaper and feed. They care for the ill child, get vomited on, excreted on. They share the anxiety of the first hair cut, immunizations, dental visits, the first day of nursery school, day care or kindergarten. Parents go through the child's first date, the first rejection and love lost. They share success and failures, dreams achieved and dreams shattered. They support the child in marriage, childbearing and child rearing, separation and divorce, and much much more.

Reciprocally, the child shares more different and extensive situations with the parent than he does with his peers and other adults. It is the parent that is present and accounted for when things go well and when things go not so well. In good relationships, we learn that we can count on or rely on our parents in almost all matters, because we are very important to them. Good parents do not tell their children that it is not their department and refer to another. They attempt to help in any and all areas to the extent that they are able and guide their child to others when matters require more expertise.

Intensity

The degree of involvement between parent and child is usually greater for each than it is with others with whom they interact. This involvement may be hostile or loving. It may be healthy or unhealthy. It may be mutually supportive or antagonistic. Regardless of the nature and quality of parental involvement with the child, it is nonetheless typically intense. Feelings of love, hate, admiration, scorn, and so forth are intense feelings. We love no other the way we love our children, nor are we so easily upset and moved to anger as when our children behave in certain undesirable ways. No one is more unfair in the child's eyes than the parent who will not allow the child to have his way.

Consistency or Sameness

Parents and children develop consistent patterns of behaving with one another. These patterns emerge as each behaves more or less in the same way in relation to each other. These patterns of interpersonal interaction create a certain consistency or sameness in how parent and child interact with one another. Each is able to predict how the other might typically behave. Each can predict what the other is thinking and what each might say in a given situation. Each measures his own behavior in relation to how the other is expected to behave. Consistency in interaction makes this possible.

Variability

Great variability exists in parental care of children. This varies from extremes of parental neglect, abuse and exploitation to extremes of parental acceptance, positive involvement and growth enhancing stimulation. Likewise, children may show significant variations to how each responds to basically the same kind of treatment. To a given interactional situation some children respond with great joy and enthusiasm, others with indifference, and still others with great annoyance. There is obviously great variability in the quality of the parent and child relationship and the responses to parent and child interaction.

Responsibility

Parents, children and society recognize that the parent has primary responsibility for the child in terms of his care, supervision and general behavior. This responsibility is not readily given up by the parent nor nonchalantly taken away by social institutions which have the capability to do so.

Parental rights, as well as responsibilities, are often regarded as primary and often take precedence over children's rights, which are typically regarded as secondary at best. Many social institutions are designed to preserve this relationship first and foremost. Case work decisions, Family Court judgements, etc. are often biased in favor of the parent. This state of affairs has necessitated the appointment of a "child advocate" to participate in such decisions and serves as the child's legal representative to minimize the biased nature of many of these proceedings. The attitude of our culture in general shows a highly biased attitude in favor of the parent. Typically people will believe the parent before they will believe the child's account of a situation.

Parents are often granted these special rights, privileges, and considerations because it is widely accepted that the parent bears major responsibility for the child's upbringing. Such responsibility, it is believed, should yield comparable rights, privileges and special considerations, which accrue to the parent.

In conclusion, these are the salient attributes that characterize the psychological parent and child relationship. Such attributes may also be found in other important interpersonal relationships but often not to the same degree or intensity. As stated at the end of Chapter 1, the establishment of a psychological relationship is of primary importance to the success of any parent and child relationship. Once established, it must be maintained at a particular level of quality; for it is the quality of the psychological parent and child relationship that forms the foundation for successful parenting. The quality of this relationship will significantly influence parental effectivenesss, which is the focus of the next chapter.

Through the remainder of this book, any reference to the parent or the parent and child relationship shall imply either a psychological parent or psychological relationship, unless otherwise noted.

References

1. Goldstein, J., Freud, A., and Solnit, A. *Beyond The Best Interest Of The Child* (New York: The Free Press, 1973).

2. Schickendanz, J., Schickendanz, D., and Forsyth, P. *Toward Understanding Children* (Boston: Little Brown & Company, 1982).

Activities

1. Identify the person you regard as your *primary* psychological parent and explain why this person has primary status.

2. Identify the person you regard as your *secondary* psychological parent and explain why this person has secondary status.

3. If applicable, identify the person you regard as your tertiary psychological parent and explain why this person has *tertiary* status.

4. Do you believe the concept of the psychological parent should or should not be applied in decisions of child custody or child placement? Explain your position.

5. List some attributes, features or aspects that characterize parent and child relationships of good quality.

6. List some attributes, features or aspects that characterize parent and child relationships of poor quality.

7. Explain or describe the attributes, features or aspects you have identified in 5 and 6.

8. Explain why you consider these productive or counterproductive to the parent and child relationship.

9. Explain or describe what in your personal or professional experience supports your point of view?

Chapter 3

Factors Influencing Parental Effectiveness

There are many factors which influence the establishment of the psychological parent and child relationship and help to maintain it over time. Once firmly established, these same factors will continue to influence the ongoing growth and development of the relationship and the quality of interactions that characterize it. Invariably, these same factors affect the parenting process and overall parental effectiveness.

PARENTAL EFFECTIVENESS

Effectiveness is the ability to produce a desired effect. Parental effectiveness is the ability to parent effectively thereby producing a desired effect with reference to the child, the parent and their shared relationship. Some parents seem to enjoy greater success and satisfaction in parenting than others. These differences in success are the result of a complex interactive process involving many factors.

Effectiveness Is Subjective

Furthermore, success in parenting may be a highly subjective matter. For example, if I raise children that are secure enough to express their thoughts and feelings to me, even when they are contrary to my own views, I may believe that I have been succesful. However, another parent might consider my children highly opinionated brats, who have little respect for their parent. That person's view of my effectiveness as a parent might be very different from my own. Indeed, I may be regarded as a failure by that person.

Importance Is Relative

There are many factors which may influence parental effectiveness. Some of these may be considered more important than others with respect to the influence they exert on parental effectiveness. Some of these may even be viewed as essential to parenting success. When we use the word essential, we typically mean that which is necessary to success in parenting or that which is indispensable or a chief point or aspect of parenting or even a leading principle.

Some of these *essentials* might even be regarded or considered to be *prerequisite* to parenting. That is, they are required before one parents. When the words required or requisite are used, we are referring to that which is necessary or needed or indispensable. The prefix "pre" means these are required before a person actually begins the parenting process.

To ponder what is essential is to also ponder what qualities or attributes adults must possess in order to parent successfully. These are inextricable notions. In order to parent successfully, the adult must have some special attributes, which give the parent a decisive advantage in parenting. The possession of these attributes will maximize (but not insure) the parent's potential to parent successfully. The lack of one or more of these will minimize the parent's potential to parent successfully.

What do you consider essential? What qualities do you believe the parent must possess in order to be successful in parenting? Do you consider any of these to be prerequisites? Are these qualities inherent or acquired? What does your personal experience tell you about their relative importance?

FACTORS INFLUENCING PARENTAL EFFECTIVENESS

Four Categories of Factors

These many factors may be classified into four broad categories of factors. Each category contains many factors or variables, some with sub-factors. The importance of any one or more of these is relative. Nevertheless, the quality of the parent and child relationship and the relative success in parenting may be largely attributed to one or more of these.

Parental effectiveness in large measure is influenced by
  1.) characteristics of the child,
  2.) characteristics of the parent,
  3.) the stage of family development and the structure of the family unit, and
  4.) the many and varied situations or circumstances that the child and parent find themselves part of or influenced by.

Each of the many factors that may be involved, separate and apart from one another, may have significant influence on the relationship and the parenting process. For example, a parent who is hostile and impatient will have a profoundly different impact upon parent and child interaction than one who is nurturing and patient.

Likewise, a child who is temperamentally active and sleeps minimally will present a very different profile than one who is lethargic and requires frequent naps throughout the day.

A given parent and child relationship that is tainted with or disadvantaged by poverty may lack things that are regarded as given by one that is imbued with or advantaged by affluence. Single parenting may be a very different experience than co-parenting with a spouse who shares a large measure of parenting.

Dynamic Interaction

These factors in and of themselves may contribute significantly to parenting outcomes. Therefore, in no way is there any intent to minimize the singular or individual impact any of these may have. However, in order to have a more comprehensive understanding and accurate picture of the parent and child relationship and the parenting process, the dynamic, interactive consequence of these must be recognized. In global terms, the parent and child interact with each other within the context of the family unit. The parent, child, and family unit are part of a larger matrix or culture. All may be influenced in varying degrees by situational or circumstantial conditions that are part of their interaction with one another.

The dynamic interactive consequence of one or more of these factors influences interaction and the parenting process. The manner in which these variables interact and the dynamic result or consequence of that interaction will in large measure account for the subtle yet significant differences that can be observed in the parent and child relationship. These differences may be significant manifestations of the quality of a given relationship as compared to others when all else appears to be similar or when there are many other common variables.

Given these general observations, the effects that each factor has singularly and/or interactively is illustrated by the following diagram. Note that this diagram illustrates only the interactive relationship of the broad categories. Recall that each broad category contains many factors and sub-factors or variables which may vary significantly in influence from one parent and child relationship to another. This diagram does not illustrate the interactive relationship of particular variables. Nevertheless, some of these will be identified and discussed in this and subsequent chapters.

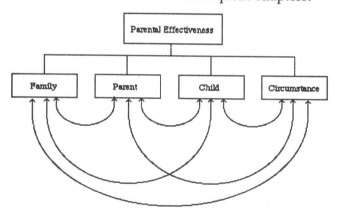

These factors are part of an interactive system. As in any system, there is a set of component parts. These parts are the broad categories with their many factors or variables. These component parts will interact with and influence one another to a greater or lesser degree. This dynamic, interactive process must be kept in mind because we shall look more closely at each of these in a more or less separate fashion in order to keep the ideas comprehensible and chapter size manageable. Separate chapters shall be devoted to each of these broad four categories of factors that directly influence parental effectiveness. However, before a closer look is taken at each of these, a brief and general view will be taken

of the developmental stages of the child, of the parent, and of the family and their dynamic, interactive relationship, as well as the situational or circumstantial factors which come into play.

Developmental Stages: Child, Parent and Family

The consideration of developmental stages applies not only to the child and parent but also to the family as an entity. The child and parent progress from one stage of development to another. The family unit has it own unique developmental life cycle also. The developmental status of the child, the parent and the family interact with each other in unique ways within the context of the larger culture. The developmental status of each may be synchronous or asynchronous, complementary or non-complementary in their interactions. Likewise, the needs of the child, parent and family may be synchronous or asynchronous, complementary or non-complementary.

Each will make the other more or less complete and contribute to feelings of success and satisfaction or feelings of failure and dissatisfaction. Each will have needs that will have to be satisfied by the other. Under favorable circumstances, the child's developmental status complements that of the parent and family and visa-versa. Within this complementary relationship, each has needs that the other is able to satisfy substantially. Each is able to give to the other what each needs. Thus each emerges with a sense of fulfillment and completeness. Each become more fully human and civilized.

Child's Developmental Stage

The developmental status of the child varies as he grows and learns. As the child's developmental status changes, his needs change and his behavior changes. The following are common categorical descriptions used to denote a person's developmental status. Each description suggests certain aspects about the person in terms of his characteristics and needs and what is important to each during these respective times or developmental periods.

Each framework serves as a guide to not only what the person is like but also what the person is likely to need in order to grow and develop well. Each framework may suggest ways of behaving on the part of the child, parent and culture that will maximize the growth and development of each. Similarly, each framework may suggest behaviors to avoid or not engage in as these are counterproductive to healthy growth and development. Erikson's and Piaget's stages are depicted below - next to the developmental periods - to illustrate how they coincide with each other temporally.

Parent's Developmental Stage

The developmental status of the parent varies with growth and learning. Along with these changes varies the parent's needs, capabilities, etc. The following common categorical descriptions are used to characterize the developmental status of the parent. Each description suggests certain aspects about the parent in terms of his or her characteristics and needs. These descriptions are not mutually exclusive. Often more than one term may be used to describe the parent as in the case of a single, adolescent, first-time parent. Two such alternative views are depicted below.

Developmental descriptions

adolescent parent
young adult parent
middle aged parent
elderly parent

Circumstantial descriptions

parent with partner
single parent (parent without partner)
first-time parent
experienced parent

Although these descriptions carry with them certain implications about the needs and capabilities of the parent, these inherent assumptions must be placed within a more comprehensive and meaningful framework. One such framework would be that of Erik Erikson. His theoretical framework is a *developmental* and *interactional* one. It looks at the developmental status of each person and how interaction with others produces growth and development that moves the persons involved in either a positive or a negative direction.

Out of this framework certain questions emerge about the parent. Where is the parent developmentally in terms of Erikson's notions of growth and development? To what extent has the parent accomplished the psychosocial tasks suggested by each of Erikson's stages? But most importantly, where is the parent especially in terms of the following Eriksonian stage descriptions?

Erikson's stages

Stage 5 - Identity vs. role diffusion/confusion
Stage 6 - Intimacy vs. isolation
Stage 7 - Generativity vs. stagnation and
    self-absorption
Stage 8 - Integrity vs. despair

Developmental periods	Erikson's stages	Piaget's stages
1. infancy	1. trust vs. mistrust	1. sensorimotor
2. toddlerhood	2. autonomy vs. shame & doubt	
3. pre-school	3. initiative vs. guilt	2. pre-operational
4. school age	4. industry vs. inferiority	3. concrete operations
5. pre-adolescent		
6. adolescent	5. identity vs. identity confusion	4. formal operations
7. young adulthood	6. intimacy vs. isolation	
8. middle adulthood	7. generativity vs. stagnation and self-absorption	
9. senior adulthood	8. integrity vs. despair	

Family Structure and Developmental Stage

A similar developmental and interactional viewpoint can be applied to the family, which is a growing and changing entity with substantially complex interactional outcomes. As individual members of a family grow and change, their characteristics and needs change within the family structure. These changes result in changes in the family unit. This dynamic process of change modifies the fabric of the family unit. Hence the family as a developmental entity changes as a consequence of individual change. As the family changes in its basic character, structure and composition, it in turn exerts an influence on the growth and development of individual family members. In effect, the family unit simultaneously is changed by and changes the members that comprise it.

Sometimes these interactive influences are profound as with the death of a family member. Hence the structure of the family is altered. The size of the family is reduced by one. If the deceased family member was one parent of a two-parent family, the family structure is changed from a two-parent family to a one-parent family. If the deceased is the parent in a one-parent family, the children may be left parentless. A grandparent's death may herald in the change from an extended family structure to a nuclear family structure.

But more often, changes are subtle as when the youngest child moves from dependency on the parent to dependency on the self. The child who grows in self-sufficiency will require less time and effort from the parent. This greater freedom for both alters the nature of their interaction and relationship. Subtle changes are often gradual and occur over an extended period of time. Consequently, their impact on individual and family development is often not pronounced and in many cases may even go unnoticed.

Simultaneously, the developmental status of the family is modified by these changes in interaction and relationships, because the family now has a child who is more self-sufficient. In the process the family unit is transformed from one with dependent children to one with independent, self-sufficient members. At a future period the child may even be more able to make a significant contribution to the family unit as he begins to help with family chores, etc. At such time the child's status within the family shall change in accordance with these contributions.

The family's needs, characteristics, capabilities, resources, etc. vary with these changes. A family that has experienced the vocational advancement of the parents may have at its disposal greater financial resources than it had when the parents were just beginning their careers. Conversely, a family may experience a significant drop in its financial resources if the main provider were to suffer a job loss, extended illness or some other incapacity.

These are just a few of the many situational or circumstantial factors or conditions that may affect individual development and family structure and/or development. Other concomitant gains or losses may be seen in status, self-esteem, social contacts, etc. Such gains or losses may have varying degrees of influence on family interaction and relationships. All of which, shall effect the status of the family as a unit to some degree.

One way of viewing the family's development is in terms of its life cycle. You will note that this is a child-oriented or child-centered way of defining the stages of family growth and development. There are other ways of viewing the family. This is but one framework.

Family life cycle

Stage 1 - Newly established family or
    the newly wed stage
Stage 2 - Childless family or
    primary couple stage
Stage 3 - Family with young children
    (infants, toddlers, and preschoolers)
Stage 4 - Family with school age children
Stage 5 - Family with pre-adolescent
    and adolescent children
Stage 6 - Family with young adult children
Stage 7 - Launching period: children are
    prepared for and begin to leave home
Stage 8 - Empty nest period (children absent)
    or secondary couple stage
Stage 9 - Single-parent empty nest
    (death of spouse)

Situational or Circumstantial Factors or Conditions

Death, separation, divorce, military service, job, etc. can result in separation of a married couple at any time during the family life cycle, thus creating prematurely a single-parent family situation. Likewise, death, separation, marriage, military service, job, education, etc. can result in the separation of the child from the parent or the separation of a child from his siblings.

The time at which a separation occurs, the nature of the separation, the meaning it has for those involved can greatly alter the nature and quality of family interaction and the type of interpersonal relationships that follow. The individual development of the child, parent and the family unit and their respective needs and characteristics interact in highly unique ways to produce highly unique outcomes.

People and families have many things in common. The commonality of our experiences explain why we are in many ways like each other in our thinking, feeling, and more. Yet people and families also have different ways of responding to and coping with life's offerings. These different reactions account for why people and families are like some but unlike others. Of course there are unique or extremely distinctive ways some people and families behave. These distinctive responses make each person or family unique or like no other.

Parents, children and families are influenced by a multitude of situational and circumstantial factors and conditions. These often originate outside of the family unit but nevertheless have significant influence on what transpires within the family between parents and children, between marital partners, and between siblings.

These factors and conditions include institutions like school, church, organized crime, etc. Also included here are sociological events and movements such as popular demonstrations, the feminist movement, the civil rights movement, etc. Acts of God and nature - flood, earthquake, and the like - play their decisive role in altering family life and living. Local, state and national conditions of unemployment, the availability of affordable housing, community resources and services, etc. are influencing factors. The general mood or attitude of communities and the culture as expressed in the incidence of suicide, alcoholism, drug abuse, prejuduice, violence, etc. influence happenings within the family unit.

Separate chapters shall be devoted to each of these four categorical areas as each area has a significant influence on parental effectiveness. In the specific chapters that follow, a more detailed discussion will be offered on certain parental characteristics, specific characteristics and needs of the child, family structure and family stages, and the situational and circumstantial factors or conditions which may affect family life and living and parent and child interaction.

COMPLEMENTARY STAGES COMPLEMENTARY NEEDS AND NEED SYSTEMS

Under ideal circumstances, the child and parent should be in complementary stages with respect to their personal development. Likewise, they will ideally have needs that are also complementary in nature. Children by nature are dependent upon and require adult care, supervision and nurturing. Normally the child needs to be and is usually ready to be parented. However children are not always ready or able to receive such care, supervision and nurturing because of the special nature of their circumstance. An extreme example would be infantile autism: The infant simply does not respond as the typical infant does to adult administrations. When such circumstances exist, parent and child interaction may be significantly affected.

With respect to adult development, adults must be ready to provide the care, supervision and nurturing that children require. Adults typically show this readiness when they begin to express genuine care and concern for others, especially young children. This attitude expresses the positive concern and major thrust of Erikson's seventh stage of psychosocial development - "generativity." Ideally parents will have entered the stage of generativity when they begin parenting.

Prerequisite for Parents: Readiness to Parent

However, many parents begin parenting before arriving at this point developmentally. A case in point is the adolescent parent, who would typically be primarily and substantially involved with identity and possibly intimacy issues and concerns. It does not mean that they are doomed. Some adolescent parents parent well and their children grow and develop well. In these cases, the adolescent parent has shown a capacity to behave in a generative fashion. *Therefore, the minimum requirement on the part of the parent would be a readiness and willingness to enter the stage of generativity and behave in ways that are consistent with its positive concerns and behaviors.*

Prerequisite for the Child: Readiness to Accept Parenting

Almost all children come into the world ready to be parented. Their very dependent nature necessitates that someone care for them. Usually they are ready to respond to these administrations.

However, some children come into the world not quite ready to receive the typical administrations of parents and to respond favorably to them. For example, some children are born prematurely and require special tratment, which may interrupt or delay the normal or typical interactions that often take place between parent and child when they come together in this new way.

Another example would be the child who is born with a significant handicap or other physical conditions that interrupts or delays normal parent and child interaction. Likewise, some children are born with fetal alcohol syndrome or drug dependency.

Infantile autism is another exceptional example. These exceptions modify typical parent and child interaction because the child is simply not ready for the normal adminsitrations of the parent.

However, under most situations the infant child comes ready to be parented. Degree of readiness will vary significantly among older children and their situation or circumstance.

Recall the discussion of the foster child and the step-child. Previously existing problems, attitude and so forth can influence the degree to which the child is ready to be parented and is able to respond appropriately to parenting.

Prerequisites for Family: Readiness to Receive and Integrate the Child

Also, readiness to receive the child for care and to integrate him into the matrix of the family must exist on the part of the family as a whole and on the part of the individuals that comprise it. Family members' willingness and readiness to do so will be largely influenced by their individual stage of development and the family's stage in the family life cycle and the structure of the family unit.

The family's developmental status, as well as the developmental status of individual family members will be an important influencing feature and will affect the family's acceptance and readiness for child rearing. Family structure will also affect this process and either facilitate or impede the child's acceptance and integration into the family unit. These variables shall be discussed more fully in other chapters.

Prerequisite for Society: Readiness to Support Parenting

At the societal level, a culture shows its readiness for child rearing by the provisions it makes which support the child rearing efforts of the families which comprise that culture. Conversely, a culture shows its lack of readiness by the provisions it fails to make or the obstacles it creates. A culture's orientation to children and families is important. The quality of life in any culture is significantly influenced by its support of children and their families. Cultures that care for their young and manifest that care in the support systems they create, enjoy a higher quality of life.

In summary, the child has a need to be parented. The parent has the need to parent. The culture has the need to support parenting if it is to survive and enjoy a high quality of life.

All benefit when all are ready, willing and able to enter into this important partnership and each contributes its fair share to the goal of raising healthy children. These respective stages and needs are considered complementary because each participant in the interaction requires the other for completion. Each become more whole as each interacts constructively with the other. Each becomes more fully human as each contributes to the other's personal growth and development. This perspective is regarded as a *developmental* and *interactional* one and shall be the point of view employed throughout the remainder of this text.

Activities

1. Identify and describe one parental characteristic or quality that you believe is essential for the parent to possess in order to be an effective parent.

2. Identify and describe one characteristic or quality a person should possess before becoming a parent.

3. Identify and describe one family characteristic or quality that you believe is essential for the family to possess in order to promote health growth and development of family members.

4. Identify your family's current stage of development using the family stage descriptions provided. Note that more than one stage description may apply.

5. Choose one parent-child pair and identify the stage of development that best describes each member of that one parent-child pair, using the stage descriptions provided.

6. With respect to the same parent-child pair, identify what you consider to be each person's most important need, characteristic, concern, issue or problem.

7. With respect to the same parent-child pair, are these needs, concerns, issues or problems being adequately met, addressed, solved or resolved, in your view? Explain why or why not.

Chapter 4

Parental Characteristics

OVERVIEW OF THE PARENTAL ROLE

Before reviewing these various parental characteristics, an attempt shall be made to place parenting in perspective. The role of parent is among the most significant of roles a person can assume in life. The impact the parent has on the child is most significant. That role will be describe in general terms. The framework for generalizing about the role of the parent is borrowed from Boyd McCandless and is taken from his analysis and description of the role and function of the school in American society. Since the school was given or acquired many of the functions originally performed by the nuclear or extended family, this framework is very consistent and compatible with parental and familial roles and responsibilities. Consequently, I believe, only minor variations will be noted between the two.

The parent's functional roles encompass four broad areas. They include roles pertaining to the following functions: **1)** maintenance, **2)** actualization, **3)** skills training, and **4)** cultural transmission.

Maintenance Function

The parent should engage in behaviors that maintain the child's well-being and promote his physical and non-physical growth and development. With respect to physical well-being, the parent should provide care, supervision, and protection, which will insure the child's physical growth and development and safety. This involves many behaviors which include assuring that the child receives proper physical care, diet, medical preventive care and treatment as required, and that the child's physical environment is safe. The many parental behaviors involved are intended to

43

maintain the child's physical well-being or safety and generally promote physical growth and development.

With respect to non-physical well-being, the parent should provide care, supervision and protection that will maintain the child's emotional and social well-being. The parent should provide an environment that is happy, challenging and self-fulfilling to the child. The emotional climate or atmosphere of the parent and child relationship and familial setting are important to the child's psychosocial-emotional growth, development and well-being. Parental behaviors that help the child "feel" safe, cared for, loved, and trustful will also maintain the child's non-physical well-being and promote his non-physical growth and development over time.

Actualization Function

In a climate that maintains the child's physical and non-physical well-being, the child is also to be helped to become all he is capable of becoming in positive ways. This is self-actualization as Abraham Maslow intended it. The parent engages in behaviors that are intended to help the child achieve personal happiness, self-acceptance, realistic self-esteem, pride in himself, pride in his individual accomplishments and capacities, and the ability to make the most of his potentialities.

The parent helps the child achieve self-actualization in part through using non-contingent positive reinforcement and unconditional positive regard. This simply means that the child is accepted as a worthwhile individual, is liked rather than disliked, and although the child may be reprimanded or punished for what he does or does not do, he is not reprimanded or punished for what he is. It also means that confidence in the child is expressed as is confidence in his potentialities even though the child may flounder or even regress.

The child's individual goals are not blocked if they are positive or constructive goals, even though these goals may not be highly regarded or desired by the parent. Nonetheless, the parent gives encouragement and support. What the child has to say, what he thinks or feels is regarded as worthwhile by the parent. The

parent does not attempt to negate or invalidate the child's thoughts and feelings even though the parent may have to provide another point of view for the child to consider in order to help the child grow in a healthy manner.

Skills Training Function

The parent endeavors to help the child acquire and develop the skills needed to function successfully in society. Since the school plays a major role in helping the child learn to read, write, and compute, the parent essentially plays an encouraging and supportive role with respect to the acquisition of these skills. However, the parent plays a major role in helping the child acquire and develop the social or interpersonal skills necessary for getting along with people and learning how to be a constructive member of society. These skills are often referred to as "prosocial" skills.

Since the parent is the child's first teacher, training in this area is initially provided in the home setting as the parent attempts to help the child learn how to get along with family members and become a constructive member of the family unit. Learning to share, to be helpful, to be considerate of others, to express one's thoughts and feelings positively and constructively, to be assertive, to be mindful of others' rights, to be independent, to be responsible are some of the many skills or prosocial behaviors the parent attempts to help the child acquire and develop. These skills will help the child become both a helpful and a competent member of the family unit and the society at large.

Even though the parent may come to rely on the school and other social institutions to provide assistance in these matters later in the child's development, the parent maintains primary and major responsibility for helping the child develop the social and interpersonal skills required for competent functioning.

Cultural Transmission Function

The parent intentionally or unintentionally imparts or transmits the culture to the child. This includes the culture of the society at large and the culture or sub-culture of the family unit. The parent transmits his or her knowledge and interpretation of the culture as he or she has come to know it, its traditions, history, beliefs, values, expectations, etc.

At one level the American parent helps to make Americans of her children. At another level, the parent helps to make hyphenated Americans of her children by attempting to preserve in varying degrees the uniqueness and diversity of the child's ethnic origins. In so doing, the parent imparts a major American cultural value by seeking to impart the commonalities of the greater American culture and yet valuing and preserving the diversity of the child's ethnic origins.

In a given American family, the children are exposed to the greater American culture and their ethnic sub-culture simultaneously to a greater or lesser degree. For example, the Jewish-American family may participate in the non-religious customs and pageantry of the Christmas holidays while simultaneously practicing the religious customs associated with Hanukkah. By this participation, the child simultaneously develops his American and Jewish identity.

PARENTAL CHARACTERISTICS

Parents possess many characteristics or attributes or liabilities that are directly involved in their parenting efforts. The possession of some are beneficial. The possession of others are not beneficial. Some change over time while others may remain relatively unchanged. Some characteristics are part of who the parent is physically, intellectually, psychologically, socially, emotionally, morally, spiritually, and so forth. Some of these attributes are acquired or learned and others are unlearned or genetically determined. These variables include but are not limited to such things as attitudes, values, beliefs, expectations, thoughts, feelings, physical health, mental well-being, knowledge, and skill.

Parental Feelings

There are many feelings that are associated with parenting. Some are productive and some are counterproductive. Some are positive and some are negative. Some feelings are intense and others are minimal. Of the many feelings that fill the landscape of parenting, *love is primary and paramount.*

Parental Love for the Child

Children need adults who love children. Love for the child by the parent includes feelings of affection, strong liking, good will, benevolence, charity, devotion, strong attachment, delight, admiration, caring, and concern. The parent's ability to give or express love for the child in appropriate ways will greatly influence the very special love relationship that exists between the parent and the child. Likewise, the parent's ability to receive expressions of love for the parent by the child is equally important. The parent and child relationship is a love relationship. They are not acquaintances or friends who merely like one another. They are people who share an intimate relationship. They are people who love and need one another.

Love between the parent and the child, in part, is the consequence of ongoing care and supervision provided to the child by the parent. This love is nurtured by the child who responds appropriately or positively to parental care and expressions of love. A noted child psychiatrist, Richard Gardner points out that a human relationship cannot be called "loving" if it is one-sided. Both parent and child must be able to give and receive love appropriately and adequately. This notion underscores the reciprocal nature of parent-child love.

Parental Expression of Love and Affection

Young children are concrete in their view and understanding of the world and their relationships. Therefore the parent's love for the child must be expressed in concrete not abstract ways. Children need words and deeds that express parental love in ways that children can understand. Children need to be touched with tenderness, hugged and kissed. Children need to be told that they are loved and that they are special to the parent. Children need to be told they are valued and prized. Parental behavior needs to support these words in concrete ways. Children want their parents to play with them, watch them perform, teach them how to do certain things that the child values. Children want their parents engaged in their lives. They need contact with their parents.

Quality and quantity: Quality of interaction is important but children need appropriate expressions of parental love and affection in sufficient quantity. Parental absence or low availability is counterproductive to assuring children that they are loved. Parents who have limited contact with their children because of work or other bonafide reasons, may have at the base of this outside commitment, strong love, caring and a desire to provide well for the child. However, children's preference would be typically to have contact with the parent, even at the expense of things that make life somewhat better materially. Children grow best with an abundance of psychological comfort. Physical comfort is no substitute.

Parental Unconditional Love

Children are loved because they are worthwhile human beings who happen to be in our care. We value children because they are people and because they are mankind's future. They are special in many ways and we love them for that. Children should not have to behave well to be loved well. They do not have to have the same point of view as their parents to be loved. Children must be loved unconditionally.

Parental love for the child should be substantially or predominantly unconditional. Realistically, we cannot expect parental love to be completely unconditional. Obviously, we have more positive regard for the child when he is cooperative rather than uncooperative. Our thoughts and feelings are more favorable when children follow our good advice. But they will not always be cooperative. They will not always take our advice and act on it constructively. Yet we love them, and care for them, and want what is best for them, because our love for them is substantially unconditional.

They do not have to be perfect. We settle for good enough because we love them for the most part without condition. There are no strings attached. There are no preconditions.

There is no "pre-parenting agreement" entered into by parent and child. Yet, no parent loves the child completely unconditionally. Healthy parents understand and acknowledge this. However, a substantial portion of parental love and affection must be unconditional.

The Genuinely Loving Parent

Parents who have the capacity to give and receive "genuine" love in appropriate ways will greatly nurture the parent and child relationship. A large measure of genuine love is unconditional love. In *Understanding Children*, Richard Gardner describes genuine love of the parent for the child as follows:

> The genuinely loving father and mother frequently experience a warm inner glow when they are involved with the child. I say "frequently," because there are inevitable times when the parent will have hostile feelings toward the child. He enjoys giving the child pleasure, and the child's delighted response produces in the parent even greater joy. And the cycle spirals upwards. The loving parent is interested in the child's welfare and becomes upset when the child's health or well-being is endangered. He has found a healthy balance between what the child wants and what he thinks is in the child's best interest. He respects the child's requests but complies with them only insofar as it benefits the child that he do so. He does not consider the child indebted to him for the sacrifices and deprivations he may suffer in the child's upbringing, but considers the gratifications he derives from the *process* of child rearing to be his primary reward.
>
> The loving parent recognizes as well that his feelings toward the child are not pure affection, and he is comfortable with this ambivalence. He can accept the periods of hostility that the inevitable frustrations and resentments of child rearing often evoke, and he accepts too the fact that he may not be equally responsive to the child at different stages in their relationship. (Some parents do better with dependent infants, others with the school-aged, and others with adolescents.) Yet in spite of these variations in the intensity of this involvement, the loving parent still derives deep gratification from the various stages of the child's growth. He has pride in his youngster's accomplishments both because he has contributed to the child's ability to achieve them and because he is happy for the child's own gratifications regarding them. (p 32-33)

The Pseudo-loving Parent

Parents who are less able to or unable to express genuine love will resort to other modes

46

of expression. These other modes of expression, in part, are what Richard Gardner refers to as "pseudo-love" or "pseudo-loving mechanisms." Pseudo love contains a large proportion of conditional love.

> The pseudo-loving parent exhibits behavioral patterns that only ostensibly manifest affection but that basically do not. The deficient parent uses pseudo-loving mechanisms to conceal from himself and others his inability to provide his child with meaningful affection. There is no parent who does not exhibit, at times, one or more of these forms of interaction with his child. If, however, many of these patterns are present or if they are exhibited frequently, then there will probably be significant difficulty in the relationship between the parent and the child.
>
> The manifestations of parental pseudo-love described here do not exist in pure form; there is often significant overlap. In addition, a parent rarely exhibits only one of these mechanisms in isolation; rather one usually sees several in combination. Although a particular pattern originates with the parent, the child's behavior soon plays a significant role in determining both its perpetuation and the form it may take. In addition, constitutional factors may be operative. For example, an innately passive child is more likely to comply with a parental pseudo-loving maneuver than the child who is innately more aggressive. As the child grows older, the pattern becomes one in which both parties contribute to its perpetuation - complaints to the contrary notwithstanding. (p 34)

Richard Gardner describes a variety of common pseudo-loving behaviors which are counterproductive measures when engaged in frequently. Reading his book, *Understanding Children*, especially the first chapter, "Parent - Child Love" is strongly recommended.

The genuinely loving parent will do much to strengthen the bonds of love between the parent and the child. Furthermore, the parent will serve as a good role model for the appropriate expression of love and other closely aligned feelings. The child who lives with a genuinely loving parent will learn how to appropriately express his feelings of genuine love and affection.

The parent who is limited in her ability to show genuine love will minimize her potential to strengthen the bonds of love between the parent and the child. The parent will not only

serve as a poor role model for the expression of genuine love but also will provide the child with a prototype for interaction that will limit the child's potential to form healthy relationships should the child fashion himself after the parent.

The Effects of Psuedo-love and the Deprivation of Love

Richard Gardner confirms this perspective in his discussion of the effects of pseudo-love and the deprivation of love. He states in part the following:

> Most psychological disturbances that therapists deal with are, in part, the result of difficulties in the parent-child love relationship. Although many factors are involved in bringing about the various types of psychological disorders, most share in common the deprivation of parental affection.
>
> The parent-child relationship serves as a model for all the child's future involvements; and since the child tends to generalize, he will anticipate from others the same kinds of responses he received from his parents. If his relationship with his parents has been basically gratifying, he will tend to seek and anticipate similar such gratifications from others. On the other hand, if one or both of his parents profess affection but, either overtly or implicitly, reject the child each time he reaches out for it, he will come to distrust assertions of love and become anxious when they are offered. The psychiatrist Harry Stack Sullivan referred to this phenomenon as the "malevolent transformation." Ostensible benevolence becomes transformed into malevolence for the child has become conditioned to experience pain when affection is allegedly being offered. In extreme forms of rejection, where the parent is more overtly rejecting or abandoning, the child develops even stronger feelings of antipathy and alienation from people. Once again he generalizes from his experiences with his parents and assumes that others will react to him in a similar manner. The parent-child relationship, therefore, determines a whole range of possible degrees of involvement with others - from the intensely intimate to the very distant. (p 61)

The child who experiences insufficient genuine love and too much pseudo-love will be significantly handicapped in the interpersonal relationship realm. The child who experiences an abundance of genuine love and a minimal amount of pseudo-love will be advantaged as he establishes and maintains interpersonal relationships.

Children need an abundance of genuine love to grow and develop well. The effective parent does not and need not use deprivation of parental love and affection. Nor is it used to influence child behavior. The effective parent's love and affection helps establish rapport which forms the foundation for constructive parental influence in guiding and influencing the child's behavior. <u>But love alone is not enough!</u>

Parental Knowledge, Skill and Personhood

Success in any endeavor can be largely attributed to a person's knowledge and skill with respect to that endeavor. This is also true of parenting. However, another variable must be considered when addressing interpersonal interaction of the parenting kind. Namely, who the parent is as a person or the parent's personhood will have significant influence on the parent's capacity to form a relationship and maintain it over time.

Personhood includes who a person is physically, intellectually, socially, emotionally, morally, and spiritually. Personhood includes the attributes and liabilities that are part of those characteristics which comprise or define who we are as people or which are collectively referred to as personality. Our personhood includes a constellation of factors which include but are not limited to our attitudes, values, beliefs, expectations, goals, thoughts, and feelings.

These three dimensions - parental knowledge, skill, and personhood - interact in varying and unique ways to influence parental effectiveness or success in parenting. In our closer look at these, please keep in mind that these parental attributes shall interact with the child, family, and situational or circumstantial factors while simultaneously interacting with one another.

Parental Knowledge of Child Growth and Development

The parent has much knowledge about many things. Some will influence parenting and others shall not. A parent who is a skilled carpenter may or may not be a skilled parent. A highly educated physicist may know little about children. A poorly educated parent may possess profound insight about how children grow and develop and what they need at various times throughout their development.

Children need adults who are knowledgeable of how children grow and develop. Children need adults who are sensitive to their needs and are aware that the needs of children change as they grow and develop. The knowledge base under consideration includes all aspects of children's growth and development. This includes understanding of the physical, intellectual, emotional, social, and moral growth and development of children. A parent who is knowledgeable of these many aspects is better equipped to parent. A parent who has limited understanding or insight is handicapped by this knowledge deficit.

Parents acquire what they know about children either *formally* or *informally*. What they assimilate is a function of the quality of the source and the parent's ability to learn and make use of what is learned. <u>The ability to use what is learned to promote the growth and development of the child is skill or the application of knowledge.</u>

Formal Sources of Knowledge

Sometimes knowledge is acquired through formal educational means. Classes in child development, parenting, child management, preparation for parenthood, etc. may be helpful sources of information to the parent or prospective parent. Career preparation in teaching, child care, nursing, pediatrics, social work, and other aspects of human services can also contribute to establishing an appropriate knowledge base for understanding children and parenting them successfully.

Sometimes this knowledge is acquired as an outcome, product or by-product of receiving a human service such as receiving guidance or counseling, rehabilitative services, psychiatric services, self-help group services, etc.

These and similar experiences are considered formal sources of knowledge concerning children and parenting. These various sources are considered formal sources because the person engages in an intentional and deliberate effort to acquire information that is regarded as helpful to the understanding of children and parenting.

Informal Sources of Knowledge

Not all knowledge is acquired as a deliberate effort with the intent to learn something specifically related to children. Some sources of information about children and parenting are acquired informally. That is, there is no deliberate effort to engage in the process of learning in order to acquire information or add to an existing knowledge base. People nevertheless acquire knowledge of how children grow and develop informally as a consequence of or as a by-product of other experiences or endeavors. These experiences include but are not limited to being parented, providing care and supervision to the children of others as in the case of looking after siblings or baby-sitting for relatives, friends, and others.

Recipient parenting: One of the primary informal sources of information about children and parenting is having been parented. Recipient parenting is being or having been on the receiving end of another's parenting behavior. The way others parent and have parented us will influence the way we parent or shall parent to some degree. Certainly the quality of that parenting will have a significant influence on a person's parenting behavior. The model that is provided to us by our parents as they parent us plays a profound role in our ability to parent. If that model is a good model, we are advantaged by it. If that mode is a poor model, we are disadvantaged by it. Nevertheless, a substantial portion of what each person knows about parenting is acquired indirectly as a recipient of parenting. What a person knows about children and parenting is often a reflection of the kind of parent that person has and the kind of parenting that person has received.

It is not surprising then that we often find ourselves parenting our own children in ways that are similar to the ways we were parented by our parents. Our parents serve as models, for the better or for the worse. We often model or imitate their parenting behaviors, intentionally or unintentionally. If our parents were good models, both we and our children are benefactors. If our parents were poor models, both we and our children suffer the consequences.

To some extent we parent well because we were parented well. In part we may parent poorly because we were parented poorly. Certainly it is true that some people who were parented poorly break free of their poor parental model and raise their children in a most competent and capable manner. Likewise it must be acknowledged that having a good parental model does not insure that one will parent well when one becomes a parent. There are many intervening and influencing variables that either maximize or minimize the basic influence the parental model has had on each of us.

Nonetheless, each of us is certainly influenced in some measure by the type of parenting received. The extent of that influence partially explains why some people seem to parent rather "naturally" and are effective without a great degree of forethought and deliberation. Likewise, this also explains why we often say or do the same things our parents said and did even though we may have strongly vowed not to say or do such things to our children when we become parents.

Child care experience: Another major informal source of information is a person's experience in caring for children. This experience may be significantly varied and have different degrees of child care responsibility and opportunities for learning about children and parenting. Within the context of the family of origin, a person may have responsibility for the care and supervision of younger siblings. Likewise, a person may have baby-sitting experience wherein information is gained in the care and supervision of non-sibling children who may or may not be related.

Job training and employment opportunities involving children are also experiences that provide the opportunity to learn about children and apply that knowledge. Of course the most direct and realistic form of child care experience is the actual parenting of one's own children. However, it must be kept in mind that this experience is very specific and may not be representative, in certain instances, of the care of children in general. For instance, different children of the same parent within the same family structure can present very different parenting challenges. Regardless of the quantitative and qualitative differences of these varied experiences, each represents a legitimate informal source of information about children and the parenting process.

Parental Knowledge and Behavior Are Connected

The possession of or lack of knowledge pertaining to children will have an effect upon parenting. For example, knowing that children do not gain control of sphincter muscles much before eighteen months of age would suggest that toilet training (specifically bowel training) must wait until the child at least has conscious control of the muscles in the bowel area. Not knowing this might result in a parent attempting to toilet train the child long before he has the physical capability to behave as desired. Beginning such training before the child is ready generally leads to frustration on the part of both parent and child.

Parents must have an appreciation for the concept of "readiness" and a sensitivity to the child's individual state of readiness. Readiness is influenced by many factors and exists on different levels. These varied levels of readiness must be considered by the parent. They must complement one another if the child is to learn to behave in a manner that is desired.

For example, the child may be physiologically mature, enough to manage and control bowel movements. However, the child may not be emotionally ready to cooperate with the parent or have a willingness to voluntarily give up what is such an intimate part of him. In this case, the child is ready at one level or in one domain but not in another. Consequently, the child is not ready to be toilet trained. The child needs to be helped or motivated to cooperate with parental wishes and separate from his personal product. Not until the child has this willingness will a state of readiness to be toilet trained exist. If the child is not ready, the parent may simply have to postpone this requirement until such time the child is ready.

The parent must be knowledgeable of the growth and development of children in general and sensitive to the nuances of the individual signs of readiness, and other significant milestones in children's growth and development. But knowledge is not enough!

Parental Skill

Skill is the application of knowledge. Children need adults who have the ability or skill to use their knowledge to promote the growth and development of children and meet their needs adequately and appropriately as they progress. Children need adults who are sensitive to the cues or signals that children send out and who are able to respond to these messages appropriately. This ability is known as "parental responsiveness." Adults who use their knowledge to understand children and what children are communicating through their actions are better able to apply knowledge in a way that benefits the child and parent. This ability is skill. Skill is the application of knowledge.

The parent must have the skill to use what is known to promote growth and development. For example, the parent may ignore what she knows about toilet training and begin toilet training long before the child is ready. For whatever reason, the parent lacks the ability to use what is known about children in general and the child in particular. Consequently, she is unable to promote the child's growth and development or enhance her position in relation to the child. A skillful parent will use her knowledge to benefit the child and in turn will benefit herself. But skill is not enough!

Parents must be able to provide adequate and appropriate care and supervision to the child. This includes basic care and supervision that is intended to keep the child healthy, safe, and to minimize risks to the child. Consequently parents feed, clothe and keep their children clean. They arrange for medical care and treatment when needed. They engage in preventative practices to avoid illness, accident, and unnecessary or unwanted, potentially harmful circumstances from confronting the child.

Child Care and Child Rearing

Parents provide a wide array of services to their children to keep them healthy, safe, and growing well. This is basic child care. However, a full belly is not enough! Children do not live by bread alone. A clean and dry bottom is not enough! Children do not thrive simply because they are squeaky clean. A safe physical environment is not enough! Children must "feel" emotionally safe also. That which goes beyond basic child care is child rearing.

There are many other things that parents must provide to their children in order to insure healthy growth and development in all areas of children's growth. The parent must have the capacity to implement and follow through with many important child rearing behaviors that go beyond the provision of basic care and supervision over an extended period of time. In addition to providing basic child care, the parent must provide consistent and reliable guidance, moral training, values acquisition and development, education, etc. The etceteras are the many things that parents do beyond providing basic care and supervision and maintaining the child's physical safety. The etcetera is the substance of child rearing as contrasted to child care.

Parental Follow-through With Child Rearing Behaviors

Having knowledge and skill is not sufficient. The parent must also have the ability to implement and follow through with certain child rearing behaviors. For example, a parent who recognizes that a child is ready to be toilet trained must have the skill to provide the guidance and training that is required. Being able to recognize the signs that indicate the need for a bowel movement is necessary. Being able to help the child recognize these signs in himself is part of the training. Helping the child express his need once he has learned to recognize these signs in himself is also required. The parent must be able to help the child gradually assume greater responsibility for self-care and skill in managing the many tasks required.

These and many more tasks are involved in helping the child manage and care for himself with respect to toilet training. The parent who is less skillful or less able to manage these varied aspects will be less successful at toilet training, even though a certain level of knowledge is presumed to exist. The parent who has the ability to apply what is known effectively has skill in parenting. But that skill must be applied over a period of time to achieve a desired effect. This sustained effort, along with its accompanying knowledge and skill, is

follow through. But follow through alone is not enough!

Parental Attitude

There are many attitudes associated with parenting. Some are appropriate and productive, while others are inappropriate and counterproductive. Our attitudes concerning children and parenting permeate what we do in relation to children. Therefore, children need adults who have the correct attitude. In fact, having the right attitude includes having a variety of closely related attitudes that effect our practices with children. There are four closely related attitudes: 1.) having a child-centered attitude, 2.) being person-oriented, 3.) being concerned about what is in the child's best interest, and 4.) being an advocate for the child.

A Child-centered Attitude

First, children need adults who are primarily child-oriented or child-centered rather than adult-oriented or adult-centered. A child-centered attitude is the right attitude. Parents who have a child-centered attitude understand that children are special human beings who have special needs and characteristics and require special consideration. These parents also understand that as children grow and develop, their needs and characteristics change. Because they understand that children are different from adults, child-centered parents will strive to understand where the child is developmentally and what he needs in order to grow and develop well.

The parent who "child-proofs" a home understands the nature of the very young child and makes accommodations that are intended to safeguard the child. This parent has a child-centered attitude. In contrast, another parent may insist that child-proofing the home is merely acquiescing to the child and may explain her position not to child-proof the house thusly, "Quite frankly, it's a lot of bull shit. The child has to learn to live in my house without always getting into things and touching this and touching that." This latter parent has an adult-centered or adult-oriented attitude. Such a view is not conducive to effective parenting.

51

A Person-oriented Attitude

Secondly, children need adults who are primarily person-oriented rather than thing-oriented. A person-oriented attitude is the right attitude. The parent who is person-oriented places higher value on people than on material things or possessions. Young children by nature are "mess-makers." They spill, bump, scratch, misplace, clutter, rearrange their environment. The healthy child does not do this with malice. It is merely how young children interact with their environment and learn. Recognizing this, the person-oriented parent attempts to create an environment that is fit for and responsive to the young child.

When things are unintentionally blemished, broken, or lost, the parent does not find cause to torment the child even when the item is a treasured one. Although the parent may be genuinely and legitimately upset, the parent strives to place the incident in proper perspective with higher value being placed on the child. The parent who is more highly oriented toward things and material possessions will have greater difficulty reconciling the incident.

In The Best Interest of the Child Attitude

Thirdly, children need adults who behave primarily in ways that are in the best interest of the child. Being primarily concerned with what is in the best interest of the child is the right attitude. What is good for the child is more important than what is convenient or easy or expedient for the parent. For example, it is easier not to discipline the child. Disciplining requires more time and energy than not doing so. However, the parent who is primarily child-centered will discipline the child because the parent realizes that it is in the child's best interest both immediately and in the long term.

The parent who is predisposed to ease may not discipline the child when required. This parent is not behaving in a way that is in the best interest of the child. The parent who repeatedly avoids disciplining the child may help create a child who is demanding and unmanageable. Such unacceptable behavior may cause others to avoid interaction with the child and result in his social isolation. This is hardly in the child's best interest.

An Attitude of Child Advocacy

Fourthly, children need adults who advocate for them. Children need adults who are willing and able to work on their behalf in order to obtain for them what they need to grow and develop well. The parent must be an effective advocate for the child both within and outside of the family context.

Advocating for the child within the home environment: Within the context of the family unit and family life, the parent must behave in ways that assure that the child gets what he needs to grow, develop, and learn well. This includes but goes beyond the basics of proper care and supervision. The parent must help the child gain access to family resources and fair treatment from other family members.

The parent may also have to protect the child against abuse, neglect or exploitation by other family members. The parent will have to intercede during sibling interaction on behalf of the child, when a sibling is harassing the child verbally and/or physically. The parent will have to intercede during parent and child interaction on behalf of the child, when the other parent has gone too far or overboard in punishing the child.

There are many other common circumstances that require parental intervention during the normal course of family interaction. Of course, there are extreme situations also involving such complex problems as child abuse, neglect, incest, etc. The extent that the parent can intervene successfully on behalf of the child is the extent to which the parent is an effective advocate for the child.

Advocating for the child beyond the home environment: The parent may have to advocate for the child outside the context of the family unit and family living. Within the context of the immediate neighborhood, the playground, the school, etc., the parent must also be willing and able to advocate for the child. The parent's ability to do so will assure for the child a safe environment; fair treatment; access to services; protection against abuse, neglect, or exploitation; etc. The parent who is willing and able to intercede on behalf of the child is an effective advocate for the child and has the proper attitude.

Having a child-centered attitude, being person-oriented, behaving in ways that are in the child's best interest, and being an advocate for the child is having the proper attitude. But simply having the proper attitude is not enough!

Parental Thoughts

Parents ponder and subscribe to many thoughts concerning the nature of children and the role of parenting. Some thoughts are appropriate and productive. Other thoughts are inappropriate and counterproductive. Some thoughts represent vestiges of the past while others reflect the most current thinking concerning children and parenting. Some thoughts reflect clear and healthy ideas concerning children while others reflect unclear and unhealthy notions.

The ideas, notions or thoughts that we have concerning children and parenting will create a certain mindset that will influence our behavior toward children. The parent who subscribes to the dictum, "Spare the rod and spoil the child," will raise the child accordingly. This parent's ideas about child management will invariably lead to the use of spanking and other forms of corporal punishment as a means of training the child. In contrast, the parent who does not subscribe to this idea will seek non-corporal and non-punitive means of managing and training the child.

Parents may have very different notions about child rearing and each will be influenced by these different ideas so as to develop very different means of managing and training the child. These diverse means will lead to qualitatively different kinds of interaction between the parent and the child. Each type of interaction will come to have a different feeling tone and meaning attached to it. Consequently, diverse notions of child rearing may not only result in qualitatively different modes of interaction but also result in qualitatively different feelings associated with parenting and being parented.

The parent who may have to spank the child frequently may develop a reservoir of hostile, angry feelings toward the child and parenting. The child who is the recipient of corporal punishment may also develop a reservoir of negative feelings toward the parent and toward being parented.

In contrast, the parent who is able to manage the child in non-punitive ways will be less inclined to develop an accumulation of such negative feelings. This parent is more likely to develop a reservoir of positive feelings of competence, cooperation, effectiveness, etc. concerning parenting and regarding the child. The child who is managed non-punitively is less inclined to develop negative feelings toward the parent about being parented.

These dissimilar feelings about parenting and being parented are the outcomes of parenting and being parented with very different mindsets.

Parental Values

Each person regards certain things as having great worth, utility, or importance. Such things we hold in respect, high regard, and admiration. These are the things we prize or value highly. A parent's values will influence many aspects of parenting behavior and will directly influence the goals parents have for their children's growth, development, and behavior. Some parental values are child-centered and some are adult-centered. This divergence of where the value is placed leads to significant differences in parenting behavior.

Child-centered Values

Some parental values are child-centered values. The value is focused on the child or predominantly associated with the child and is regarded as in the child's best interest. For example, a parent may value independence or self-reliance. This value may guide the parent to behave in ways that facilitate the acquisition of independence or self-reliance in the child. Such a parent will encourage the child to do for himself, choose for himself, and decide for himself and will positively reinforce the child's efforts to do so in a variety of ways.

When the child insists on doing something himself, the parent cooperates. When the child shows interest in deciding for himself, the parent guides the child through the decision making process. When the child is looking for a choice, the parent helps the child find an alternative that the two can live with happily. When the child seems ready for greater independent functioning, the parent will encourage the child toward that end.

When the child's actions do not turn out well, the parent will support the child and encourage the child to try again later. The values the parent has guides the parent's behavior toward a goal of greater independence and self-reliance in the child.

Adult-centered Values

Some parental values are adult-centered values. The value is focused on the adult or parent or predominantly associated with the parent and is regarded in the parent's best interest. A parent who has an adult-centered value may value dependence or reliance on the parent. Such a parent will not encourage the child to do for himself, chose for himself, or decide for himself. Rather, the child's behaviors that are dependent in nature will be reinforced and efforts on the part of the child to be independent or self-reliant will be discouraged and possibly even punished. The parent's underlying assumption is that it is in the parent's best interest to have the child remain dependent on the parent. Independent children may be perceived as threatening, challenging, time consuming, etc. Such are not convenient for the parent.

When the child comes to the parent to have things done, the parent cooperates. When the child shows hesitancy in deciding for himself, the parent will make the decision. When the child is looking for an alternative, the parent will provide the child with a choice the parent prefers. When the child seems ready for greater independent functioning, the parent will discourage such tendencies.

When the child's efforts toward independent functioning do not turn out well, the parent will be reassured that the child is not capable and this will cause the parent to continue to exercise parental domination over the child's choices, decisions, and behaviors related to independence and self-reliance. It may very well be more expedient, easier, and less stressful for the parent to maintain the child's dependence. This is perceived by the parent as being in the parent's best interest.

Parental Goals

People have various ideas of what a good child is or should be. In a general sense, these are the parent's goals or what the parent wants to achieve. As was suggested earlier, there is a certain value associated with that achievement or goal. Parental goals for their children involve how parents want their children to behave, think, feel, and believe. Some parents want their children to behave in a kindly and considerate manner towards others, think clearly and rationally, feel a sense of belonging to the family of man, and believe in man's capacity to solve human problems in a positive or constructive manner.

In contrast, some parents want their children to do it to someone else before it is done to them, to be mindful that people will take advantage of you or use you whenever possible, feel that people befriend others only for self-serving purposes and believe that man is incapable of solving human problems in a positive or constructive manner. Therefore, any means justifies the end that serves you best. Every man for himself... The survival of the fittest...

Such divergent goals will certainly lead to significant differences in parental behavior and parent and child interaction. The goals parents have in relation to raising their children and how they go about achieving these goals for child rearing have an important impact on the parent and child relationship and success in parenting. Success in achieving certain goals depends on many factors. Of great importance is the parent's capacity to select, implement, and follow through relative to these goals.

Four main components are involved in this process. They involve 1) the goals themselves, 2) the techniques parents believe in and use to accomplish these goals and values, 3) the parent's capacity to use these techniques effectively, and 4) the parent's sense of achievement in relation to these goals and values. Each of these shall be discussed herein.

Goals Vary as to Facility

Some goals are relatively easy to achieve. Other goals are somewhat more difficult to accomplish. Some goals which are more difficult to achieve are difficult for a variety of reasons. Some goals by their very nature are more complex and all-encompassing and may take years of interaction and learning to be accomplished by the child. Becoming a physician takes many years of education, considerable effort and motivation and ongoing support and encouragement by the parent. Similarly, the child must also make a considerable commitment in time and effort.

Learning to tie one's shoe, although significantly eventful at the time it is accomplished, requires considerably less time, effort and parental support and encouragement. Similarly the child makes a correspondingly less considerable commitment in time and effort to learning to tie his shoes.

Goals as Sources of Problems

Some goals may even cause problems for the parent or child or both. The parent who expects academic excellence for the child may have to monitor the child very closely and provide considerable tutoring if the child's ability and/or motivation does not match parental expectations. The parent may not only work very diligently at accomplishing this goal but also may feel frustration and disappointment if the child falls short of the parent's expectations.

From the child's perspective, the child may feel excessively pressured to perform above his ability and/or motivation level. He may experience frustration and anger toward the parent as a consequence of feeling the failure of not being able to meet parental expectations.

Goals Change in Value and Rank

Some goals change in value or desirability over the years. These changes are a function of the developmental level of the child, the parent, the family unit, and the social matrix of which they are a part. A parent with high housekeeping standards may have to make some accommodations in accordance with the age and development of the child. As the child grows and develops, he may become more capable of maintaining the house in accordance with parental standards.

A parent who has limited experience with children may not have a reasonable or realistic level of expectancy for the child. Such a parent might underestimate the capability of the child and initially behave over-protectively and thereby limit the child's behavioral opportunities. As the parent spends greater time with the child and converses with other parents, a more realistic level of expectancy may emerge. This might result in the parent behaving less over-protectively and providing more behavioral opportunities to the child. Thus the parent may change from emphasizing goals that are limiting to emphasizing goals which offer the child greater opportunity to accomplish things that are more appropriately suited to his developmental level and capabilities.

The family composition may alter parental goals in subtle or significant ways. A parent whose goal is to spend a great deal of time with the child in mutually satisfying activities may find that this may not be as possible because of family size, for example. A family with three or four young children may usurp most of the parent's time and energy providing basic care and supervision. The many activities the parent had planned for the children individually and in groups may no longer be as feasible for the parent given the family's composition and resources. Due to such constraints, the parent may have to make adjustments in this goal and learn to be satisfied with a lower level of involvement with the children.

The social matrix of which the parent, the child, and the family are a part will also affect parental goals. Changes in cultural values, beliefs, expectations, technology, etc. will influence parental goals for the child and family life. For example, as the culture move toward more egalitarian attitudes and practices toward men and women, career opportunities will change for males and females. More parents today will encourage their female children to become doctors rather than nurses. Fewer parents today will discourage their male children from becoming nurses. Consequently, the goals parents have for their children will in some measure reflect changes in the society at large.

Parental Beliefs

Generally speaking every person has a reservoir of beliefs which reflect how we think, feel, and behave. A belief is something we accept fully as true even though it may not be true or proven. A belief functions as a firm persuasion of the truth and we often put our faith in what we believe. We have beliefs about many things including what children are like and how they should be raised. These beliefs concerning children and parenting influence what we think and feel and how we behave. These beliefs manifest themselves in a person's child rearing philosophy, practices, and more.

The parent who believes that "children are to be seen and not heard" is likely to behave quite differently than the parent who believes that children have a right to and should be encouraged to express their thoughts and feelings in appropriate and acceptable ways. Each parent is likely to have a qualitatively different relationship with her child because of these markedly different beliefs. Likewise, each child is likely to feel quite differently about himself and his parent as a consequence of how the parent concretely behaves in relation to the child based upon a particular belief or belief system.

With respect to child rearing philosophy and practices, the parent who believes that the child has a basic tendency to develop bad habits that will get out of control is likely to be somewhat suspicious and compelled to monitor closely the child's actions. In comparison, the parent who believes that the child has the basic capacity to learn and mature without pressure or protection from the parent will feel more optimistic and less pressured to watch the child's every move. By further comparison, the parent who believes that the child is constitutionally delicate, weak or extra vulnerable is some way will be more inclined to behave protectively and may even limit substantially the child's actions.

If the above beliefs are merely artifacts (and they rarely are), it is less easy to predict their consequences for child growth, development, and behavior. However, if each of the above beliefs is part of a cluster of similar beliefs (and they usually are), then it becomes representative of a larger system of child rearing ideology and practices, which have predictable effects upon the child's growth, development, and behavior. When these beliefs are part of a larger system or mindset, they concretely influence and manifest themselves in not only the goals parents have but also the techniques they use in child rearing.

Child rearing philosophy and practices and their effects upon children and parents is such a significant factor that further discussion will take place about this singular factor as the main topic for consideration later in this text.

Means - ends Beliefs *or* Techniques

The goals parents have in relation to raising their children and how they go about achieving these goals have an important impact upon the parent and child relationship, the parenting process, and success in parenting. Parents believe that certain methods or techniques will be effective in helping them accomplish their goals while other methods will be less effective or not effective. This is the means-ends belief connection. Those means are what are commonly referred to as child rearing techniques or methods. Consequently, parents select and use certain techniques and reject and do not use others based upon these beliefs.

Seven Commonly Used Techniques

Parents employ many techniques or methods as they raise their children and attempt to accomplish their goals relating to child rearing. These many and varied techniques can be classified and placed into one of seven commonly used technique categories or classifications. Most parents will not use the categorical headings identified herein when describing the methods they use. Nevertheless, their techniques will fit into one or more of these broad classifications. The reader may have to do some critical analysis, translation and classification to place his or her own techniques into the proper category. Common references will be identified in each category to help this process.

The findings of a variety of researchers and the experiences of various practitioners suggest

56

that parents believe in and use a wide range or variety of methods or techniques. Parental descriptions of their practices also vary significantly. Nevertheless, many of these methods can be included in one or more of the following technique categories.

The seven commonly used technique categories to be described are:

1) the non-intervention technique,
2) the modeling technique,
3) behavior modification methods,
4) motivational modification methods,
5) situational modification methods,
6) environmental manipulation techniques,
7) natural and logical consequences

The Non-intervention Technique

The parent who uses these techniques believes that by using various non-intervention strategies the goals for child rearing will be accomplished. The parent who uses this technique will do nothing because she believes that the child will outgrow inappropriate or undesirable behavior. The parent believes that the child will behave in an appropriate or desirable manner when he matures. The assumption here is that there are certain inevitable periods (the terrible twos, for example) or behaviors (nose picking, for example) that are part of the typical growth and development of children. Children outgrow these periods or behaviors and so the best thing to do is to do nothing or to ignore these. Do not focus any unnecessary attention on these and do not attempt to intervene because these are typically short-lived and pass with time.

The best thing to do is nothing or to ignore behavior. The parents capacity to use this approach effectively will depend upon the parent's ability to do nothing or ignore or "screen out" inappropriate or undesirable behavior. Parents vary significantly in their capacity to do so. Certain child-like behaviors quickly annoy some adults. Others are not adversely affected by these same behaviors. The parent's tolerance level or limit is a crucial element here. Some parents have greater tolerance for particular behaviors than others. These differences are significant differences when the non-intervention technique is employed.

Parental judgement or sensibility is also important in using this technique effectively. Some behaviors are so inconsequential that they certainly can be ignored. Nothing needs to be done about these. Some behaviors may require some form of intervention or attention by the parent. These are certainly judgement calls that will be influenced by the parent's value system, belief system, and many others variables. Of course, there are behaviors that have consequences for present and future growth and development. These cannot be ignored. Common sense and good judgement mandate that the parent do something. However, parents vary significantly in their ability to make good judgements about their children and child rearing. If common sense were in fact common, most of us would possess it. Unfortunately, many seem to lack good judgement or common sense too frequently when it comes to child rearing.

The Modeling Technique

The parent who practices this method believes that if the parent sets a good example, the child will imitate the behavior of the parent. The parent assumes that the child's degree of identification with the parent will be great enough to motivate the child to want to be like the parent. Thus the child will mimic, copy, or imitate parental behavior. Psychoanalytic theory refers to this as the "identification process." Social learning theorist suggest that children's observation of other's behavior and their subsequent imitation (subject to the child's interpretation) of that behavior is a main feature of children's learning and socialization. Regardless of theoretical perspective, children are influenced by the models that are part of their life experiences and they do assimilate and manifest the behaviors they observe to some extent.

The parent who believes in the modeling technique would not subscribe, at least consciously, to the dictum, "Do as I say, not as I do." Rather, the parent believes that the child will learn by the parent's good example. Such a parent would likely believe that "actions speak more loudly than words," especially parental actions that are in full view of the child.

The parent's capacity to implement and follow through with this technique will be a function of the parent's ability to be a good role model. Parents who are gentle and loving can expect their children to assimilate these characteristics. Parents who are abrasive and unloving can less likely expect their children to be gentle and loving people. Strong evidence exists for a wide array of behaviors. Parents who smoke are more inclined to have children that will smoke, despite parental efforts and advice against smoking. Children who live in a family where violence and other strong-armed techniques are used to influence the behavior of family members, will often demonstrate aggressive characteristics in their interactions with others. Children who live with parents who respect themselves and others will learn to respect themselves and others. <u>Children indeed learn what they live!</u>

Children will assimilate both the good and poor models for behavior that are part of their life experiences. Of course, what children see on television and in the movies, hear on the radio, read in the paper and books, etc. is part of their life experiences. Violence as seen on television has a considerable impact on children's behavior. The research data is overwhelming in this regard. Children's behavior becomes more aggressive after viewing aggressive behavior on television. Children exhibit more pro-social behaviors when the television they view incorporates pro-social values and demonstrates these in concrete behaviors.

Behavior Modification Methods

The underlying belief in using behavior modification techniques is that the child's behavior can be changed if the parent appropriately reinforces the child's behavior. Through the use of positive and negative reinforcements or rewards and punishments, the child's behavior can be modified to satisfy parental expectations. Parents have different names for the reinforcement contingencies they employ. Some of the more common names given to positive reinforcements are rewards, goodies, promises, hugs and kisses, bribes, warm fuzzies, approval, compliments, a pat on the back, etc. Some of the more common names given to negative reinforcements are punishments, chastisements, reprimands, admonishments, cold pricklies, being grounded, being sent to one's room, taking

away privileges, withdrawal of love, the silent treatment, etc.

The more sophisticated parent will utilize other behavior modifying approaches such as extinction procedures, shaping behavior methods, systematic desensitization techniques, and possibly other more involved modalities that have been the outcome of the study of learning theory and its applications.

However, these various techniques, simple or more complex, are as good as the user is able to employ these skillfully and effectively. The parent's knowledge of and skill in using these techniques will be a significant factor in the successful use of behavior modification methods. Of course, the child's individual response to the method that is used will also be a factor to be accounted for as not all children respond in the same way to a particular technique. What works very effectively with one child may have little or no effect upon another, even within the same household.

Motivational Modification Methods

The underlying belief in the use of motivation modification methods is that the child's behavior can be changed if his motivation or desire to behave in certain ways is changed. The underlying goal is to change motivation and more acceptable behavior will follow from that.

The parent who believes in the effectiveness of this technique is inclined to talk to the child more and use verbal persuasion, reasoning, or explanation in order to change the child's underlying motivation or desire to behave in certain ways. Some parents who employ this method will verbally coax, cajole, coerce, use guilt or even threaten in order to influence the child. The application of "reverse psychology" is seen among the various techniques found in this category. A former student succinctly described her approach with her children by stating that "sometimes my children need an attitude adjustment, so we talk."

Regardless of the actual approach used, there is a reliance on the use of the power of words rather than physical might. Parents who believe in these methods talk frequently with their children. These parents have a tendency to be more verbal. Their children likewise show very good verbal or linguistic development. Such children are often observed using words to modify the parent's position to one that is more favorable to what the child wants. Children certainly learn what they live.

The parent's ability to use words effectively, to be persuasive, and so forth are important features of the parent's capacity to implement and follow through with motivational methods. Words in general and certain words in particular have great influence on some children. However, some children are minimally influenced by words. Parental action has far greater effect on the latter children. Hence, we can see that the parent's effectiveness in using these techniques is not only a function of parental capabilities but also a function of who the child is and how he responds to the motivational modification methods employed by the parent.

Situational Modification Methods

The assumption or belief underlying the use of situational modification methods is that certain situations, which children find themselves in or are part of their condition, influence their behavior. The parent believes that by modifying the situation or changing the conditions desirable behavior can be achieved.

For example, such a parent would realize that children sometimes experience stress when they are separated from their parents for extended periods of time as when attending nursery school. The parent would attempt to minimize the stress of separation and ease the transition from being at home with the parent to being at nursery school with other adults and children by visiting the nursery with the child to help him become familiar with the surroundings and the people in it. The parent may also spend an extended period at the nursery school on the child's first day of full attendance to further facilitate the child's comfort with the new environment and his eventual separation from the parent.

Likewise, the parent who subscribes to this technique would look for causative factors in changes in the child's behavior. A child who is unusually cranky may be tired, becoming ill, or may be bored. The parent would be mindful of

such conditions and would take these into consideration or attempt to change these conditions to the extent possible. Therefore, the parent would strive to help the child nap, provide appropriate medication, or find something interesting to occupy the child's time. These causative factors would be not used as excuses for the child's behavior but rather would be used to explain atypical behavior in the child and would serve to guide the parent's behavior as she attempts to help the child behave well.

The parent's ability to use these methods effectively would be influenced by the parent's ability to assess the role of potential contributing factors, determine their relative influence upon the child's current behavior, and manage effectively those that seem to be operative. The parent must be realistic, know what the child's typical behavior is under given circumstances, and be sensitive to the verbal and non-verbal messages or cues that child provides about his status. The parent must also be able to determine if the child's behavior has been affected favorably by adjustments in the situation or conditions that seem operative.

Environmental Manipulation Techniques

Some parents believe that the child's physical environment affects his behavior in both positive and negative ways. Environments that are planned with children in mind are less likely to precipitate poor behavior in children and more likely to facilitate positive behavior.

Nursery schools, day care centers, Head Start programs, and other early childhood education programs are typically designed with the child in mind. These settings are established with the intent to promote constructive growth, development, and behavior in children. Such environments have many child-sized fixtures such as tables, chairs, toilets, wash basins, etc. which make it easy for the child to function independently and feel a sense of being in control of himself. Such accommodations make it easy for children to behave well.

The parent who appreciates the connection between the structure of the environment and the child's behavior will be more inclined to child-proof the home, install coat and towel racks at a suitable height for the child, and make other adjustments in the child's physical environment that will facilitate desirable behavior and minimize undesirable behavior.

The parent's sensitivity to the child's predicament, a willingness to make such accommodations now rather than wait until the child grows out of or into the environment, etc. will play significantly with respect to the parent's capacity to use this technique effectively. Parental attitude, creativity, resources, understanding of children, etc. are other important influencing variables.

Natural and Logical Consequences

Parents who use these techniques believe that children learn from the natural and/or logical consequences that are part of the child's interaction with the world of people and things. Sometimes parents behave and sometimes they do not. Sometimes the natural occurrence of events teach. Sometimes interactions with others teach the child.

Natural Consequences

Natural consequences are those consequences of the child's behavior that occur naturally as an outcome of the child's interactions with the world. These outcomes have the potential to teach the child how to or how not to behave. A parent might advise a very young child several times not to touch a hot radiator but may have limited success in helping the child to understand "Hot. Don't touch!" However, during an unsupervised moment, the child may touch the hot radiator and learn immediately and fully the meaning of the words, "Hot. Don't touch!" The unpleasant feeling associated with touching the heated radiator is the natural consequence of the child's behavior and teaches the child what the parent's words were unable to teach.

Logical Consequences

Logical consequences are consequences that are imposed by the parent or are the result of parental behavior or lack of behavior. The parent shall behave in a prescribed, agreed upon fashion under a given set of circumstances vis-a-vis the child's behavior. The child understands that the parent shall not or is not obligated to behave in a given situation with respect to the child's behavior or lack of behavior. Sometimes the parent behaves and sometimes the parent does not and this is understood by both parent and child.

Differences Between Logical Consequences and Behavior Modification

An important distinction needs to be made and understood between the reinforcements employed as part of the behavior modification technique and the consequences that are part of the logical consequence approach. A logical consequence is arrived at through understanding of the circumstances and agreement by both parent and child that the future logical consequences are fair or reasonable and shall be honored by both parent and child. The child plays a direct role in establishing the consequences and setting the parameters for the parental and child behavior.

In contrast, the child is not consulted nor is his understanding of the circumstances crucial, nor his agreement necessary for reinforcement (reward or punishment) to be administered by the parent, when such behavior is part of a behavior modification contingency.

When the logical consequence technique is employed, the parent and child enter into an agreement after discussion of the matter of concern. The child agrees to behave in a certain way and likewise the parent shall also behave in a specified manner concerning the matter. If the child fails to behave in a way agreed upon, parental response is predetermined and expected as the logical consequence of the child's failure to comply with his part of the agreement. If the parent fails to comply as agreed, the parent is then in default. Neither party can change the terms of their agreement without mutual consent. Unilateral changes cannot be made. A unilateral change will invalidate the agreement and render it null and void.

A case example:
Jennifer wants a pet dog. Her parents are willing to cooperate with her but do not want the dog to become their responsibility. Jennifer and her parents discuss what is involved in having and caring for a pet

60

dog. Jennifer agrees that she will be responsible for feeding the dog each day, giving it appropriate exercise and keeping the doghouse and surrounding pen area clean.

Both parents are reasonably assured that Jennifer understands and is capable of performing her tasks; yet, they realize that she may need a few weeks to learn the routine well enough prior to assuming complete responsibility. The parents agree to instruct Jennifer to assist her in acquiring mastery of these chores. Furthermore, the parents agree to assist further by purchasing the dog food, paying for immunizations and building a suitable dog house and pen.

Jennifer also agrees that should she not be able to fulfill her responsibilities, the dog shall be returned to the pet store and she shall have to reimburse her parents for the cost of immunization, and building the dog house and pen out of her own savings. This is what she agrees to. Her parents agree not to assume responsibility for the dog should Jennifer fail to care for the dog as agreed upon. Furthermore, the parents agree to follow through on the plan to return the dog should this not be a viable arrangement.

If Jennifer is able to uphold her end of the agreement, she shall enjoy the favorable consequences of having a pet dog. Should Jennifer be unable to care for the dog as prescribed and required, the consequence shall be loss of the pet and a portion of her savings. If Jennifer follows through as planned, she shall learn the rewards of responsible behavior. If she does not follow through, she shall learn the consequences of irresponsible behavior.

With respect to either outcome, the ability of Jennifer's parents to implement and follow through with this agreement shall teach Jennifer the meaning of contracts and their associated responsibilities. Failure on the part of the parents to follow through will teach Jennifer irresponsible behavior and that agreements need not be honored.

Believing Is Essential

The belief that a particular technique will assist in accomplishing a given goal for child rearing is essential to making a choice of techniques to be employed. However, a belief in any one or more of these techniques is not enough to accomplish successfully the task of parenting. The parent must be able to put beliefs into practice. A strong persuasion or

belief that the parent can do so is often essential or a prerequisite to success.

A case example:
I recall vividly an experience I had as a family practitioner. I had been working with one particular family over a period of time and had come to establish a good relationship with both the parent and children. The parent had confided in me and seemed ready to work on some of the problems she was having with her six-year-old son in particular. I had begun to provide some advice and guidance which she seemed to put to effective use.

Based on these preliminary good results, mother identified a problem she wanted help with. With the problem in mind, I developed an intervention plan involving the use of behavior modification techniques. As I began to present the plan she seemed initially interested and responsive. However, as I began to provide more detail as to how this plan would be implemented, she stopped me and said, "I won't do that! That sounds like bribery to me and I won't bribe my children to get them to behave!"

Her perception was that the positive reinforces that I suggested might be used with her son were nothing more than payoffs or bribes for good behavior. She stated further "I don't believe in that and I won't do it, John. Do you have any other ideas?" She was willing to continue to work on this problem with my assistance. However, she did not believe in this approach and could not bring herself to employ these particular techniques.

No matter how effective a given technique might be for managing a particular problem, the parent must believe that this approach is consistent with his or her overall system of beliefs. If a technique is perceived to be not consistent, the parent may reject its use.

Believing Is Not Enough
Skill Is Necessary

The techniques or procedures parents believe will help them accomplish their child rearing goals must be used effectively or competently. Therefore the parent's capacity to implement and follow through with these techniques and use them appropriately and wisely will play a major role in helping the parent parent successfully.

The parent's strengths and weaknesses in using any one of these techniques will weigh heavily in the effective utilization of those techniques regardless of the strength of the parent's beliefs. A parent who smokes, drinks, and eats excessively is a poor model for good health practices. A teacher who yells frequently, is sarcastic and critical and speaks primarily to reprimand is a poor model for constructive communication. The mother who warns the child "Wait until your father gets home!" is not making effective use of reinforcement contingencies which rely heavily upon immediacy for effectiveness.

Such considerations underscore the importance of skill in parenting. It is not enough to believe in certain techniques. Parents are effective because they are able to use the techniques they believe in competently or skillfully. Just believing in them is not enough. <u>Parental beliefs must be supported by appropriate parental behavior</u>. For in parenting, parental behavior speaks more loudly than parental beliefs.

No One Technique Is Enough

Some parents favor one or two techniques and have a tendency to use these predominantly in their child rearing. And although there is nothing inherently right or wrong with this, it seems that the more effective parents employ all or most of these techniques during their parenting careers. Knowledge and skill in utilizing all these techniques will enhance the parent's chances for success.

This is especially true when one considers that different children respond differently to the various techniques. Furthermore, a given child may respond differently to a particular technique during various periods in his development. Therefore, the use of another technique may be more suitable and productive in either case. Notwithstanding preferences and strength of beliefs, it is the wise parent who develops knowledge and skill in using a wide variety of child rearing techniques, because <u>no one technique is enough</u>!

Parental Expectations

Parents anticipate that children will behave in certain ways. They look upon certain things as likely to happen within the context of parenting or in relation to the child's growth and development. These anticipations and likelihoods are part of the expectations parents have in relation to their children and parenting.

These expectations may have a powerful influence on a variety of aspects of child rearing. These expectations will influence what we do or not do, feel or not feel, believe or not believe, etc. The parent who expects cooperation from the child will anticipate cooperative behavior from the child and look upon the child as capable of joining the parent toward some common effort or goal. The parent who expects cooperative behavior from the child will experience a positive feeling tone in anticipation of the child's cooperative behaviors.

In contrast, the parent who expects the child to be uncooperative will anticipate uncooperative behavior and will look upon the child as capable of making the task more difficult or even working against the parent toward the goal. The parent who expects non-cooperative behavior from the child will experience a negative feeling tone in anticipation of the child's uncooperative behavior.

Expectations are powerful influences upon children's actual behavior and these expectations can actually shape or precipitate certain anticipated behaviors. The data pertaining to teacher expectations and children's academic performance is compelling. Research in this area has demonstrated that teacher expectations can affect student academic performance. For example, consider a teacher who has two different classes of children whose academic performance is statistically the same. The teacher is told that one group will be the best class she has ever had. They are bright, interested, easily motivated, and just a pleasure to teach. The teacher is told that the other class will probably be the worst she has ever had. They are obtuse, not interested in much of anything, difficult to motivate, and just extremely frustrating to teach.

The class that is described favorably, performs as expected. These children prove to be bright, interested, easily motivated, and a pleasure to teach. The class that is described unfavorably performs as expected. These children are obtuse, disinterested, difficult to motivate, and highly frustrating. The children's academic performance is significantly different. The group labeled "bright" performs significantly better than the group labeled "obtuse." In fact the latter group's performance is academically poor.

Expectations are powerful determiners of children's behavior in the parenting context as well. Parents who expect parenting to be difficult, typically find it so. Parents who expect the child to be troublesome, typically experience child behavior that is troublesome. In contrast, parents who expect parenting to be challenging yet rewarding often report it as such. Parents who expect children to behave primarily in positive ways, rarely report troublesome child behavior. Parental expectations concretely influence parent and child interactions and the perception each develops as a consequence of these interactions often reflects those initial expectations.

Realistic and Unrealistic Expectations

Any given expectation must be put into proper perspective. There are some basic questions we need to ask in this regard. Is the expectation the parent has for the child reasonable and realistic given the child's developmental level and past experience? Is the expectation unreasonable and unrealistic considering the child's past performance in this particular regard?

Reasonable expectations are usually met by the person for whom the expectation is held. A parent who has a reasonable and realistic expectation for the child will find the child capable of behaving in the manner expected. The parent who has reasonable and realistic expectations for himself or herself with respect to parenting will be able to meet those expectations and will generally have a feeing of satisfaction and accomplishment.

Unreasonable and unrealistic expectations are sources of problems in parenting. The parent who has unreasonably and unrealistically high expectations will find disappointment in the child's behavior. Likewise, the child may feel frustrated by his inability to meet parental expectations and angry with himself for his lack of competence. The parent who has unreasonably and unrealistically low expectations may have a different impact upon the child. The child may feel unchallenged and unmotivated. The parent may feel disappointment in the child's lack of interest, desire and productivity. Expectations

that are too stringent are sources of trouble as are expectations that are not challenging enough.

The parent who realizes that the young child will not be highly competent when acquiring a new skill will expect considerable messiness when the child begins to feed himself. The child, the high-chair, the floor, etc. will not be examples of neatness and cleanliness. The parent may have to accept temporarily less antiseptic surroundings until such time as the child gains in skill and mastery.

In contrast, the parent who expects the young child to be neat and clean during this phase of his learning to be self-sufficient may become frustrated by and annoyed with the child's lack of skill. Furthermore, the parent may be unwilling to put up with the temporary negative impact upon the environment. Such a parent may not be able to tolerate the messiness and insist upon feeding the child, thereby minimizing parental frustration but also minimizing the child's opportunities to gain in skill and competence and acquire the associated feeling of mastery.

Such limiting behavior on the part of the parent certainly limits the disruption of the environment. However, it also limits the child's growth and development in very important areas. In contrast, parental behavior that is enabling, allows the child to acquire the experiences that he needs to grow and develop well in certain areas. Reasonable expectations tend to promote growth and development. Unreasonable expectations tend to stifle growth and development in children.

Parental Health Status

The health status of the parent may significantly influence the parent's ability to parent well or in ways that the parent desires. The parent's health status may limit or make impossible various kinds of interactions with the child. Reciprocally speaking, parental health may limit or make it impossible for the child to behave in certain ways toward the parent.

Parental health may vary from time to time as is typically the case and may show variations that are normal or typical of healthy adults in general. The changes that result in parent and child interaction are usually of an ephemeral nature. A return to normal interaction is usually forthcoming. However, some health changes may be of longer duration and may be temporarily debilitating as to alter parent and child interaction temporarily. A return to normalcy is usually anticipated. There are also parental health problems that may be more severe and relatively long-lasting or even permanent. The latter variety would usually have a more profound impact on parent and child interaction and return to normalcy may not be realistically anticipated. In such cases parent and child interaction is significantly and sometimes permanently changed.

Physical Health Status

The physical or physiological condition of the parent is one dimension of parental health status. A parent who is physiologically healthy and possesses an adequate level of physical energy and stamina may engage in more and varied interactions and activities with the child than a parent whose physical health is poor.

The parent's good physical health may permit the parent to wrestle on the floor with the child, engage in bicycling, play ball, and participate in the latest dance craze with the child in the privacy of their home. Such interactions have great potential for establishing a reservoir of positive feelings between the parent and the child and these serve to further strengthen their relationship.

In contrast, a parent's poor health may limit, restrict, or even prevent the parent from engaging in such activities. This would limit the quantity and quality of mutually enjoyable shared experiences thus minimizing opportunities to further strengthen their common bond.

The age of the parent may have similar influences upon parent and child interactions. A younger healthy parent may be able to engage in more vigorous or strenuous activities than an older parent. Even though an older parent may be healthy, the aging process decreases energy, flexibility, strength, etc. These normal outcomes of growing older may server to limit is some ways the type of interaction the parent may feel (physically

and/or psychologically) comfortable engaging in.

Parental Use of Physical Ill Health, Handicaps or Disabling Conditions

How the parent uses his physical ill health, handicap or disability is a significant dimension of parent and child interaction. Some parents are realistic about their limiting conditions and try to help the child develop a realistic view of the parent's status. Such a parent would typically strive to minimize any negative impact her poor physical health status might have on the child and try to maximize the positive aspects of the interactions they are able to have.

A case example:
One such parent, a multiple sclerosis victim, comes to mind. This parent and her spouse have worked diligently at helping their children understand the nature of the mother's condition and the impact it might have on them as individuals and on family life and living. Due to her increasing debilitation, the father and children have had to progressively assume greater responsibility for their self-care, the care of the mother and the home environment. The mother has managed to continue to do things she is realistically capable of doing and has avoided misusing her condition to receive unnecessary or unrealistic service from her spouse and children.

This mother has been an outstanding example of independence, self-sufficiency, and determination notwithstanding her handicapping condition. The children have benefitted from this circumstance by becoming increasingly more independent themselves, self-sufficient, helpful and cooperative.

Interestingly, all three children have planned careers in human services. One is striving for a career in exercise physiology, another works with the elderly in an intermediary care facility, and the youngest, although less certain, has thoughts of pursuing a nursing career.

In contrast, another parent with the same condition might misuse the handicapping condition to manipulate her spouse and children into providing unnecessary service to her, to control their lives and increase her power or influence by using her dependency. Such parents become excessively manipulative, demanding, and controlling. These characteristics typically generate anger, resentment, guilt and other negative feelings in the spouse and children. These feelings contribute to an accumulation or reservoir of negative, counterproductive feelings in the spouse and children which serve to lessen the quality of their relationship with one another. Conceivably, these children might be expected to develop very differently than the children in the case example provided above.

Psychological Health Status

The psychological condition of the parent is another important health consideration. A parent who is emotionally healthy and happy is likely to engage in and share more constructive interactions and activities than a parent who is emotionally unhealthy and unhappy. A parent who feels good about herself and her role as parent will generate more positive feelings and will be better able to create a constructive emotional climate in which children grow. A parent who is secure in her goals and values, especially those pertaining to child rearing, will be less threatened when children challenge her. A parent who is loving and caring and capable of expressing these characteristics in appropriate ways will help develop children who feel loved, cared for, and capable of reciprocating these feelings.

In contrast, the parent who has many mood swings or is acutely or chronically troubled psychologically will be less capable of creating an emotionally happy and healthy environment. A parent who has low self-esteem and is uncertain of her role as parent may give her child real cause for contempt and contribute to a role reversal where the child takes charge. A parent who is insecure in her goals and values for child rearing will be more inclined to have the child challenge her position or disregard her entirely. A parent who is unable to express love and caring in constructive and positive ways will do little to show her child how to constructively express these feelings. Furthermore, her child is likely to feel unloved and not cared for by the parent.

Parental Use of Psychological Ill Health, Handicaps and Disabling Conditions

The parent may use his psychological ill health, handicap or disabling condition in a variety of ways that may significantly influence the amount and quality of parent and child interaction. Parents differ as to how realistically they are able to manage their psychological condition and how well they can minimize negative influences.

The parent that experiences many mood swings may strive to recognize when major shifts are occurring and manage these as appropriately as possible. Such a parent may recognize that using certain medication during these transitional periods helps minimize the degree of divergence and length of disparity and helps return the parent to a more stable state. Likewise such as parent may encourage the child to spend a weekend at a friend's or relative's home or make other arrangements for the child so as to minimize the negative impact upon parent and child interaction. This parent has learned to live with her mood swings and manage them in such a fashion as to lessen the chances of their having an adverse effect upon the parent and child relationship. Providing explanations to the child at a level suitable to his understanding is extremely helpful in assisting the child to manage what he experiences.

In contrast, a parent who has not learned to recognize the emergence of a major mood swing may find herself caught up in it before she is able to manage it with medication and make arrangements for the child. Consequently, the two may find themselves engaged in negative interaction with possibly neither understanding why nor being able to curtail or redirect their interaction in a more positive direction. Regular occurrences of this type would contribute to the accumulation of many negative thoughts and feelings in both. These would serve to diminish the quality of their interaction and relationship.

The parent who is chronically ill or incapacitated will be less able to maintain regular positive interaction with the child. This may cause a pattern of avoidance or withdrawal in either or both thus minimizing further their chances of maintaining regular positive interaction. Some psychological conditions precipitate particular kinds of negative interaction. The parent who is chronically angry may be excessively hostile and abusive to the child verbally and/or physically. Such treatment will cause the child to experience a variety of negative thoughts and feelings which in turn contribute to the build up of hate, resentment, aggressiveness, shame, guilt, vengeance, etc.

Some psychological conditions or manifestations thereof may lead to a pattern of negative interaction which may lead to extreme forms of neglect, abuse, and sexual exploitation. These extreme interactional consequences of parental psychological ill health result in severe damage to the child and the parent and child relationship. Considerable psychotherapuetic intervention is often required to nurture the child back to a more normalized state of psychological well-being himself.

Child Advocates, All

Those who genuinely love and cherish children, especially professionals who work with children and their families, will be sensitive to such possible extreme conditions and will learn to recognize the signs or indicators of these conditions. To help in this regard, Appendix B and Appendix C contain a listing of such signs and the community resources that may assist us further in this aspect.

If one cares, one will be motivated to find out. Knowing directs our actions. To act is to put the child's best interest first. These principles apply to all who come in contact with the child whether they be parent, relative, professional or casual acquaintance. The true test of our love for children is in the actions we take or fail to take on their behalf. *We all are and we all must be advocates for children.*

References

1. Gardner, R. *Understanding Children* (New York: Jason Aronson, Inc., 1973).

2. McCandless, B. *Children: Behavior and Development*, 2e (New York: Holt, Rinehart and Winston, Inc., 1967).

Chapter 5

Characteristics and Needs of the Child

The intent of this chapter is <u>not</u> to provide an overview of child growth and development. To do justice to such an undertaking would require that this chapter become a book in itself. This is beyond the scope and intent of this chapter, which is to simply put the child in his rightfully important position as an influential member of parent and child interaction.

Some crucial elements of who the child is, what he needs and what role he plays in interaction shall be identified. In simple terms the child is not only influenced by the parenting he receives but also influences the parenting he receives. Likewise there are some concerns and issues that are closely associated with the child and these also influence and are influenced by parent and child interaction. Some of these important related concerns and issues shall also be identified and described in this chapter.

CHILDREN'S ROLE IN INTERACTION

Children Are Proactive

The child is a proactive member of the interactional team. The child is not a passive member in the relationship. He is not someone who simply responds or reacts to parental behavior. In fact, the child, even during infancy, plays a very active role and often initiates or terminates interaction as a full member of the interactional team. More accurately, the child is both reactive and proactive in his interactions with the parent and his environment of other people and things. Events certainly happen to the child. But the child also causes things to happen to himself, others and things within his influence. Parents of toddlers come to this realization quickly and fully.

Children Have Power

Never underestimate the power of children. Some parents are amazed to find out how much influence or power young children have. Despite the fact that the infant remains significantly dependent upon the care, supervision and good will of the parent, the infant can bring a smile of joy to a parent or a lament like "He doesn't love me!" The child has the ability in subtle ways and through barely discernable behaviors to create a state in the parent of complete satisfaction and joy or utter frustration and ill feelings.

New parents recognize very early in their relationship with their infant children that the infant has an amazing repertoire of behaviors and abilities, at first underestimated by the parent, that produce a wide range of parental thoughts and feelings. Some of these thoughts and feelings come as a great surprise to many novice parents. The surprise can be pleasant: "I can't believe how much joy she has brought into my life and how fulfilled as a person she has made me feel!" The surprise can be negative: "If she continues to refuse to go to bed, I swear I'll place her for adoption!"

Children Are Influential People

The impact that children may have on parents must also be underscored. A particularly expressive child may do a great deal to help the parent become more expressive of her thoughts and feelings, especially those pertaining directly to the child and their shared experiences. The child sets an example that the parent follows. The child frees or liberates the parent to be more fully expressive of her thoughts and feelings. Thus we can see that the child is not only influenced by the parent but also influences the parent in considerable ways.

Children Are Complex Beings

The child's characteristics and needs are components of a complex interactional system. The child has many characteristics and needs which singularly and in concert with one another influence the amount and kind of interaction that takes place between the parent and child. Some of these characteristics and needs are inborn. That is they are inherent features of who the child is at birth and shortly thereafter and what will be long after. Some of these characteristics and needs are acquired or learned as the child interacts with people and things in his environment over time. It is this complex interaction of the child's inherent make-up and environment over time that produces the unique individual each child becomes.

THE ROLE OF CHILDREN'S CHARACTERISTICS AND NEEDS IN INTERACTION

Inborn and Acquired Characteristics Interact

These many and varied characteristics and needs are not isolated, independently functioning phenomena. They are component parts of a total system. Each shall exert an influence and be influenced by the other and possibly be modified by the others to a greater or lesser degree. Furthermore, these characteristics and needs are part of a greater system - the child himself, who provides direction, will power, unique interpretation, etc.

For example, an inborn characteristic such as temperament may be strengthened or modified by interactional experience. Likewise, a learned characteristic such as skill at playing a musical instrument may be significantly influenced by the child's inherent musical propensities. Yet if the child is lazy or lacks stamina, he may not engage in the devoted practice musical skill requires. As a consequence, the child's musical potential may go unrealized.

The Child's Characteristics and Needs Influence Parent and Child Interaction

Likewise, the child's characteristics and needs are placed in an even larger interactional system, namely, parent and child interaction. The parent and child shall simultaneously influence and be influenced by their shared interaction. The child's characteristics and needs shall influence how he responds to parental behavior. The child's characteristics and needs will influence how the parent will respond or behave toward the child. A child with significant musical ability, who learns to play a musical instrument may well create a great amount of joy and pride in the parent.

On the other hand, the child who does not develop such musical ability, may contribute to feelings of disappointment and resentment in the parent. Furthermore, the parent may often chastise the child for wasting his talents and gifts and suggest that the child should feel guilty for such squander. This may be especially true if the parent were lacking in such ability or opportunity; yet, had a strong desire to be musically proficient.

CHILD'S CHARACTERISTICS

The Child's Knowledge, Skill and Personhood

Like the parent, the quality of the child's interactions will in large measure also be influenced by what the child knows or does not know, what he is able or not able to do, and who the child is as a person. The child brings to his interactions with others the many and varied characteristics of his unique humanity. The child is a person too and the quality of his relationship will be influenced by this undeniable fact.

Child's Interest and Knowledge

A child who has an interest in knowing certain things and acquiring specific kinds of knowledge may stimulate interaction with the parent in favorable ways. The parent may be positively impressed by the child's interest in and thirst for information about a particular matter. This may serve as motivation for the parent to spend time with the child, allocate family resources to support the child's interest, which collectively contribute to the quality of their interactions with one another. The child's interest and the parent's positive response to it serve to create an accumulation of many positive shared experiences and feelings. And these shared experiences and feelings cement

their relationship or bind them together more strongly.

A child who is disinterested in matters that might stimulate interaction with the parent will have fewer opportunities to share in experiences that strengthen the quality of their relationship. Likewise, a child who shows interest in matters that the parent does not value may pick up messages from the parent of disapproval, which will lessen feelings of good will between them.

As a consequence of such positive or negative interactions, the child may come to know different things about himself, others, interpersonal relationships, and the physical things in his environment. The knowledge the child acquires as a consequence of these interactions will influence the person he becomes and the kind of interactions he shall experience.

Child's Skills

The child may acquire or fail to acquire certain skills that will directly influence his interactions with people and things. The abilities range from basic self-care to more complex interpersonal interactional skills to abilities as a learner, doer, and producer.

The child's interactions with the parent may facilitate or impede the acquisition of certain skills. For example, a child whose parent encourages appropriate verbal expression and models effective modes of verbal communication may contribute greatly to the child's ability to express himself and communicate effectively with others. In contrast, a parent who fails to encourage or actually discourages appropriate verbal expression by the child and is a poor model herself may do very little to help the child develop skill in this area.

Child's Personhood

Who the child is as a person will greatly influence the child's capacity to form a relationship with the parent, maintain the relationship and be parented over time. The child's personhood is comprised of the same constellation of characteristics that define any personality. These include but are not limited to the child's temperament, attitudes, values, beliefs, expectations, goals, thoughts, feelings, concerns and issues.

These features of the child's personality exert a similar influence as do these same features in the parent. For example, a child who believes that the parent is on his side will behave significantly differently than the child who believes the parent is his adversary.

Children who expect service from the parent will behave differently than those who value their self-reliance and self-sufficiency and serve themselves. Not only will these two children come to expect and have different kinds of interaction but also their expectancies will influence their personality development. The child that expects that things will be done for him may develop a strong inclination to procrastinate. He may have learned that if he waits long enough, someone else will do it for him.

By contrast, the other child does what he needs to do for himself when it needs to be done. As a consequence, he learns to not only be self-sufficient but also to be efficient and expedient regaring his duties and responsibilities.

The child's attitudes, values, beliefs, expectations, etc. which pertain directly to being parented emerge from and are shaped by parent and child interaction. These will be of primary concern and shall have a direct influence on the quality of the parent and child relationship and the unique growth, development and behavior of the child.

Child's Perceptions

The child will form perceptions of the world of people and things as he interacts with his environment. These perceptions will, in turn, influence his interactions with people and things. For example, a child who perceives the parent to be nurturing and supportive will have a significantly different life experience than a child who knows the parent to be not nurturing and not supportive. Each child will develop significantly different perceptions of human interaction.

The first child may develop a significant sense of trust and feelings of security in knowing that the parent is dependable in her nurturing and support. He will learn to count on these parental behaviors. Consequently the child's feelings of security and general well-being are strengthened when the parent predictably behaves in ways that are consistent with the child's perceptions of the parent.

In contrast, the child who perceives the parent to be not nurturing and not supportive will emerge with a different view of the relationship. This view will be confirmed each time the parent behaves in a non-nurturing and non-supportive manner. The child will learn that he cannot depend on the parent for nurturing and support. As a consequence the child may lack feelings of trust and security and his general sense of well-being will be compromised.

Temperament of the Child

Temperament refers to the natural disposition of a person. It often includes not only physical disposition but also the perceptual or interpretive learning style of the person. People differ in terms of their activity level. Some are high energy people who are often "on the go." Some are less energetic and some are even lethargic. People differ in the amount of sleep they require. Some young children require a nap each day as part of their daily routine. Some children rarely seem to need to take this time out from their generally busy daily routine. Some children are very perceptive and quick to learn or figure out things. Others seem to require more time and tutorial input from others.

Temperament is often used to explain or excuse child behavior. A parent may comment that it is the child's temperament that explains his behavior or conversely that the child's actions are the consequence of his temperament. Generally the role or impact of individual temperament is recognized by most parents.

Parents will often report on the regularity or persistence of their baby's temperament or more accurately, behavioral state. Some parents characterize their infants as being fussy and crying often. Other parents describe their infants as easy-going and crying very infrequently. Babies are born with a wide variety of temperaments or behavioral states. Babies differ greatly to the extent that they are active or inactive, awake or sleeping, irritable or pleasant (non-irritable), attentive or inattentive, responsive or unresponsive, cranky or content (non-cranky), proactive or passive, etc.

The temperament with which the infant meets the world has significant influence on his interactions with his caregivers. An infant who is highly irritable and difficult to calm may generate much anxiety and tension in the parent. Anticipating negative interaction, the parent may begin interaction with the child in a heightened state of anxiety or tension, which when perceived by the child may escalate the child's level of irritability, which in turn makes it a greater challenge for the parent to calm the child.

In contrast, the child who is easy-going and easily pleased may help elicit feelings of satisfaction and competence in the parent. The parent of an "easy" child approaches interaction in a state of relaxation and with feelings of competence, which in turn may be perceived by the infant as reassurance and confirmation of his easy-going, easy-to-please nature.

As can be seen by these examples, the child's temperament simultaneously influences and is influenced by the parent's response to the child. The child's temperament in some instances is reinforced by parental behavior, in some instances exacerbated by it, and in some limited cases changed by parental behavior.

Physical Characteristics

Children's physical characteristics play an important role in their interactions with their parents. Physical attractiveness is always an asset regardless of age. Despite the fact that most children are found appealing to most adults, some children are especially attractive. As a consequence of this good fortune, the child is likely to receive much positive attention and praise. The child comes to learn that others regard him as attractive and this view by others contributes positively to the child's image of himself. When told of his attractiveness, this young child often responds, "I know."

Unfortunately, some children have the misfortune of being less physically attractive because of the genetic roll of the dice, ill health or accident. We can certainly think of extreme cases like the elephant man, the child portrayed in the movie, Mask, etc. Their physical appearance had a significant impact upon how others responded to their appearance and interacted with them.

In less severe cases, children are told with some levity added, how "funny looking they are." Please keep in mind that these comments, no matter how innocuous they may seem to others, send a powerfully negative message to the child which he often internalizes.

A person I know well, who happens to be a very attractive individual, was told often by her father that she would never be as beautiful as her mother. Other negative remarks were made about the musculature of her arms, and other features of her physique. Despite her actual attractiveness, she grew up believing that she was unattractive. This belief had a significantly negative impact on her self-concept development and other features of her personhood. During her adulthood these negative images still remain powerfully operative, despite the many compliments from others about her actual attractiveness.

The child who shares a physical likeness with another may be advantaged or disadvantaged by it. If the likeness is of someone who is admired and loved, then the child may be given positive messages about that likeness: "You are so good looking, just like you father." If one is reminded of someone who is despised and for whom much animosity still exists, the messages given to the child may be very negative. "When you pout like that, you remind me of my sister who used to get her way by doing that. When you do that, I could slap your face."

Exceptional Characteristics

Exceptional characteristics are those atttributes or liabilities that are exceptional or extraordinary. They include such things as handicapping conditions and disabilities such as physical handicaps, sensory impairments, learning disabilities, mental retardation, physical and psychological health conditions or impairments. They also include special interest and abilities such as intelligence, musical virtuosity, artistic talents and gifts, and the like.

Handicapping Conditions and Disabilities

There are numerous conditions which may handicap or disable the child. The degree of the handicap or the extent of the disability varies from condition to condition and from individual to individual. Physical handicaps and sensory impairments may be included here. Limitations in mobility and flexibility are conditions which can influence significantly parent and child interaction. Limitation in hearing, sight, etc. require special measures.

Physical handicaps: A child who has impaired mobility may require special attention and care-giving from the parent. A child who has poor muscle control may have to be fed and dressed by the parent to a much greater extent than more normal children. Some children may even require an intense degree of service throughout the child's life. Some children may require wheelchairs and/or other appliances to live a more normalized life. The net result is that the child depends more on the parent for assistance. Consequently, parenting is more time and labor intensive with children who have physical handicaps or disabilities.

Sensory impairments: Children with sensory impairments that are not discovered, may suffer from this lack of discovery. I remember vividly the child who was regarded by his parent and day care teachers as a behavior problem. He would not listen to them. They would have to repeat the rules often and he would still not abide by them. His parent and teachers would have to shout at him otherwise he would ignore them. He would yell at them and his playmates. When I was called in to consult with the professional staff, my questions about his hearing drew blank faces. A hearing test was arranged and revealed substantial hearing loss. He was fitted with hearing aids and his behavior changed completely. He behaved like a different child.

Learning disabilities: Learning disabilities can have similar influences. It is important to point out that despite the child's intelligence, he may have difficulty learning in one or more areas. There are many different types of learning disabilities with many different causes. Some are apparent but many are not. As a case in point, consider the child who seems reasonably intelligent but is not doing as well as expected in his school work. Teachers may characterize him as having the potential but not performing well. He may appear to not be paying attention or concentrating on his school work. Such reports cause the parent to admonish the child for not paying attention in school and not being more careful in his school work.

Mental retardation: Mental retardation manifests itself in varying degrees and is caused by either system or environmental conditions or a combination thereof. Having a child who is mentally retarded changes the course of parent and child interaction and family life profoundly and presents to the parents and other family members a significant challenge. Some families respond favorably to this challenge, while other families respond unfavorably. Meeting this challenge can enhance the lives of all. Not being able to meet the challenge may alter family life and relationships significantly.

I recall one couple who gave birth to a child with Down's Syndrome, which is also known as Mongolism, and which is caused by an extra #21 chromosome (systemic in origin). The husband was unable to come to terms with the fact that a child of his suffered from this condition. He blamed his wife and her gene pool. He was unable to accept the child and enjoy the kind of interactions he had enjoyed with his other children. The marital and family relationships progressively deteriorated and the couple eventually divorced.

However there are many families that respond positively to the challenge of having a mentally retarded child. The television program, "Life Goes On" is one of my favorites. It portrays a family with a Down's Syndrome child, Charles "Corky" Thatcher. The actor, Christopher Burke, who plays this part is in fact a Down's Syndrome person. This series depicts a family who has responded to the challenge and met it with great success. The television viewers are given a glimpse of the impact on family life and living, the devotion of the parents, and the disproportionate focus of their time and energies to support this child.

We see how this challenge impacts upon siblings, and raises serious concerns for the child's potential to manage his life in the future when the parents are no longer able to give their support. But most importantly, we see their shared successes, how their lives have been enhanced, and the potential to live productive lives that exists for mentally retarded individuals. It is a heart warming program that inspires and gives hope; but it is not a fantasy. It is a representation of the lives of many real people whose lives and relationships are profoundly influenced by a child who is mentally retarded.

Physical and Psychological Health

Children's physical and psychological health status may vary considerably. Their health status may be influenced by conditions present at birth (congenital) or that are acquired later. Regardless of the origin of such conditions, the child's health status is modified and this change exerts an influence on parent and child interaction.

Physical Health

Children that are born premature come into the world in a delicate and vulnerable condition. They often require special measures to help them survive their incomplete gestation. The special attention they receive and the very real risks that confront them, shapes how parents come to regard them. The parent is struck by the child's very delicate and vulnerable state. Certain extra special measures must be employed and precautions taken. These special requirements begin to structure the way the parent interacts with the child.

Many children survive premature birth and become very healthy, very normal children. However the parent's mindset has been formed and it may not be easily changed to incorporate the fact that the child is out of danger and that all is well with the child. A substantial portion of such parents are not able to free themselves of their original view of the child. As a consequence, they continue to perceive the child as delicate, vulnerable and requiring special protection. Hence the child's original health status, regardless of how it has changed and improved, continues to influence how the parent views the child and parents him.

Emotional Impairment

Our emotions are complex matters that we learn to manage as we grow and learn over time. For a multitude of reasons, some children don't show the same response repertoire and ability to manage their emotions in socially acceptable ways. This inability to manage feelings successfully interferes with and impedes relationships, learning, and healthy growth, development and behavior in general.

Infantile autism has been mentioned in an earlier chapter as well as the problems that some foster and adopted children bring to their relationships from previous relationships. For example, a foster child may have been abused. As a consequence, his ability to trust others has been seriously impeded. He is reluctant to "get close" or allow others to form a relationship with him. He resists, strikes back verbally and physically and generally exhibits much negative behavior. Parenting him is difficult for the foster parents no matter how well intentioned or devoted they may be. This child's emotional impairment unequivocally influences the kind of interaction he shall have with others.

Special Interest and Abilities

Children show many different kinds of interest and abilities. Some of these children are referred to as talented or gifted. Some may even be call child prodigies. These special interest and abilities cover the full range of human experience. Music, athletics, scholarship, art, drama, writing, mechanics, human relationships and diplomacy are some examples of the areas where some children are exceptional or extraordinary.

The child who is especially interested and capable in athletics may serve as one example. The child may spend much of his time shooting baskets in his yard. He has the good fortune to have a basketball hoop furnished by the parent. Basketballs would seem to be items that last a long time but they do not when they are bounced hundreds of times each day, day after day. Hence the parent finds it necessary to replace the basketball on a regular basis.

But there is not just the commitment of financial resources to support the child's special interest and ability. The child wants the parent to shoot baskets with him, pass the ball to him in a certain way so that her can refine his skill at receiving the ball. The child wants the parent to serve as an opponent so he can learn how to make a basket even when someone is trying to prevent him from doing so. Of course, the child wants the parent present at games, to cheer him on, to praise his proficiency, to encourage him when his performance is not up to par, to commiserate with when the team loses, and to share in the joy of winning. The child's special interest and ability influence in concrete fashion how the child and parent will spend their time together and what will be the focus of their interaction.

To conclude this section, these child characteristics and conditions profoundly change the thrust and focus of the parent and child relationship, the types of experiences the parent and child can share and the kind of interaction they shall come to know together.

CHILDREN'S NEEDS AND NEED SYSTEMS

Children Have Many Needs

Children come into the world dependent on the care and good intentions of others. Initially, children have many needs that they are not able to satisfy themselves. Consequently much of their dependence during their early years consists of relying on others to adequately and appropriately meet their needs until they develop the capacity to fulfill their own needs.

One of the important reasons we want to learn about children is to better understand what they need and how to meet their needs at various stages in their development. Parents and child care professionals are in the "needs meeting business" where children are concerned. The study of the growth and development of children can assist parents and

child care professionals in their efforts to learn about children and ascertain what their needs are and how best to meet them.

There are some helpful models that serve to guide us in this search. A few will be discussed in this chapter. But first it is necessary to define in general terms what a need and need system is before looking at some specific examples.

Needs Defined

A need is a constitutional or acquired necessity, or want, which is appeased by recurrent satisfactions. The word constitutional refers to those needs that are part of the child's basic biological nature, such as the need for food or sleep. Acquired needs are those that are learned or are come by later as a consequence of learning. Some have a need for power and control. These are needs that have been acquired as a result of the unique interactions the child has experienced with his significant others and the physical environment.

We all have a need for power and control but how these manifest themselves can be very different from person to person. For some it is simply a matter of being independent, self-sufficient and making decisions for ourselves. Others must dominate people and things to feel they have power and control. Generally, learned needs are more greatly influenced by the unique interactions people have and thus show far greater variability.

A need can be a necessity, requirement, craving or want. A need may also be something useful or desired that is lacking, such as being in need of more information before making a decision. It may be also a lack of something that is wanted or deemed necessary. For example, the child may need more positive attention.

Regardless of our attempt to define, a need is something that has to be appeased, satisfied, met, or fulfilled again and again, repeatedly. Once is not enough. We don't eat one meal to last a lifetime. Nor is one night's rest sufficient. These need satisfying mechanisms are repeated again and again. They occur and reoccur repeatedly. Needs require ongoing, regular appeasement. Needs require recurrent satisfaction.

Need System Defined

A system is a set of components which interact with each other. Each component influences the other constituents and is influenced by the other components to a greater or lesser degree. All systems - biological, mechanical, social or psychological - have these three essential parts or features: **1.**) a set of components, **2.**) interaction with each other, and **3.**) mutual or reciprocal influence. A need system is a set of needs (components) which interact with each other and influence each other in various ways in varying degrees.

Maslow's Hierarchy of Basic Human Needs

Abraham Maslow's hierarchy of basic human needs is one good example of a need system. What is especially interesting is Maslow's integration of needs that are of biological, social and psychological origin. Maslow's schema is usually represented by a pyramid with the most basic of human needs set at the base. The more sophisticated, complex and psychological needs are found at the top. These needs are set in hierarchical fashion. That is there is an ordering, ranking or grading of these needs.

This is a need system that shows and undergoes a process of increasing complexity and sophistication. The needs at the base are more basic and rooted in human biology. As one ascends the schema, we note that the needs become rooted in sociology and psychology and become more complex. The more human needs are influenced by experience or learning, the greater the potential for complexity and variation.

Physiological needs: The most basic of needs are those rooted in human biology or physiology. This category of needs includes the human organisms need for biological homeostasis, food, water, air, elimination of waste from the body, physical comfort, shelter and general individual survival. Also included in this group of needs are the needs for touch,

sex and procreation, which is group survival or survival of the species.

Safety needs: The next level in Maslow's hierarchy or rank order is safety needs. Included in this group are needs for security, stability, structure, order, and freedom from anxiety and chaos. Out of physical comfort emerges psychological comfort. If the child is helped to feel physically comfortable, then a state of psychological comfort emerges from this good physical feeling. Many biologists believe that most human emotions or feelings have their origin in human physiology. The experiences of trauma victims lend considerable support to this notion.

Belongingness and love needs: In my opinion, much of what makes us more fully human is seen at this next level. People need love, affection, belonging, affiliation, family and friends. Humans are social beings who become more fully human within the context of good human interaction. People need people and need to be with people. When we are with people who treat us kindly and care for us, we feel loved. We belong to them and they belong to us. These are our connections or roots. These are affiliations we need. Knowing we have a place in the world contributes to our sense of well-being. It is a good comfort that strengthens our feelings of security. Knowing we belong adds to our sense of worth and contributes to the satisfactions of the next level.

Esteem needs: Much will be said throughout this book about esteem, especially self-esteem and the closely related human aspects of self-worth and self-concept. People have esteem needs. These include self-esteem, esteem of others, achievement, recognition and dignity. Each are variations of our value, worth or worthwhileness as people. Being loved attests to our value. Loving others strengthens our connections to them. It feels good to be held; this is a basic need. But it also feels good to be held in high regard, to be valued, to belong, to be loved; this is a higher more complex need.

Self-actualization needs: Here we find the ability to direct one's life, find fulfillment and meaning. These are existential notions. But quite simply Maslow has described this as a process of becoming all we can become. To that notion I would add the positive, constructive force or potential that exists in all humans. To extend and redefine what I believe was Maslow's intent, I would suggest that self-actualization is the process of becoming all we can become in a positive way.

This is not a process that is ever finished. There is no final product. Recall the lyrics from a song by Spiral Staircase: "I love you more today than yesterday but not as much as tomorrow." Self-actualization is being more today than one was yesterday but less than one shall be tomorrow.

Parenting is a case in point. As we gain in experience, knowledge and skill, we become more capable as parents. As we learn how best to promote the growth and development of others, we become more fully human or self-actualized. Consider Erik Erikson's notion of generativity: creating, producing, promoting, parenting. The concepts of self-actualization and generativity are mutually supportive phenomena. They serve to illustrate the dynamic, interactive and mutually influential relationship of different needs and need systems.

In conclusion, Maslow's hierarchy of needs is one important framework or system of needs that can help us understand what children need. There are other important ones such as those offered by Erik Erikson and Jean Piaget. These in particular give us much insight concerning children's needs and how best to satisfy or help satisfy those needs. More will be said of these two theoretical frameworks immediately.

Child's Developmental Stage

The developmental status of the child varies as he grows and learns. As the child's developmental status changes, his needs change and his behavior changes. The following are common categorical descriptions used to denote a person's developmental status. Each description suggests certain aspects about the person in terms of his characteristics and needs and what is important to each during these respective times or developmental periods.

Each framework serves as a guide to not only what the person is like but also what the person is likely to need in order to grow and develop well. Each framework may suggest ways of behaving on the part of the child, the parent and the culture that will maximize the growth and development of each. Similarly, each framework may suggest behaviors to avoid or not engage in as these are counterproductive to healthy growth and development. Erik Erikson's and Jean Piaget's stage descriptions are shown below as examples of such developmental stage descriptions.

Developmental periods	Erikson's stages	Piaget's stages
1. infancy	1. trust vs. mistrust	1. sensorimotor
2. toddlerhood	2. autonomy vs. shame & doubt	
3. pre-school	3. initiative vs. guilt	2. pre-operational
4. school age	4. industry vs. inferiority	3. concrete operations
5. pre-adolescent		
6. adolescent	5. identity vs. identity confusion	4. formal operations
7. young adulthood	6. intimacy vs. isolation	
8. middle adulthood	7. generativity vs. stagnation and self-absorption	
9. senior adulthood	8. integrity vs. despair	

Stage Descriptions
As Need Descriptions

I want to propose a different way of looking at and using these stage descriptions. These stage descriptions can be regarded as statements of what children need in order to grow and develop well. For example, let us convert Erikson's first stage - trust vs. mistrust into a need statement rather than viewing it just as a stage description.

The conversion would be something like this: What the child needs in order to grow and develop well is to develop a basic sense of trust in himself and others. He also needs to overcome feelings of mistrust in himself and others. If he accomplishes these primary psychosocial tasks or satisfies these needs sufficiently, he will move to the next level. His need at the next level will be to develop a strong sense of autonomy and overcome feelings of shame and doubt. The child satisfies these needs not alone but with the help of parents and other significant people.

A similar conversion can be made with Jean Piaget's stage descriptions. For example, let's take one of the many characteristics of children during the preoperational period - egocentricity. One aspect of this characteristic is that the young child has a tendency to view things from one perspective, his own. This is a cognitive as well as a social disadvantage. In order to grow and develop well the child needs to become less egocentric or substantially overcome this tendency. If he is able to do so successfully, he learns to take into consideration other perspectives and other points of view. This represents both cognitive and social growth. As the child gains greater and greater flexibility in his cognitive and social perspective, growth is promoted.

Children Need Adults

Children are initially very dependent upon their parents to satisfy their many and varied needs. But children eventually learn to depend upon themselves more and parents less. This shift is a sign of their growth or increasing maturity. Nevertheless, children rely on parents to satisfy their needs and guide them as they learn to satisfy these themselves or find other adults to fulfill their needs. As children expand their circle of social encounters, other people like child care professionals, teachers, youth group leaders, etc. play an increasing role in children's need satisfaction. Children unequivocally need adults, but not just any adults. Children need adults who have special qualities.

Children Need Adults
Who Are More Fully Human

Self-actualization is the process of becoming more fully human, and that is good. In order for children to get off to a good start in this process, they need adults who are more fully human themselves. Children need certain things from adults and society and the environment within which they grow. But the most important ingredient is adults. Children need adults. But they need adults who have certain attributes, humanness is one.

Children Need Adults
Who Love Children

Children need adults who can provide genuine, unconditional love that is expressed in concrete ways that children understand and that creates a feeling of being loved in the child. Children need adults who provide appropriate and adequate care and supervision. This goes a long way toward satisfying children's physiological needs and creating feelings of comfort and safety. This is child care.

Children Need Adults
Who Have Knowledge and Skill

Children need adults who are skillful and knowledgeable concerning how children grow and develop and what they need at various ages and stages in their development. This includes all aspects of their development: physical, emotional, social, intellectual, moral and spiritual. Children need adults who have the ability to meet children's needs adequately and appropriately in these diverse areas.

Children Need Sensitive Adults

Children need adults who are sensitive to the cues or signals that children send out and are able to respond to these messages appropriately so that the growth and development of children is promoted. Children need adults who can implement and follow through on their child rearing behaviors. Children need adults who are able to promote their growth and development in the many diverse areas mentioned. This is child rearing.

Children Need Adults
Who Have the Correct Attitude

Children need adults who are child-oriented and people oriented. Children need adults who behave in ways that are in the best interest of the child. Children need adults who are good advocates for them and can obtain or help obtain for children what they need to grow and develop well.

Children Need Good Advocates

Advocates are people who work on behalf of children to insure that children get what they need to grow and develop well. Being a good advocate for children requires knowledge of what children need to grow and develop well and special skill in motivating people and systems to provide to children what they need.

This knowledge is obtained through careful study and observation of children. This special skill is obtained by studying and working with the people and systems that affect the lives of children. Some people and organizations have devoted themselves exclusively to this one function.

Social work professionals have a special name for this knowledge and skill base; they call it "community organization." This is a formal part of the education and training of social workers.

Unfortunately, it is not typically part of the education and training of parents or child care professionals. It should be. Since it is not, it is necessary for parents and child care professional to educate themselves. Part of being a good advocate is to assure the child of his rights.

CHILDREN'S RIGHTS

Children Have Rights
That Need To Be Assured

Children have certain rights that must be preserved and applied. Some of these rights are statutory and some are implied or assumed. Nevertheless, children often need adults to assure them of their rights. Children have a right to be free of abuse and exploitation. Children have a right to be fed and provided with adequate health care. Children have a right to have their concerns addressed in legal hearings concerning child custody, protective services, etc. These are not privileges; these are rights that every child has and should be assured. As parents and child care professionals, we must be well informed of these and what our personal and professional responsibilities are in relation to these.

Children Need Adults Who Are
Aware and Supportive of Such Rights

Children need adults who take the time to educate children about their rights and also help them learn how to assert themselves relative to these. Children need adults who will respect, honor and protect these rights and come to their assistance when these rights are being infringed upon by others. Likewise, children need adults who will set limits when the child infringes upon the rights of others. Children need adults who have these special concerns and devotion.

There have been various and numerous governmental bodies and committees, commissions, professional organizations, groups, etc. which have attempted to articulate the many and varied rights that should be assured children. Because of space limitations, just one of these efforts shall be offered as a representative sampling to provide the reader with a sense of their focus and to stimulate thought on the subject. The following statement of children's rights is from the New York State Youth Commission:

CHILDREN'S BILL OF RIGHTS

For each child regardless of race, color or creed

1. The right to the affection and intelligent guidance of understanding parents.
2. The right to be raised in a decent home in which he or she is adequately fed, clothed and sheltered.
3. The right to the benefits of religious guidance and training.
4. The right to a school program which, in addition to sound academic training, offers maximum opportunity for individual development and preparation for living.
5. The right to receive constructive discipline for the proper development of good character, conduct and habits.
6. The right to be secure in his or her community against all influences detrimental to proper and wholesome development.
7. The right to the individual selection of free and wholesome recreation.
8. The right to live in a community in which adults practice the belief that the welfare of their children is of primary importance.
9. The right to receive good adult example.
10. The right to a job commensurate with his or her abilities, training and experience, and protection against physical or moral employment hazards which adversely affect wholesome development.

NEED SATISFACTION AND GROWTH

Need Satisfaction Is Crucial To Growth

Children need adults who recognize the crucial role they play in satisfying or helping to satisfy children's needs. Need satisfaction has a significant positive influence on the growth and development of children. Unmet needs play a significant role in undermining or limiting children's growth and development.

When Needs Are Met

What happens when children's needs are met adequately and appropriately? There are three general and basic, positive outcomes.

Needs Are Replaced When They Are Met

As needs are met or satisfied in an adequate and appropriate manner, they are replaced by higher, more complex, more sophisticated needs or the attention is shifted to other aspects and concerns. Recall Maslow's hierarchy. A child who is severely weakened by hunger cannot play and frolic with other children. He is not concerned with such affiliations. He is focused on his hunger. Feed this child, nurture him back to reasonably good health and he will soon want to play with his agemates. Need satisfaction leads to replacement by more advanced needs or allows the child to change his focus on such needs.

Growth Proceeds In A Positive Direction When Needs Are Met

As needs are met or satisfied in an adequate and appropriate way, growth and development proceeds in a forward direction. Positive direction is given to the child's growth and development. Once feed adequately, the child above seeks social affiliation. His contacts with others will help create the connections he requires to feel he has a place in his culture. He is beginning to feel he belongs and is loved by others beyond the immediate family. His growth and development is moving in the proper, positive direction. Need satisfaction gives positive direction to the child's growth, development and behavior.

Growth And Development Are Promoted As Needs Are Met

Meeting or satisfying children's needs adequately and appropriately promotes growth, development and constructive behavior. This is the key to growth promotion. Meeting children's needs is not "spoiling" them. Not meeting their needs is what "spoils" them. To spoil is to damage or impair. When needs are not adequately and appropriately met, children are damaged and their growth and development is impaired. Meeting children's needs promotes their growth, development and behavior.

This is the simple, straightforward truth as to why it is crucial that parents and other adults learn what children's many and diverse needs are and acquire the knowledge and skill that will help them meet children's needs adequately and appropriately.

When Needs Are Not Met

What happens when needs are not met adequately and appropriately? There are several general and basic, negative outcomes. The extent to which the outcome is negative is a matter of degree. The severity of the outcome is a function of the degree of deprivation. Deprivation is not having or not having in sufficient quantity what is needed to grow and develop well. When children's needs are inadequately and inappropriately met, a condition or state of deprivation often exists to some degree.

Need Replacement Is Prevented Or Impaired When Needs Are Not Met

When needs are not met adequately and appropriately, one of three levels of difficulty may be noted.

1. The need is not replaced when it is not satisfied: The most severe condition or worst case scenario is that replacement by higher, more complex, more sophisticated needs may not occur. A concrete example is the extreme degree of starvation that exists among young children in Ethiopia currently. Many will simply not survive. There is such a severe degree of deprivation that the child's body has been so damaged and impaired that he can not make it out of the extreme condition he is in, even if food were to be made available in adequate amount and variety.

2. Need replacement is difficult when satisfaction is lacking: The less extreme outcome is that there may be difficulty satisfying these needs because the child is not quite or adequately ready to accept, assimilate and accommodate to the next level of development or to the next level in the need hierarchy. When deprivation exists, need replacement is tenuous or questionable or

difficult. Despite this, some children will make it, but not without damage or impairment. There will be some Ethiopian children who will begin to respond favorably when food is given. Recovery may be slow and difficult but will be achieved. However, many who survive will be impaired to some degree so that optimal growth cannot ever be achieved.

3. Temporary stagnation takes place when needs are not met: The least negative outcome is that some children will stay put momentarily. They may stagnate or get stuck in place or get fixated for a period of time when needs have not been met adequately and appropriately. A child who is showing a significant degree of dependent behavior may take a longer period of time to acquire self-sufficiency skills that will contribute to his independence and lessen his dependence. Progress may be minimal and may take longer to manifest itself. But eventually, slowly, with difficulty, the child emerges less dependent and more independent.

Negative Direction In Growth May Result When Needs Are Not Met

When needs are not adequately and appropriately met, three variations in direction may be noted. Growth and development may not proceed in a forward, positive direction. Rather, the direction of growth and development is negative or backwards.

1. Negative direction in growth occurs when needs are not met: The worst case scenario in this instance is that growth is turned in a negative direction. Some Ethiopian children when given food will not be able to assimilate the food given because the degree of damage to the digestive system is extensive. An attempt to digest the food may cause severe pain, which may cause the child to enter a convulsive state, thus worsening his condition. The child's growth is forced in a negative direction. The same would happen to a child who is punished for dependent behavior. He may show even greater dependency.

2. Regression may result when needs are not satisfied: Children sometimes regress when needs are not met properly. They become more immature or more infantile. A child who feels threatened by a newborn sibling and is not able to obtain the attention he desires may begin to show behaviors that he outgrew a long time before. He may wet his pants, ask to be fed or dressed. His behavior has shown regression to a former, less mature level of development.

3. Positive movement is difficult when needs go unmet: Even when some children move forward in large measure, their forward movement may not be a smooth, easy movement. More than the typical difficulty is seen with unusually long pauses and occasional regressions and equivocations. The child is moving in the right direction, but he seems to stumble and fall often and his struggle to get up, recover and continue is noticeable beyond what is typical of his agemates, whose needs have been more properly satisfied.

Diminished Growth Promotion Is The Result Of Unsatisfied Needs

When needs are not adequately and appropriately met, the promotion of growth and development suffers. Two variations are noted here depending on the degree to which needs have not been adequately and appropriately met.

1. Growth is not promoted when needs are not met: In extreme cases growth is simply not promoted. This is indeed a worst case scenario that happens occasionally. The more extreme examples have been given using starving Ethiopian children.

Let's take a more likely situation where the parent has promoted or reinforced dependent behavior in the child and consequently the child shows a significant degree of dependence. The child has reached a certain arbitrary age and the parent decides that the child must begin to be more self-sufficient and behave less dependently. The parent's efforts to now suddenly encourage independent behavior in the child meets with resistance from the child. The parent becomes frustrated and punishes him for his dependent behavior. Punishment makes matters worse and the child shows even greater dependency on the parent. Punishment

is escalated and so is the child's dependency. The child's growth has not been promoted in the least. In fact, his growth has been impeded by inadequate and inappropriate measures, such as the use of punishment.

2. Minimized growth promotion may result for partially satisfied needs: Growth may not be promoted in an optimal fashion. Let's take the case cited above regarding dependent behavior. Let's say that in this instance the parent does an excellent job encouraging and supporting independent behavior but continues to punish dependent behavior. The positive reinforcements for independent behavior and the negative reinforcements for dependent behavior work at cross purposes. The child begins to show more independent behaviors but the punishments for dependency continue to interfere with a more optimal path toward independence.

Taking the punishment out of the equation and ignoring dependent behavior and refraining from encouraging it will optimize the child's acquisition of independence and facilitate his outgrowing his dependence. This approach would tend to optimize the promotion of the child's growth, development and behavior.

Spoiling By Others Is The Result Of Improper Need Satisfaction

Spoiling children is to damage or impair them. When needs are not met adequately and appropriately, spoiling may occur. Spoiling is largely the consequence of two errors in the parent's attempt to satisfy the child: *substitution* and *excess*.

Need substitution: One, spoiling is the result of adults substituting other needs and/or need satisfiers for what is really required by the child. We spoil the child when we substitute inappropriate need satisfiers for appropriate need satisfiers.

If a child is in need of parental affection and wants the parent to spend time with him, a toy given in place of the parent to keep the child constructively occupied will not suffice. What the child needs is time with the parent. What the child needs is the parent's attention and show of affection. A computer and a computerized chess game is no substitute for a game of chess with the parent.

Caution: Material possessions do not spoil children unless they are offered in lieu of what is really needed. The child who is given a computer and then spends many enjoyable hours learning to use it under the parent's tutorialship and receives much positive reinforcement from the parent about the progress he is making is receiving more than the benefits the computer has to offer.

As the child gains in proficiency, he learns to play some games on his own and then offers to teach the parent, who enthusiastically accepts. They enjoy many hours playing these games together and sharing one another's expertise and special interest. Each learns from the other and each holds the other in high regard.

This child is advantaged by this possession not spoiled by it. He is not spoiled by it because it was not offered as a substitute for the parent. It is a material possession that maximizes parent and child interactions not minimizes it.

Excess: We spoil children when we over do the meeting of needs. Over doing is inappropriate practice. Limits must be set in meaningful and appropriate ways. Providing too much service to children often reinforces dependence, helplessness, and diminished self-sufficiency. Parents must learn what measure of service is required and what measure is excessive.

We can never love children too much, if our behavior is appropriate and is a manifestation of real, genuine love. However pseudo-love is another matter. It is a manifestation of an inability to provide genuine love and affection. "Smother love" can do what the name implies, smother the child. We can give children the material advantages of affluence without spoiling them if such items are not given in excess to the point that they are devalued or given as substitutes for parental love and affection. We can give children an abundance of hugs and kisses without their being inappropriately sexual or incestuous.

Self-spoiling Occurs When We Are Unable To Meet Our Own Needs

Sometimes unmet needs become replaced by other needs, need systems, and/or need satisfiers that are more readily available to the child. Need substitution and excess take place. However, in this case, the child himself performs the replacement not the adult. It is typically overdone, excessive and leads to poor growth and development because the original need has not been adequately and appropriately satisfied.

Food is a common substitute here: Food in place of love. Food in place of something interesting to do. Often the wrong kind of food is consumed in excess and this leads to poor growth and health. Obesity would be one of a number of severe problems resulting.

I am an example of occasionally using food as a substitution. When I am bored, I find myself eating excessively. What is really needed here? I am lacking something interesting to engage my time and energy. For lack of something better to do, I eat. This is another form of the "substitution game" that takes place when children are spoiled, because they are given something other than what they really need. But in this case the person himself performs the substitution, self-spoiling of a sort.

Excessive Demanding Is Common When Needs Are Not Met

Sometimes when needs are not met adequately and appropriately, excessive demanding by the child may occur. Excessive demanding indicates that needs are not being satisfied. Children demand: "Love me, not him!" Pay attention to me, not her!" "I want this; I want that; I want, I want..." Give me this; give me that; give me; give me..."

Despite the excesses the child may be able to obtain for himself by demanding, there does not seem to be any satisfaction. This is so in part because what he is given is not what he really needs. In part it may be because the child has not learned to ask for what he actually needs. In this case the parent may be well intentioned but also frustrated that what has been given does not seem to satisfy. Among other things, the child may need to learn to recognize what he really needs and find ways to express those needs in order to maximize chances of having them met.

Obsessive Or Compulsive Behaviors May Develop When Needs Are Not Met

Sometimes unmet needs lead to obsessive and/or compulsive behavior in the child. Obsessive behavior is besetting or dominating action that is persistent. Such behavior includes actions, feelings, ideas or the like, which the child can't seem to escape. Compulsive behavior is similar. It is behavior that is compelling or a strong irrational impulse to carry out a given action.

Children who feel the deprivation of love or are not certain that they are loved may become obsessed with hearing that they are loved: "Tell me you love me! Again! Again! Every time you sit next to me, tell me you love me!" You do love me don't you? Don't you? You forgot to tell me. Remember, every time you sit next to me, tell me."

When children's behavior is overdone, excessive, overboard or compelling and it takes on a certain pattern or regimentation, then it is indicative of obsessive and/or compulsive behavior. The pattern is repeated often. When the pattern is not allowed to be repeated or is disrupted, the child reacts very adversely. This adverse reaction is an indicator of obsessive/compulsive behavior.

For example, a child may require three bed time stories. He may insist on the same three stories, in the same order each time. When a change is made in the number or sequence, the child becomes extremely agitated. He may have difficulty falling asleep, if his routine or pattern is upset or changed.

A distinction needs to be made between ritualistic behavior and obsessive/compulsive behavior. Rituals and ritualistic behavior are typical childhood behaviors. They are usually short-lived. Children are not especially upset when they are interrupted or changed. In fact, some ritualistic behaviors may be a positive or helpful indicator of the child's development.

Case study example:
I recall when my daughter was a toddler. She had many stuffed toy animals of various sizes. For a brief period, whenever I would lie down on the couch, she would stop whatever she was doing and go to her room and bring out the largest of these and place it on top of me and snicker. Then she would return to her room and bring the toy that was the next smaller in size and place it on top of me next to the largest. She would repeat this procedure until all were piled on me next to each other in perfectly descending order.

When this was completed she would snicker even more heartily, clap, and tell me I looked silly. Then she would begin to return them to their original location in her room, one by one in exactly the opposite order in which they had been placed on me. When this ritual was completed, she would return to whatever she was doing previously or engage in something different.

This type of behavior was revealing about her ability to order or seriate, her memory capacity, and her ability to reverse her thinking. If I had to answer the telephone during this ritual, she was not upset or disoriented in any way. When I returned, I would help her reestablish the conditions prior to my leaving and she might continue. At other times she would begin playing with them or might have begun to return them to her room.

As parents and child care professionals, we must learn to distinguish between typical childhood ritualistic behavior and bonafide obsessive behavior or compulsive behavior. Obsessive and compulsive behaviors usually indicate that needs have not been met adequately and appropriately.

Needs Are Transformed Or Distorted When Needs Are Not Satisfied

Sometimes unmet needs become transformed or distorted when they are not satisfied adequately and appropriately. Promiscuity instead of love and intimacy. If it is over done; it is excessive (quantitatively). Quantity is no substitute for quality, especially with respect to love and intimacy. Of course, such an example would not be characteristic of young children.

In young children, we find that the child's need for gaining attention in constructive ways can be transformed or distorted. Young children may use misbehavior as a means of getting attention. Misbehavior is a distortion of the behavior originally designed to get the needed attention. Possibly the child was not able to get the attention or degree of attention he desired. He may have been ignored or quickly dismissed by the parent or teacher. However, he discovers that misbehavior gets and maintains attention for a longer period of time. Children don't distinguish between positive and negative attention. Attention is what they desire and attention is what they get, be it positive or negative. The child does not make a conscious decision to seek negative attention. He simply takes what he can get, even if it is negative.

Young children may also show very rigid behavior when playing with other children. This may be so because structure and limits are not imposed on the child at this time by the adults. It is something the child needs and imposes upon himself. This same behavior may be a reflection of the child's need to be in charge or in control, possibly because he is not given the opportunity to exercise his own emerging autonomy in the presence of the significant adults in his life.

Young children sometimes insist on doing something again and again and may not be able to stop without adult intervention. The need and enjoyment of repetition is normal among young children. In these instances, the child's need to repeat seems excessive and compelling.

Some young children become excessively helpful and compliant because of a tremendously strong need for acceptance and/or fear of rejection. These are often children who are exploited or victimized by other children and adults. It is natural and healthy for children to want to please and be liked. But when this places the child at a disadvantage and leads to his exploitation, then the bounds of normal behavior have been exceeded. Normal, healthy behavior has been distorted and transformed into a behavior that is no longer normal and healthy.

A Deprivation Mindset May Result When Needs Go Unmet

Sometimes unmet needs leave a person with an overwhelming sense of dissatisfaction or feeling of deprivation. A void, emptiness, barrenness or incompleteness is felt.

Sometimes this creates a strong desire or want that leads to excessive or unrealistic expectations, which cannot be satisfied. Sometimes there is acceptance or resignation on the part of the child that his needs will never be satisfied.

An example is loneliness and isolation in the absence of love and affiliation. There may be a strong longing for love and affiliation: "When will I be loved?" "Is there no one for me?" There may be resignation: "No one loves me!"

Children with a deprivation mindset will express it in a variety of ways: "No one will be my friend." "Nobody likes me." "No one will play with me." The child may resign himself to this fact and may give up trying. Giving up leads to further feelings of loneliness, social isolation, estrangement, hopelessness, pessimism, a minimization of interpersonal contact, and an orientation toward things rather than people. These feelings and behaviors fuel the cycle of increasing alienation.

Children show a deprivation mindset by giving up or they stop trying. They withdraw from people and interpersonal involvements. They minimize their contact with people. These behaviors in turn minimize chances for satisfying affiliation, belonging, and love needs. The child's withdrawal is counterproductive to satisfying such needs.

Rejection, Refusal, Denial Are Common When Needs Are Not Adequately Met

Sometimes unmet needs cause people to reject or refuse what they need most. This is a "defense mechanism" or denial. It may be expressed very openly by some: "Leave me alone! I want to be by myself." "Who needs love? Not me. I can live without it." It may be expressed by refusal to seek help that is needed. The adult alcoholic may deny that he is an alcohol troubled person by his refusal to seek assistance. Constructive change begins only after the alcoholic recognizes and admits to the problem. These denials are learned early in life.

We hear children shout, "I don't want to be your friend! I don't want to play with you!" Children tell us firmly, "I don't want you to hold me!' Children will advise forcefully, "Leave me alone! I don't want to play!" Such behavior alienates children from others. Such behavior minimizes opportunities for positive interaction. The result of this rejection or refusal on the child's part minimizes the child's chance of getting what he needs. When these behaviors and attitudes persist, they create people who may be emotionally distant or cold, aloof, rejecting, uncooperative, unapproachable, insensitive, uncaring, and incapable of giving love in a mature way. One cannot give what one does not have.

To conclude, these are some of the many negative outcomes when children's needs are not met adequately and appropriately. Fortunately in most instances these negative outcomes are reversible and more positive outcomes can be obtained.

In order to have positive outcomes, children need adults who know what children need and how to satisfy those needs adequately and appropriately. Toward that end then it is necessary for parents and human service professionals to become knowledgeable about the growth and development of children and to learn how to promote good growth, development and behavior in children.

WHAT WE KNOW
ABOUT CHILDREN'S NEEDS

In summary, what do we know generally about children's needs and their relationship to growth, development and behavior? The following summary can serve as a guide to understanding the needs of children and their relationship to growth as well as the role adults have in need satisfaction.

Children's Needs Change
As They Grow

Knowing where children are developmentally can provide us with some valuable clues about what children will most likely need at different periods in their development.

Children's Needs Change
In Predictable And Logical Ways

This is because children grow and develop in a predictable and logical manner. The stage descriptions offered as examples chronicle this regularity and predictability. Being familiar with these is extremely helpful. Knowing how children grow and develop helps us anticipate and predict how their needs will change from period to period.

Growth Proceeds
When Each Need Is Adequately
And Appropriately Met

To meet needs or help the child meet his needs is to promote growth and development. Parents and child care professionals are in the needs meeting business. The extent to which adults meet children's needs is the extent to which the child's course of development is optimized. The extent to which adults fail is the extent to which the child's growth and development may be limited or impeded.

Children Often Tell Us
What They Need Or Don't Need

Sometimes they tell us directly and positively: "Pick me up!" Sometimes they tell us indirectly and negatively. They may tell us they need attention through their misbehavior. They may tell us they need to work on becoming more independent when they insist, "Me do!" When they work on becoming more than they are at the moment, they are self-actualizing at that point in their development.

Adults Must Attend To What
Children Communicate About
Their Needs

Adults need to learn to perceive accurately the messages or signals children send to us about their needs. We know that children communicate what they need or don't need to adults. But their ability to communicate is sometimes limited. Therefore, adults must learn to understand children's messages and cues and respond to them appropriately and adequately.

For example, most children will generally retreat when the adult voice is stern of tone. Yet another child may attack when a stern voice is used. We have to be able to determine what the behavior means for this particular child. For most it is flight. For some it means fight.

Adults Must Minimize The Use Of Punishment

Adults must avoid or minimize the use of punishment when children are showing needs or behaviors that are not desired. For example, when children cling, they generally have dependency needs. Satisfy these. With proper satisfaction, the clinginess will eventually go away. Don't punish the child for his dependency. Punishment tends to strengthen dependency rather than weaken it. Satisfaction of the need in addition to encouraging more desired behaviors will move the child forward in his growth and development.

Stage Descriptions Are Helpful Guides To Children's Needs

The child development knowledge base can provide adults with some useful guidelines for knowing what children need during various periods and how to best meet these needs. The stage descriptions offered as examples are but a few of many helpful frameworks.

Our experience as parents, child care and social service professionals can help also if we learn how to observe children's behavior carefully and interpret it accurately.

References

1. Erikson, E. *Childhood and Society* (New York: W. W. Norton & Compant, Inc., 1950).

2. Erikson, E. *Identity: Youth and Crisis* (New York: W. W. Norton & Compant, Inc., 1968).

3. Schmossing, Youkeles and Burger. "Maslow's Hierchy of Human Needs" in *Human Services in Contemporary America* by , p 3.

4. Salkind, N. *Child Development* (New York: Holt, Rinehart and Winston, Inc., 1990).

Chapter 6

Family Structure
Family Life Cycle

THE AMERICAN FAMILY

The American family has undergone considerable change, which is to a large measure a reflection of changes in American culture itself. These changes exert their influence on family life and living. It is a Herculean task to understand well the nature of these changes and the many contributing factors, some closely associated with family life, some distantly removed.

A Changing Profile

In 1980 I was selected by the governor of Rhode Island, Joseph J. Garrahy to serve on the state planning committee for the first White House Conference on Families. The committee's task was to determine who would represent the state and how they would participate. In order to do this the committee decided to develop a profile of the American family and compare and contrast that to a profile of the Rhode Island family in order to answer the many questions that emerged. For example: How representative was the Rhode Island community of the larger American community? How do the percentages of single-parent families compare?

In search of the answers the committee members learned many things that often surprised and sometimes stunned. For example, we learned with shock that less than 17% of American families conformed to the "traditional" family profile: a working husband, a wife at home, two or more children. Many of us had predicted between 40% and 60%. This was based on the general understanding that in 1955 about 60% of American families fit the traditional profile. A few pessimists in the group ventured an estimate of around 25%. Had we been sleeping? Why were

91

we so "out of touch?" In 1989 a joint study conducted by Harvard University and Massachusetts Institute of Technology suggested less than 11%. Data from the 1990 Official U.S. Census Report indicate that approximately 9% meet the traditional criteria. Times have been changing and so has the American family.

Currently one half of all two-parent families are either "blended" or step-parent families. More than half of America's fifty-two million children under eighteen years of age have spent part of their childhood in a single-parent family according to the U.S. Census Bureau.

Kenneth Labich in an article in *Fortune* magazine presented the following statistical profile in describing the changes in the American family. In 1970 85% of American households consited of two parents; 11% were mother only; 1% were father only and 3% consited of neither parent. In contrast, in 1990 72% of American families consisted of two parents; 22% were mother only; 3% were father only and 3% had neither parent. In 1970 29% of children under five had working mothers. This percentage increased to 53% in 1990. For children between six and seventeen years of age, 43% of their mothers were in the labor force in 1970 and 66% in 1990.

Not All Change Is Negative

However, not all changes need to be viewed as negative. Some changes are indeed positive ones. What is also changing is the view of Americans about the American family and what constitutes it. Along with such changes has evolved changes in tolerance and imagery. Our personal and professional practices have also been modified. Today more than ever before, foster and adoptable children are being placed in single-parent homes. Today more than ever before, we recognize that gay and lesbian people make good parents too. Today more than ever before, race and religion are only minor considerations in placing children.

Increasingly American males seem to be taking a more direct role in parenting their children and in helping care for the home environment and share in the tasks that were previously the almost exclusive domain of

females. Increasingly, single-parent homes are headed by males. It seems that men to some extent have also benefitted from the various "liberation movements." Their mates and lovers, but most of all their children have also been beneficiaries.

THE FAMILY LIFE CYCLE A CHILD-CENTERED MODEL

Indeed, there are many factors and conditions that influence the structure or appearance of the family. Regardless of these factors and conditions, and its structure and appearance, the family exhibits a life cycle which can be characterized by various stages as it grows, develops and changes. The scheme offered here is a child-centered one. That is, the stages of the family are defined in large measure by the presence or absence of children, and the ages and stages of the children who comprise the family.

Family's Developmental Stage

The family is a growing and changing entity with substantially complex interactional outcomes. As individual members of a family grow and change, their characteristics and needs change within the family structure. These changes result in changes in the family unit. This dynamic process of change modifies the structure and fabric of the family unit. Hence the family as a developmental entity changes as a consequence of individual change. As the family changes in its basic character, structure and composition, it in turn exerts an influence on the growth, development and behavior of individual family members. In effect, the family unit simultaneously is changed by and changes the members that comprise it.

Sometimes these interactive influences are profound as with the death of a family member. But more often, they are subtle as when the youngest child moves from dependency on the parent to dependency on the self. The child who grows in self-sufficiency will require less time and effort from the parent. This greater freedom for both alters the nature of their interaction and relationship.

Subtle changes are often gradual and occur over an extended period of time. Consequently, their impact on individual and family development is often not pronounced and in many cases may even go unnoticed.

Simultaneously, the developmental status of the family is modified by these changes in interaction and relationships, because the family now has a child who is more self-sufficient. In the process the family unit is transformed from one with dependent children to one with independent, self-sufficient members. At a future period the child may even be more able to make a significant contribution to the family unit as he begins to help with family chores, etc. At such time the child's status within the family shall change in accordance with these contributions.

The family's needs, characteristics, capabilities, resources, etc. vary with these changes. A family that has experienced the vocational advancement of the parents may have at its disposal greater financial resources than it had when the parents were just beginning their careers. Conversely, a family may experience a significant drop in its financial resources if the main provider were to suffer a job loss, extended illness or some other incapacity.

Other concomitant gains or losses may be seen in status, self-esteem, social contacts, etc. as a result of such changes in parental employment status. Such gains or losses may have varying degrees of influence on family interaction and relationships. All of which, shall effect the status of the family as a unit to some degree.

The Family Life Cycle

One way of viewing the family's development is in terms of its life cycle. You will note that this is a child-oriented or child-centered way of defining the stages of family growth and development. There are other ways of viewing the family. This is but one framework. The following is an outline of the stages in the family life cycle, which shall be discussed in more detail.

Family Life Cycle

Stage 1 - Newly established family
or the newly wed stage
Stage 2 - Childless family
or primary couple stage
Stage 3 - Family with young children
(infant, toddler, and preschooler)
Stage 4 - Family with school age children
Stage 5 - Family with pre-adolescent
and adolescent children
Stage 6 - Family with young adult children
Stage 7 - Launching period: children prepare
for and begin to leave the home
Stage 8 - Empty nest period (children absent)
or secondary couple stage
Stage 9 - Single-parent empty nest
(death of spouse)

Each stage has its own special concerns or focus. Each stage has its own unique development tasks to be addressed and accomplished. What takes place at each stage has direct influence on what follows in the family life cycle. Exceptional problems or concerns have their impact. Exceptional benefits and advantages have their influence. Positive and negative outcomes become woven into the fabric of the family life cycle in a similar way that they are woven into individual development.

Stage 1.
Newly Established Family or the Newly Wed Stage

The "family" begins when two adults decide to live together as a family unit. Family is initially placed in quotation marks here because my notion may be discrepant with other notions that maintain that a family is not a family until children are born to a couple. You may have heard a couple declare, "Now we are a family." I do not subscribe to that view. I believe that they were a family before their child arrived. My view is that the family is established as soon as people decide to live together as family members. Hence, this would include two or more people who live together and share their lives as we imagine occurs in the traditional family.

93

Two female friends come to mind immediately. They met in high school, went to the same college and shared a dorm room. Their friendship grew greatly during their college years. One become pregnant but decided not to marry the father of her unborn child because she realized that they were not "in love" and that he was not ready to be a father. The birth of her child, necessitated her discontinuing her college education. These two close friends decided to establish a home together. And together they raised "their" child. They have lived together for many years. The natural mother of "their" child eventually married and gave birth to a second child within that marital relationship.

These two friends continued to live together. And all three parents shared their lives and the parenting of these two children. All three became psychological parents to the two children. The non-biological mother was recently given an award for her outstanding contribution to the early childhood education field. She was unable to accept the award herself because she was conducting a workshop at a conference in another part of the country. The youngest child, now an adolescent, received the award on behalf of her psychological mother. No matter the definition, this is a family.

Stage 1 usually lasts about a year or two. The primary task facing the couple is learning to live together as a family. It is a challenging and sometimes difficult stage as it may be the first time life is experienced as an adult outside the family of origin. Each brings to this newly established relationship and living arrangement their unique history. To what extent their two life histories are compatible or not shall be determined during this stage. Some couples adjust and accommodate and strengthen their partnership. Others do not. The largest percent of divorces occur during this stage.

Stage 2:
Childless Family or Primary Couple Stage

When the "living together" matters are resolved and the couple has learned to live together successfully and as a consequence reaffirm their relationship, the second stage is entered. They are now a couple who plan to remain a couple but they are without children. It is characteristic during this stage that one or both begin to talk about having children.

Hence, stage two has two developmental tasks. One is the confirmation of the relationship. The second is the decision to have or not have children. This second decision may be resolved easily, if both wish to have children together. This decision may be resolved for the couple if an unplanned and unanticipated pregnancy occurs. If one is unsure or has decided against having children, the task of deciding is more difficult. This issue must be resolved. The couple shall decide to have children, not have children, or part company.

Stage 3:
Family with Young Children (infants, toddlers, preschoolers)

Stage three is established with the arrival of the child, regardless of the decisions made or not made in the preceding stage. This stage is defined by the presence of *young* children. The primary focus of this stage is the care and nurturing of young children. Young children are very different from school aged children. They receive the largest measure of care and nurturing from their parents within the home. Raising young children is time and labor intensive. It is for these reasons that young children are used to define Stage 3.

Raising young children can be demanding and at times stressful. These demands and stresses pose important challenges to be met and overcome. Many face parenting with little or no experience. Parenting is not an occupation for which we are typically well prepared. It is regarding these realities that the individuals and their partnership are strengthened or weakened.

Stage 4:
Family with School Age Children

It is during stage four that the child leaves the "bosom" of the family to receive care and nurturing from other adults. It is during this stage that the child enters the world of school and the influences of others - teachers and peers. This is the primary developmental task that faces the parents: They must learn to let the child go. They must learn to trust his care and nurturing to others. They will have to reconcile the fact that others will now exert a profound influence on their child. The helpful guidance of teachers is more easily accepted.

However, the profound influence of the peer group is usually unanticipated.

The child brings these influences home and confronts the parent with them. The teacher: "My teacher said." "I can do it at school." "My teachers taught me." "My teacher said I am very smart." "My teacher said I am stupid." "My teacher said you pack a good lunch." "My teacher asked me why you give me so much junk food."

The peer group: "Billy's mother lets him..." "Mommy, why don't you like Jane? What's wrong with her?" "You can't tell me! I can play with whomever I want." "Can I have supper at Joey's house. His mother said I can. She's nice."

It is during this period that the parent is bombarded with influences outside the home. Many over which the parent exercises little or no control. This is a challenge for most. It is absolutely frightening to some. It is typically the major challenge facing the family during stage four.

Stage 5:
Family with Pre-adolescent and Adolescent Children

There are challenges and there are challenges. Raising adolescent children is the most challenging of all for many parents. Preadolescents and adolescents are so strikingly different than who they were just a brief time ago. They undergo so many changes so rapidly that it is a challenge to simply keep pace with the "issue of the day." And their world consists of so much more than their teacher and a few playmates. There are "boy friends" and "girl friends" and dating and driving. Need I say more?

And the larger American culture is their influence, their era, their generation, their values. Too many parents have either forgotten their adolescence or are too acutely aware of it. Which frightens us more? And the ever increasing influence of the peer group is an ever present fact to which the parent and family must accommodate. Even younger siblings are influenced and have their opinions: "Her boy friend is such a creep." "I like his girl friend. She always talks to me and asks me how I am doing." And there are other concerns: Nike

Pumps, automobiles, my own money, sex, alcohol, drugs, etc., etc.

Stage 6:
Family with Young Adult Children

Fortunately most parents, and children, and families survive adolescence. Children become young adults and they begin to show this not only in their age but also in their interests, concerns, and general behavior. Their preoccupation is no longer with the "here and now" only. They express concern about the future: their future, their parent's future, the world's future. They are beginning to appreciate who they are and who they want to be. A sigh of relief can be heard from parents as they begin to appreciate that they have done a reasonably good job parenting and they can begin to relax somewhat. Soon their children will be on their own. It is with this realization that the child will soon be on his own that parents and families begin to change their focus. This change ushers in the next stage.

Stage 7:
Launching Period: Children are Prepared for and Begin to Leave Home

When parents come to the realization that their children are no longer children, that they will soon be leaving the nest to live outside the family unit, the family begins the developmental tasks of preparing its children for this eventuality.

There are many provisions that are made and many strategies that are employed to accomplish this task. They include working children paying room and board. College students may live on campus, or possibly off campus but away from home. The space above the garage is converted to living quarters for the young adult as a transitional measure as the child moves away from the center of the family unit. The young adult child may move in with a grandparent or other relative where a little more freedom is anticipated; yet, some supervision may still be exercised and guidance offered.

These and other strategies, often worked out through negotiation and some degree of mutual consent, begin to prepare all involved

95

for the child's eventual, permanent move out of the family domicile.

Stage 8:
Empty Nest Period (children absent) or Secondary Couple Stage

This is the stage when all children have moved outside of the family domicile. The family unit is now without children present. The task facing the couple now is learning to live as a "childless" couple again. The couple now occupies the house alone. This fact precipitates two common but different reactions in couples.

One reaction is a positive one. As the couple realizes that they no longer have the constraints and demands of child rearing, they discover that they now have more time to spend with one another.

If their relationship has remained relatively strong and positive, this is welcomed. The couple now is able to and begins to devote more time and energy to each other. For some its a rekindling of an old flame. For others it is rediscovery and revitalization. Some couples seem to fall in love again. Some even begin to behave like new lovers by holding hands, sitting close to each other, exchanging glances and smiles, etc. These behaviors sometimes embarrass some adult children and delight others: "Why don't you two act your age." "I think they are so cute together."

On the other hand, being freed of the constraints and demands of child rearing is frightening to some couples. This is one negative reaction. Especially if they have not grown strong as a couple over their years of parenting. For some couples, parenting has become a convenient diversion that has served to cover up the reality of a weakened relationship.

Some couples address this reality and confront the issues facing them. Some do it themselves while some seek the assistance of professionals. Some couples will decide to "work on" the relationship. Others will decide to give it up. Unfortunately some couples avoid the issues entirely, and progressively grow apart. There are no children to keep them busy or provide a common interest and goal.

This can be a trying period for couples. It is during stage eight that we observe the second highest incidence of divorce.

Stage 9:
Single-parent Empty Nest (death of the spouse)

If the family life cycle were uninterrupted by separation or divorce, one of the members of the couple would become a single parent in an empty nest as a consequence of the death of a spouse. The task facing the surviving member is to learn to live as a single parent in an empty nest.

Living alone is challenging and stressful. People make their adjustments in a wide variety of ways. Those that are still employed may thrust themselves into their work. Some may seek the company of their peers. Some may become involved in volunteers work or devote themselves to special social or political causes. Some may devote themselves to grandchildren. Changes in living quarters may be sought: a retirement community, moving in with an adult child. Marrying again may also be an option. There are many alternatives that can be pursued as the surviving member attempts to reconcile the developmental task at hand.

DYNAMIC INTERACTION OF INDIVIDUAL AND FAMILY DEVELOPMENT

Accepting New Family Members

A case in point that illustrates that the family unit and individual family members are influenced by the family's stage of development is when a new family member is integrated into the family structure. That new family member could be an elderly parent, an infirm relative or friend, a nephew or niece attending college locally, or a newborn. Let's take the case of a newborn.

Case study example:
Ellen, an acquaintance, brought her fourth child, a boy, home from the hospital after giving birth. Awaiting his arrival were the siblings, fifteen-year-old Melissa, eleven-year-old Nancy, and seven-year-old Steven. Their individualized response to him and the relationship that each developed with him is classically

typical considering their individual stages of development.

Melissa was politely interested but seemed more concerned with how much child care responsibility might be given to her and how soon he would sleep through the night and not disturb her sleep. In the months that followed, it was clear that this newborn was somewhat of an inconvenience and an imposition to her. Furthermore, she was more than moderately annoyed that her parents did not consult with her about having another child and she could not fathom why they would want another child in the first place.

Nancy's reaction was quite different than Melissa's. Nancy thought that her baby brother was the greatest thing since sliced bread. She could not wait to hold him, and feed him, and bathe him, etc. And she voluntarily and enthusiastically did all of these things and more. She behaved "like a little mother" and often responded to his needs before either parent would. Her attentiveness to him was acute and her behavior was very appropriate and especially loving and nurturing. Her involvement with him was so great that occasional disputes between her and her mother arose as to who would care for him. Mother sometimes had to remind Nancy that she had other things that she needed to do like school homework or household duties.

Steven's response was typical for a first grader. He found his brother interesting and was often playful with him. He treated him with kindness and gentleness but occasionally concluded that he would be more fun to play with when he was older. "He can't do much now! But he's O.K." is how he explained it to me. When his brother began to crawl that was a blessing and curse for Steven. Steven would enjoy crawling after him while Steven barked like a dog. Steven would take great delight in the joyful laughter and scurry it usually caused in his brother. Steven would also show great annoyance when his brother would crawl across a puzzle Steven was putting together on the floor, or intrude upon other such play that engaged Steven. He would sometimes pick him up and relocate him, or annoyingly shove him away, or complain about his brother's intrusive behavior, or plea for relief: "Will someone please take him? He's wrecking everything! Help!!"

Being a teenager, Melissa was much more concerned about herself and how her life might be affected. She was helpful when called upon and volunteered for little regarding her brother's care. When her mother asked for a little more help with household chores because she was tired or preoccupied with his care, Melissa would occasionally snap back at her mother with condemnation: "I didn't tell you to have another child. Why should I suffer?" This is typical adolescent behavior.

Nancy's behavior is typical for a child of her age.

She was helpful in caring for her brother and provided good care. There were occasional competitive and ownership issues concerning him; but Nancy and her mother managed to work these matters out very successfully. Nancy received much praise and positive attention concerning her role in her brother's upbringing and she was obviously very proud of her significant contribution to his care and welfare. Nancy and her brother developed an especially strong attachment to one another. For all intent and purposes, she had clearly become his third psychological parent as well as a loving and nurturing sibling.

Steven simply went about his business doing what was of most importance to him: First grade things, playmates, and protecting himself from and preserving his belongings from an intrusive toddler brother. On one occasion, Steven summed it up this way: "Whew, he sometimes gets on my nerves. But he is cute. And fun sometimes."

These responses are representative of children at these different stages of individual development. It is important for parents to understand that these responses are a function of where each child is developmentally as well as who each child is or seems to be. A case in point is the fact that Melissa was eight years old when Steven was born. Ellen recalls that Melissa behaved toward Steven in much the same way that Nancy behaves toward the newest member of their family. "What's wrong with Melissa?" asks Ellen. Nothing is wrong with Melissa. Her behavior is simply a reflection of where she is developmentally now.

In conclusion, the above family life cycle framework makes certain assumptions that quite often do not stand up in real life. It is to some measure an idealized overview of the family life cycle. In reality we must concede that any number of events can occur that would alter this model in significant ways, especially with respect to sequence or timing. Death, separation, divorce, military service, job, etc. can result in separation of a married couple at any time during the family life cycle, thus creating prematurely a single parent family situation. Similarly, death, separation, marriage, military service, job, education, etc. can result in the separation of the child from the parent or the separation of a child from his siblings.

The time at which the separation occurs, the nature of the separation, the meaning it has for those involved can greatly alter the nature and quality of family interaction and the type of interpersonal relationships that follow. The individual development of the child, parent and the family unit and their respective needs and characteristics interact in highly unique ways to produce highly unique outcomes. The commonality of our growth, the diversity that exists in us all accounts for why each of us are in some ways like all others, like some others, like no other person.

FAMILY STRUCTURE

Family Size and Spacing of Children

The number of people in the family has a signifcant influence on parent and child interaction. We know that generally American families are smaller than they were in previous generations. The number of children born has generally decreased since 1964. Interestingly, 1990 showed the highest number born since 1964.

The trends of fewer children being born and family size decreasing are due to many variables. A significant variable is econonmics. It is simply much more expensive to raise children over an eighteen year period or more. The cost of feeding, clothing and educating children is substantial. The cost of keeping them constructively occupied has also increased substantially. American families have not been able to keep pace, so they have cut back...on the number of children they have.

Quality of personal life is an important variable also. American families want to do more for and with their children. Parents want better relationships with their children. Having fewer children is seen as a way of better managing relationships, and of spending more quality time with children. These goals have also motivated parents to give serious consideration to the spacing of children also.

Today we are amazed at the larger families of previous generations. We wonder and assume: How did they ever manage? There were so many mouths to feed and egos to nurture! But we must also concede that there

was also more family support and community support. More families lived in extended families or close to extended families. Our ties to friends and neighborhood families were closer. Families depended more on one another. Family members and friends helped out. Siblings were required to assume greater responsibility for child care and household management. This is in large part how they managed the larger numbers.

It was not until the mid 1960s that the State of Rhode Island removed family economic responsibility from public assistance eligibility requirements. Prior to that time nuclear and extended family membere were required if possible to contribute to the dependent family's financial support.

There is no question that interpersonal interaction is more complex and taxing in larger families. If you are from a small family, imagine having six to twelve siblings. Imagine if you can that they are approximately a year apart in age. Imagine being a parent to six or more children. The one thing that has always impressed me among children that come from large families is the high frequency of feelings of not being loved, or cared for, or of not being of importance.

Case study example:
I vividly recall a former student of mine who is the youngest of twelve children and who exemplifies these feelings. I was attempting to illustrate the increasing complexity of family interaction as family size increases. Knowing the size of Patricia's family and having some insight into her feelings about her family and parents, I deliberately attempted to represent graphically on the chalk board in the classroom what family interaction involving twelve children might look like.

There were chalk marks every where. Some students were taking delight in my futile efforts at graphic representation, using lines with arrows to show interaction on an individualized basis for each family member. Some exclaimed, "Wow!" Pat exclaimed, "That is just like my family! And I often get lost in the shuffle. I can't get to my parents. There is too much interference. I end up going to my older siblings instead."

That semester Pat was encouraged to examine her feelings more closely and to try to understand the underlying reasons for some of them. With guidance, she came to the conclusion that she needed to assert herself more in terms of direct interaction with her parents. She attempted to avoid going to her older siblings for encouragement, support and guidance and to solicit these directly from her parents. This was a strongly established pattern that she was trying to change but she was making progress, especially at not being referred to an older sibling by her parents.

On one such occasion when her parent directed Pat to ask her sister, Pat confronted her mother with her feelings: "Don't you care about me? Don't you love me? You never have time for me and my problems!" Her mother was shocked! That single confrontation started a very important dialogue between Pat and her parents.

Pat learned that her parents were not aware of how she felt. And certainly they loved her and assured her. Who would not? Pat was so quiet, so cooperative, and so good. Her parents stated at one point, "You never have problems. You manage so well. We never had to worry about you as we have about some of your other brothers and sisters. You were our model child. We didn't think you needed our guidance."

Smaller Families
Enjoy More Interaction

Smaller families have greater potential to provide children with more direct interaction with parents. The smaller size of the family makes parents more accessible and less preoccupied with the intense care and supervision that very young children require. Spacing can help here also but that is a matter of perspective. Some parents desire sufficient space between their children so they can allocate time, energy and resources more fairly and fully. Some parents prefer to have their children close in age so they may face similar child care tasks and concerns and not have to revisit them years later. It is indeed a matter of preference.

Smaller Families
Enjoy More Quality Interaction

One thing is clear. In smaller families, parents and children generally spend more quality time with each other. The depth of their involvements with each other is greater and their sense of attachment is stonger. Parents believe they know more about what is going on in the lives of their children and have greater involvement and influence.

Children feel that their parents care for and love them and have concern for what is going on in their lives. Also children seem more inclined to solicit parental guidance when making decisions about friends, school, behavior, and many other aspects of their lives. I believe this is especially important given the trends in this culture that American families are exerting less and less influence on their children's behavior and that children are now feeling increasingly more estranged and disenfranchised from their families.

Children Raising Children

In larger families there is a tendency for parents to rely more on older siblings to assist in child care. Cooperation and helpfulness are important family values. Children should learn to cooperate and help out in a wide range of family matters. The care of siblings can be good training for parenthood. Children that receive care from persons other than the parent also learn to rely on others, not solely on parents. These are important and valuable lessons.

However, a problem arises when parents rely too much on their older children for child care and child rearing of younger children. When this reliance is excessive, we in essence have children raising children. Children need adults. Older siblings typically do not have the maturity and experience to make judgements and decisions that are in the younger sibling's best interest. There is an inclination on the part of older siblings to either provide too much service to the younger sibling, or to be overly protective, or to be too rigid in managing the younger sibling or to rely too much on physical measures in disciplining.

Older siblings who have excessive child care responsibility often feel resentment and anger toward the parent and sibling. These feelings often lead to feelings of guilt and shame as children conclude that they ought not feel this way toward their parent and younger sibling. Nonetheless, they also feel exploited.

Nuclear Families

The nuclear family is another name for the traditional family referred to earlier. Recall it consists of two parents. The father works and the mother is home caring for children and house. There are two or a few children. The nuclear family resides in its own home with two cats in the yard, etc. Today this type of family structure accounts for 9% of all American families.

Is the nuclear family another American dream? Is this an ideal? Almost all families start out with that dream or ideal. No couple, at least consciously, sets out with the notion that they will divorce. They attempt to build a life and create a dream come true together. My parents started out that way. It didn't work. I started out that way. It didn't work. And so do all couples start out that way. It doesn't work for about half. The other half make it work.

The nuclear family is what we all want for ourselves and what we all work toward. When we achieve it, we realize that we are in a small minority. When we lose it, we mourn it. It is our ideal. It is the kind of family environment where when everything is going well, children grow well. When everything is going well, parents grow well. When everything is going well, couples grow well. When everything is good in the nuclear family, the culture is healthy. These are our assumptions and they are valid and correct.

But the culture is not healthy. As a consequence, the nuclear family is not doing well. Its existence has changed from sixty percent in 1955 to nine percent in 1990. The American nuclear family is an endangered species. What are we going to do to prevent its extinction? We have many programs designed to preserve animal and plant species, and endangered locations of the earth:. Save the Snow Seal. Save the Monarch Butterfly. Save the Northern Elm. Save the Princess Pine. Save the Bay. But there is no Save the Nuclear Family program!

The American nuclear family may need a lobbyist in Washington, D.C. The American family in general may need a lobbyist. "Indeed, if the personal (tax) exemption had kept pace with increases in individual income and inflation since 1948, it would now be worth $7,781 instead of $2,050." (*Providence Sunday Journal*, 6/2/91) Major corporations take millions in exemptions and tax credits and the American worker is allowed two thousand dollars. Does the American family need a lobbyist?

The nuclear family has the capacity to devote greater time and effort to parenting and family life in general. To deny this capacity would be foolish. When everything is well with the nuclear family, we generally observe an increase in the quantity and quality of parent and child interaction. There is generally greater satisfaction with family life and living. There is generally a greater sense of family solidarity and an enhancement of individual growth and development. For those who want and achieve the nuclear family structure, the benefits are apparent.

Extended Families

The extended family is an extension of one family to include another family or to include members from another family. The first five years of my life were spent in an extended family. My mother and I lived with my grandmother and bachelor uncle on the second floor of my grandmother's house. My father was in the Navy. On the first floor resided my uncle, aunt, and cousin, who was five years my senior. Another bachelor uncle occupied the third floor by himself.

This arrangement is typical of the extended family. My maternal grandmother and grandfather (deceased at that time) were immigrants. And like so many immigrant families, the newness of the culture and economics kept families in close proximity, often in one domicile. But the majority of my grandmother's children had already left the extended family to establish nuclear families of their own. Feeling safer and more confident economically, they left the nest. They left some advantages and disadvantages of extended family living behind.

Advantages of Extended Family Living

There are many advantages of extended family living. Some have to do with security and economics to be sure. But the overwhelming advantage is in terms of relationships. In the extended family there are more people, especially adults who care and have concern for you. They are involved in

100

your life, and you in theirs. Each may provide encouragement, support, and commiseration to one another. This is available to both adults and children.

My mother is the youngest of the children. She married, became pregnant with me, and her husband left for the South Pacific Corridor to save America from the Janpanese threat. She needed much encouragement, support and commiseration and received it from a loving extended family. I was never lacking for attention. When my mother was not available, there was my grandmother, my aunt, my uncles, my cousin, and another very playful uncle, who later in my development became my psychological father. To this day, even after the death of my grandmother, and two uncles, I feel the strongest connection to those with whom I lived the first five years of my life.

Interpersonal interaction is more complex in the extended family. This complexity is similar to that found in the larger family. The major distinction is that extended families usually have a larger number of adult figures. Children who grow up in extended families have much adult interaction and input. They typically become very skillful in their social interactions with adults. They typically have exposure to three or more generations.

Such interactional opportunities help shape their mindset and personality development. Children raised in extended families are often more adult oriented and more comfortable with older individuals. They are typically more flexible in their thinking because they have learned to accomodate to more than one adult perspective, with more than one generational viewpoint.

When I first started working in the human services field, I worked as a case worker with the elderly, the blind and the disabled. I felt very comfortable with this client group and was very successful in working with them. Later I was involved in redesigning the service delivery system for the State of Rhode Island. This client group served as the pilot project for the new system.

This involvement gave me an opportunity to meet other case workers throughout the state. What I learned as a consequence of interviews I conducted still fascinates me to this day and illustrates earlier statements about how children's growth and development is affected by extended family living. I found that slightly over eigthy percent of the case workers who worked with this client group spent a portion of their childhood in an extended family.

Diasadvantages of Extended Family Living

You are never alone in an extended family. This is one of its most important advantages. But it is also one of its disadvantages. Family members can become too involved with one another, can come to rely too much on one another, can limit their social contact to just the extended family. "Enmeshment" is the technical term. This is not healthy, if it occurs. This is the major shortcomming of extended family living. Not all extended families develop this feature. Fortunately, my extended family did not.

Extended Families Reinvented: Adult Children Return Home with Children

There has been a steady decrease in the number of extended families. This country's economic opportunities have in large measure contributed to that. More families can afford to live more independently. And that independence is something Americans in increasing numbers were willing and able to pay for. Although in some small measure, some people wanted to leave the disadvantages of extended family living behind. Nevertheless, most were desirous of establishing their own nuclear family.

The trend is now showing a reversal. There is a noteworthy increase in extended family living today. A portion of this increase is the result of the recent influx of immigrant populations, who like those before them seek the security and economic advantage of extended family living. But the major two reasons for this increase is the acceptability of single-parenting and the high divorce rate, which results in single-parenting.

Adult children who have children are remaining in their parent's home. Adult children who have left the home to establish nuclear families are returning to their parent's home with children following divorce. In some cases, married couples who are having financial difficulty managing independent living are also returning to the parent's home. The need for economic and emotional support is the overwhelming force driving this trend.

This trend is not only changing the profile of the American family but also and most importantly changing family relationships and individual development. Parents who had assumed that their parenting years were over are now parenting again. This includes their children and their grandchildren. Some do it willingly; others do it unwillingly. In either case they are not without ambivalent feelings.

Parents want to help but are angry about having to help and not necessarily on their terms. They often feel the lifestyle that has evolved in their children's absence is now being infringed upon and forced to change. Children who seemed independent and to be managing on their own are not able to. There are many mixed feelings: "Have we failed them? It's not my fault! Why should I feel responsible? I feel angry. I feel terrible about feeling angry. I'am in a no win stuation, and I don't like it!"

The adult children have similar ambivalent feelings. It is not easy going back. It is not easy to admit that you have made a poor choice, that you aren't able to manage your life independently. It is an uncomfortable feeling to be in your parent's home again with children of your own, and feel like a child again. The matters are confounded if the adult child has developed a very different approach to child rearing than the parent.

The children often get confused and are torn between the two parenting figures. To whom do they owe their alliegience, to whom do they listen? And why does the child's parent seem different here?

Some have proposed that you can never go back. Indeed it may be difficult at times. But the reality is that despite these very common concerns and problems, many of these newly established extended families are managing their newly intertwined lives. Some are not just managing; they are doing well in the spirit that families are supposed to help and support their members. And the children are getting to know their grandparents to a degree that would typically not have occurred.

Single-parent Families

Single-parent families are very common and they necessitate special attention not only because of their presence but also because of the impact they have on those involved. There are some general consequences for children and parents that must be acknowledged.

Task Management

Whatever the task at hand, single-parenting requires a permanent adjustment. What it generally means is that the single parent experiences a reduction in the task that can be performed and/or a reduction in adequacy of performing certain tasks. There is limited time and energy and there is no other adult to share in these tasks. As a consequence, fewer tasks get done or they get done less well.

The single parent must assume a greater number of roles, especially if the absent parent was actively involved in parenting and household management. The single parent has sole responsibility for parenting. In some instances this may in fact be an advantage, but usually it means that important parenting decisions are made in isolation or without the input of another caring and concerned parent. Two heads are often better than one. The single parent must function without the benefit of another perspective. There is also the matter of encouragement and emotional support. This is often lacking in a single-parenting situation.

Communication

The loss of a parent of one sex produces a structural distortion in communication between the child and the adult world. Children's interaction is significantly limited to interaction with one parent. The remaining parent offers one point of view. Although this may have certain advantages, the child is limited to one adult perspective. In addition, the child may lack the learning opportunities that are inherent when the child can observe two adults communicating and living successfully together. The child is deprived of a successful role model for two-parent family living.

The single parent may be significantly limited to interaction with children, especially if the children are young and still require considerable parenting. Adults need other adults to converse with. The single-parent condition may significantly limit or reduce the necessary adult to adult exchanges. Single parents often "jump at the chance" to converse and spend time with other adults. Quite simply children cannot satisfy the adult's need for interaction with other adults. Single parents often express feelings of loneliness and emptiness.

Power Structure

The power structure in the family is altered and shifts in the direction of a monarchy. Since there is only one authority figure in the one-parent family, the child is more likely to see authority and power as personal. When something is not decided in the child's favor, he has no one to appeal to or to have hear his case. Of course, this may be seen as an advantage by the parent who does not have "the court of appeal" to contend with. Once a decision is made it is final.

Affectional Matters

Identification of source of love and affection with only one sex is likely to cause some concern. Adjustments during adult life may be impaired, particularly if the sole source of love and affection is of the same sex as the child. Children learn to relate to members of the opposite sex first and foremost as they interact with the opposite sex parent. This is not a prediction of future failure but the expression of concern for children's opportunities to learn reasonable and realistic modes of interacting with opposite sex adults.

Single parents often express concerns about meeting their personal needs as adults, especially in the sexual domain. These needs may go unmet for an extended period of time. Unmet needs usually impair healthy growth and development. Concerns about propriety, setting a good example, and living with standards that do not send mixed messages to children, especially adolescent children, are of special concern for single parents.

Dealing with Loss

Both parents and children have to deal with their loss real and imagined. For both parents, the "dream" or ideal has been lost. There is the loss of love, esteem, and the "good life" even though it may have seemed like hell just prior to separation and divorce. And typically for both there is loss of income and the former standard of living. Parents are not just affected by the loses that directly affect them. They are also affected by the losses they assume their children will suffer from such changes. Such realities and speculations make it even more difficult for the parents to deal with their loss.

Children's sense of loss typically has one focus - themselves. This is children's egocentric nature. To some extent this singular focus lessens their overall sense of loss, but be assured that this statement is not intended to minimized the child's sense of loss. It is real and significant! And although young children are especially interested in what will happen to them directly and their possessions, they are also concerned about their relationships: "Will I get to see...?" "Who will cook for daddy?" "Where is mommy going to live? Will I be able to visit her there?"

Notice how children are more more practical in their concerns. Philosophical matters, dreams and ideals are not their concerns. Young children especially don't understand such abstract adult concerns. Young children especially often have difficulty understanding what the parents may be experiencing. Again their egocentricity comes into play. Adults often do not understand this about young children and are angered by it. During this vunerable time, parents often have less tolerance for these childlike characteristics. These matters may negatively affect parent and child interaction.

Adult and child reaction to loss is quite different. Nevertheless, each experiences profound loss when the structurte of the family changes from a two-parent family to two parents living separate and apart. And this new arrangement brings with it many situations and circumstances to adjust to while trying to manage and accomodate to their respective losses. Children typically go through this process in about half the time as is characteristic for adults. Children typically take about a year and one half to resolve their sense of loss. Adult resolution typically takes about three years.

Shame and Guilt

Both children and parents express feelings of shame and guilt about the family situation. Even though single-parent families are more common and societal attitudes have become more accepting, these concerns still manifest themselves. It seems that often parents express more shame and guilt because they often feel that they put their children in this situation. But we also know that children commonly assume that they are responsible for the marital breakup. Children's shame and guilt often dissipates more rapidly than adults.

Perception of Problems

Single parents perceive more behavior in children as problematic. This may be because single parents expect that their children will suffer the loss of a parent and the changes in family life and living. Possibly it is because children initially show adverse reactions to separation and divorce. Of course there is no other parent to offer the perspective that the child's behavior is typical for children: "My brother use to do that when he was that age. It didn't turn out to be a problem." Other adults and institutions have similar expectations and often see problematic behavior in children from single-parent homes.

Intermittent Disruptions of Family Life

Family life may be disrupted when the separated or divorced parents are together or there has been a visitation of one parent or the child is returning from spending time with the other parent. This is difficult for the child and difficult for the parents. This is especially problematic if the parents differ greatly in their approach to parenting where one is overly indulgent, or overly rigid. If one or both of the parents "bad mouth" the other in the child's presence, this is especially destructive and disruptive.

Children sometimes cling to the hope that parents will be reunited. Their regular disappointment may lead to angry hostile behavior. Sometime children may blame one parent for the other's absence: "Why won't you let daddy come back? You're mean. It's your fault." These are all justifiable and understandable reactions for children but this is no comfort to the parent or child confronting these.

Different Expectations for the Male and Female Parent

The American culture has very different expectations for male and female parents. We generally expect females to provide care and be nurturing to children. When they are left alone with the job we are less generous and supportive than when a male is left alone. When males are given custody of children, we assume that the female must be a contemptible person: "What kind of mother would...?" When men care for children we treat it like it is an extraordinary accomplishment: "You change her diapers?" "You replaced the zipper on his jacket?" "You won't believe it but this guy can really cook!"

Step-families and Blended Families

One half of two-parent families are "blended" or step-parent families. A step-parent family is a family where one of the adults is a step-parent. The step-parent is the non-biological, non-adoptive parent, who becomes a step-parent as a consequence of marrying someone with children. A blended family is a family which consists of two step-parents, each with his or her own children. Each brings his or her children to the marital union to create a blended family. Sometimes these blended families remain two step-families living together. Sometimes adoption is involved where there is a legal merging of the two families. In either case, we have two families living together to form one larger family.

The blended family is family living's version of the corporate merger. As in the case with corporate mergers, some are friendly and some are hostile. The blended family is like the

"Brady Bunch" in structure. Unfortunately, it is typically not like the "Brady Bunch" in quality of family life and living. The Brady blended family was exemplary in its capacity to merge two different families and manage the intermittent problems that arose. The Brady family is also not a real blended family. However, that is not to imply that real blended families are not or cannot be successful. Many are indeed but there are significant challenges along the pathway toward success.

Step-parent families are notorious for their problems. "Cinderella" and "Hansel and Gretel" come to mind immediately. Step-parent relationships are typically difficult and poor attitude plays a major role in this difficulty. The attitude of the the parent, step-parent, children and others are influential. A good or constructive attitude can go a long way toward insuring success. Please recall or review the section in "Chapter One - Kinds of Parent and Child Relations" relating to the step-parent and child relationship.

Blended families face similar challenges. What is said for one can be said for the other. Blended families are usually made up of two previous families that ended in divorce. They typically bear the hurt and show the "fall out." There is always residue and it always has an influence to some degree. The children must establish not only a relationship with another parent but also with other siblings. How much time children have to get to know these other people varies considerably. For some children these new relationships are thrust upon them. Some parents are more deliberate and give the children and themselves considerably more time to form relationships before establishing a blended family.

The children and parents have to work through these new relationships with considerable ambivalence. But the children seem most stressed by this demand. The child often feels torn with respect to his feelings of allegiance to the non-custodial parent, especially if that parent is attempting to maintain a relationship with the child. And who does the child take direction from? There is the parent, and the step-parent, and the non-custodial parent. And what if the guidance from these three parents is substantially different? These are the major interactional challenges facing children in blended families.

The parents have their stresses also. Is the parent willing and able to relinquish total responsibility for the children and share it with the step-parent? Has this aspect even been resolved vis-a-vis the non-custodial parent? Many parents in blended families are often not willing and able to make this adjustment. The common practice when this is so is that one parent assumes sole responsibility for her children and the other parent assumes sole responsibility for his children.

"Never the twain shall meet." This approach to child management presents very serious problems to the blended family. Children are not only confused by it but also often take advantage of it. Advantage taking has a tendency to place a wedge between the two parents and the two sets of families. This approach divides the two families and keeps them divided. Both parents and children contribute to this divisiveness.

Blended Families Are Making It Work

Despite the many potential problems, there are many step-families and blended families comprised of sensible adults who are devoted to making the newly established family successful. The failure of a previous marriage may serve to motivate. The concern for the healthy growth and development of the children drives them. The opportunity for a second chance energizes them. And there is the yet unfulfilled dream or goal of the American nuclear family, retrofitted for the 1990's.

Gay and Lesbian Families

Americans are slowly coming to the realization that one's sexual orientation does not make one an effective or non-effective parent. Success in parenting has nothing to do with sexual preference or sexual lifestyle. If heterosexuality were of significance or especially well suited for child rearing, then why are there so many heterosexual parents who are simply not good parents?

In fact, research data would blow holes in the balloons of homophobics. When quality of parenting or success in parenting is evaluated and then correlated with sexual preference, the data suggest that gay and lesbian parents as a group show better performance as parents. When we examine the growth and development of children, parental effectiveness, and parent's sexual preference we find no substantial difference among the children.

Good parenting produces good growth, development and behavior in children. The parent's sexual preference is of no consequence. However, what is striking is that children of gay and lesbian parents typically show greater tolerance for diversity, especially in the human relationship realm, than children of heterosexual parents.

Quite simply, gay and lesbian people make good parents too. (And I suppose to a lesser degree they make poor parents too, but they are disproportionately fewer in this category.) The child welfare and legal professions are beginning to recognize this fact also. As a consequence there has been a steady increase in the number of foster and adoption placements made to gay and lesbian adults. These two professions and the child development profession are monitoring these placements closely in order to study the impact gay and lesbian families have on the growth, development and behavior of children. Data to date is highly positive or favorable.

This watchfulness has prompted only one concern and it is not about the children. The concern is that the attitude of the larger American culture is too slow to change in this regard. The larger culture is still highly homophobic, and unnecessarily concerned about the children. The children seem to be doing very well. Children need loving and nurturing families and in large measure, they seem to be getting these needs met in gay and lesbian families.

Joint Custody

Joint custody is where both parents are awarded custody of their children equally following their divorce. Living arrangements vary but the typical arrangement is that children spend a predetermined portion of the week, month or year residing with each parent. With joint custody, there is no custodial or non-custodial parent. Both have custody and share that custody equally in theory even though the

child may not necessarily spend an equal amount of time with each parent.

Time is not the important factor. What is important is that both parents want to remain actively involved in the parenting of their children. The relationship with the child need not end simply because the relationship with the child's other parent is legally terminated. What is also equally important is that each parent wants the other to remain actively involved in the child's life. Relationship with the child is not terminated.

The parents may no longer share a domicile or an adult love relationship. But they shall continue to share the child and parenting with its many rights and responsibilities, advantages and disadvantages. As much as I would like to see it, this can not work with every couple. Parents who can agree to this and make it work are special. They are especially devoted to their children and know and want what is best for them. They typically have a very good relationship with their children. They realize that despite the failure of their marriage, the parent and child relationship need not also fail and be terminated as a consequence. That would not be good for the child nor the parent. One significant failure of the interpersonal type is more than enough. These are some of the characteristic attitudes and beliefs that parents who choose joint custody have.

However, it takes real effort, legitimate compromise, and genuine cooperation on the part of both parents to make joint custody work successfully. It requires that both parents must learn to put their marital issues aside and focus on the child and what is best for him. This is especially difficult when there is still much hurt, disappointment, and anger in and between the adults. This is even more difficult when there are significant differences of opinion as to how the child should be raised. Proximity of living quarters is helpful. The farther apart geographically, the more difficult the arrangement of joint custody becomes.

Despite these common obstacles, joint custody can work successfully if the parents work together. This enterprise of joint custody may be among the few joint endeavors some couples are able to work on successfully together. But working for the common good is essential to success. Commitment to, concern for and love of the child are the driving forces behind successful joint custody arrangements.

References

1. Labich, K. "Can Your Career Hurt Your Kids?" *Fortune*, May 20, 1991, p 38.

Activities

1. Identify your family's current stage of development using the family stage descriptions provided. Note that more than one stage description may apply.

2. Choose one parent-child pair and identify the stage of development that best describes each member of that one parent-child pair, using the stage descriptions provided.

3. With respect to the same parent-child pair, identify what you consider to be each person's most important need, characteristic, concern, issue or problem.

4. With respect to the same parent-child pair, are these needs, concerns, issues or problems being adequately met, addressed, solved or resolved, in your view? Explain why or why not.

5. Which best describes the current structure of your family? Two-parent, single-parent, blended, step-parent, etc.

6. Which best describes the current structure of your family? Nuclear or extended?

Chapter 7

Situational and Circumstantial Factors and Conditions

There are many situations and circumstances that the child and parent find themselves a part of and influenced by. Often these factors and conditions are usually not within the easy control of the child or the parent. Sometimes they are totally outside of the parent or child's control. These factors and conditions often have their origin outside of the family and parent and child interaction. Certainly both the child and the parent may be able to accommodate to these to some extent, but often they are placed in a reactive position rather than in a proactive position. They must react to, adjust to, accommodate to the situations and circumstances they find themselves a part. Each is individually influenced. Consequently their relationship is often affected.

These situational and circumstantial factors and conditions include such things as poverty, death of a family member, chronic illness, alcoholism and drug abuse, domestic and societal violence, separation and divorce, neighborhood, community resources and support systems, peace and war, employment and unemployment, job or career, and more. The impact that these and any others may have is a function of many different things. What might be inconsequential to one family may be of major importance to another. Families and individual family members show unique reactions and varying ability to cope with a given situation or circumstance.

POVERTY

Poverty is one of the most wrenching of conditions. It impacts on family life and individual development in pervasive and profound ways. The War on Poverty has been lost. There was too little deployed and not long enough. James Hymes tells us that poverty's stronghold continues:

"In twenty years we have made no progress whatsoever in reducing the percentage of young children in its grip. Obviously we have waged the war on poverty ineffectively and given up the fight too soon." The Children's Defense Fund concluded from its examination and comparison of data since 1980 that the number of children living in poverty in 1991 has increased by two million children. CDF advises that one out of five children live in poverty.

Poverty is about many things. For individuals and families it is about not having what is needed or not having enough of what is needed. Poverty is deprivation. It is about missed opportunities. It is about being on a non-leveled playing field or lacking equal opportunity. Poverty affects the tangible and the intangible (poverty of spirit). Poverty affects parent, child and family life.

Case study example:

When I was about nine or ten I was invited by a playmate to join his Boy Scout troop. He described the weekly meetings, and various activities, and occasional camping trips. It seemed interesting so I agreed to go with him to a weekly meeting. I was encouraged to join by my other peers and the troop leader.

I learned that a fee accompanied the application, so I delayed completing and returning the form. Then I learned that a uniform was required. When I learned how much the complete uniform would cost and the amount of the weekly dues, I concluded that my family could not afford my participation in scouting.

I recall my mother asking about dues and other expenses and I remember telling her that I didn't think I really wanted to be a scout and so why waste the money. I attended a few more weekly meetings but eventually told the troop leader that I didn't think scouting was quite what I was interested in.

To this day, I can feel the hurt and disappointment because I really did want to be a Scout. It made me angry but I was not sure what I was angry about: being poor, uniform requirements, not belonging, wanting what I could not have...

Many years later a close friend became a local administrator in the Boy Scouts of America. I learned that there were those same requirements: application fees, weekly dues, uniform costs, camping trip fees, etc. It was clear to me after all these years that scouting was still very much a middle class activity. When I asked Ron if there were any troops for poor children, or scholarship programs, etc. he didn't quite seem to get what my intent was. Coming from an affluent family,

he could not understand why I was becoming angry. And what did the fact that he had a company car have to do with anything? For the next couple of weeks our relationship suffered from my childhood poverty. Fortunately, our relationship survived.

This is poverty as seen briefly from a child's perspective. What about the parent? What is it like for the parent? What was it like when my mother was unable to meet the monthly mortgage after my father left the family unit. She eventually lost her home and we had to move into a rented apartment. I can recall the frequent moves we made from one apartment to another. The rent was twenty dollars less here at the new location or the current landlord was raising the rent beyond her ability to manage financially. What was it like for her to see her children no longer have the safety of their own yard to play in or their loss of leaving established friends behind and their apprehension of making new friends in another neighborhood?

I remember the agony in her eyes and in her voice as she once more tried to explain why we had to move again, why we could not have something, why she was preoccupied, why there was nothing to eat in the house, etc. And this woman was a generous person who would figuratively and literally give "the shirt off her back." But in all that doing without and explaining why, I also remember her patience and earnest effort to explain so her children could understand and not blame themselves for their misfortune. And we children were also fortunate that she was not only kind and concerned but also resourceful. To this day I can not figure out how we managed so well with so little. She taught us to not be wasteful, to be clear about what we needed, and above all how to survive.

And so I did survive my childhood poverty but not without consequence. I know that poverty has had a profound influence on my personal development, relationships, and career choices. I know that I am a frugal person, that I am resourceful, and more. I still do not spend money easily. Many marital arguments concerned money. My first professional human service job was as a social case worker with Public Assistance recipients, poor people.

My personal examples are used to illustrate the point that poverty impacts on the lives of people in a variety of ways and that impact often has long term consequences. Ask anyone who lived through and survived the Depression of the 1930's. Listen carefully, hear its pervasive influence on their lives and personal development. And you will learn much about poverty's grip. If you have lived in poverty, you don't have to ask. You are an expert. You just need to look back at your own life and development.

DEATH OF A FAMILY MEMBER

Death is the ultimate loss. Parents and children go through a similar process of grieving. The distinction is that with children, their age and developmental level play a profound role in their understanding of death and how they behave as they go through the grieving process. Adults often want to protect or shield children from this grief. But children must be allowed and helped to experience their own reaction to the death of a family member and permitted to grieve. It is only through grieving that a person comes to live with the loss in a healthy fashion.

The death of a family member means a special relationship is lost. And as a consequence certain things change. And those changes often mean additional losses. People's reaction to these losses are unique to them but also characteristic of people in general. There is disbelief, and anger, and resentment, and self-pity, and more anger, and self-disappointment, and guilt, and shame, and more anger, and eventually (hopefully) acceptance and resolution. All are guaranteed except the later two but the latter two are essential to healthy growth and development.

We are often surprised at these feelings in ourselves and others and how these feelings manifest themselves. A grieving child yells "I hate you!" at a sibling who was often told by the deceased parent, "You're going to put me in my grave!". Adults agonize when the child asks, "Why did my mommy have to die?" What can be said in defense of the deceased person or by way of explanation to the child who asserts, "I hate daddy for leaving us! It's all his fault we have to move." And depression abounds in adults and in children. How does one deal with another's depression when one is

depressed himself. Professional assistance may be needed.

In face of this loss and in the mix of these powerful emotions, parent and child interaction takes place. The parent's temper is quick. The good behaving child is now characterized by misbehavior. The gentle child hits and speaks angry words. The passive child withdraws and sinks into depression. An insightful child tries to comfort a sibling or parent. The deceased person is blamed on one day and idealized on another. It is all so confusing at first. And still relationships must continue but they seem so difficult these days. Everyone's ability to cope is being taxed. And we don't have much experience with this nor any real preparation for this kind of loss.

One thing is perfectly clear, relationships are stressed, behavior is modified, and things are not the same and will never be the same. The latter part is difficult enough for adults to understand. But children especially have a difficult time with this. Months after a grandparent has died and the child seems to have made considerable progress in his understanding, he will ask, "I wonder what grandpa will get me for my birthday."

CHRONIC ILLNESS

Chronic illness of a family member can do much to alter the family's standard of living, attitudes toward life and living, interpersonal relationships, and more. Chronic illness can afflict the parent, child or others living in the family unit. Regardless of who is afflicted, all family members suffer to some degree.

During the current session (1991) of Congress, the Senate is once again debating a National Health Bill. Of the millions of families that are without health insurance, an estimated ten million children are involved. What this means for these children is that they will receive little or no care or care only after illness has become severe. The results of this approach are increased pain and suffering and the likelihood of lost optimal health or future disability or impairment.

Relationships suffer too and exert a profound influence on personal development and attitude. Consider the family with a child with chronic ear infections. The child is in severe pain. The pain is persistent and he becomes fatigued and highly irritable. He pleas for help from the parent. The parent assures the child that the earache will go away. But it persists. The parent is hesitant to take the child to a physician for there is no health insurance to cover the cost of the office visit or the medication that will most likely be prescribed. The parent is in conflict and feels trapped. The tendency to provide treatment for the child is blocked by the realities of the high cost of medical treatment.

The child continues to fuss and this begins to wear on the parent's nerves. The parent is angry at her inability to bring comfort to her child and even more angered that her economic condition is preventing her from doing what is in the child's best interest. The child's pleas for parental assistance are not met and he begins to loose trust in the parent's ability to provide care and comfort. He feels helpless and to some extent abandoned. The child may express his distress and perspective: "It hurts and you won't help me. You don't care." Despite attempts to reassure and comfort the child, the parent also feels helpless. But guilt and shame enter the parent's consciousness and feelings of failure as a parent follow.

Chronic illness has an impact on how other family members behave and interact within the home. Families have unique responses but there is much similarity. Those who have lived under such conditions often describe family life and living as being "like walking on eggs." They have had to be very conscious of noise and activity level. There usually is a large measure of restrictiveness: playmates are not allowed in the house; radios can not be played loudly if at all, no roughhousing, etc. Often family members feel restricted and in some instances oppressed. There is much frustration and this often leads to anger and hostility.

Family members often feel that they must leave the home in order to feel free and be themselves and express themselves more fully and robustly. As a consequence some feel alienated. The home is not their home. The infirmed person's condition controls most of what others can and cannot do. And this is often perceived as unfair and is accompanied by feelings of resentment. Guilt and shame follow.

Both adults and children have these thoughts and feelings. They simply manifest themselves differently. Children will show them in childlike ways and adults will exhibit the adult version of the same thoughts and feelings. Unfortunately when adults are stressed, they sometimes cannot understand why the child is not more understanding or accepting of conditions, or not more helpful, etc. When parents view the child as adding to the problem, interactions often take a negative direction.

The family's standard of living is affected. Chronic illness often usurps a disproportionate amount of the family's financial resources. Sometimes it leads to financial ruin. A television special hosted by C. Everett Koop, M.D., former Surgeon General of the USA highlighted health care issues. (NBC: June 4, 1991) It depicted a family with a chronically ill child who requires extensive medical care and supervision daily. The father's employment was recently terminated. He was told "off the record" that the cost of his medical coverage was too expensive for the company. The employer officially denies this.

When the family's medical coverage expires in one month, the family will have to pay the cost of care which is $26,000 per month. The father is now unemployed and cannot afford the medical insurance premium that was paid by the employer. And if the family were able to obtain medical insurance, most insurance plans would not cover pre-existing conditions. The family may be well on its way to a poverty existence. And what about the child's medical needs? The medical treatment the child now receives is keeping this child alive.

ALCHOHOL AND DRUG ABUSE

Substance abuse in this country is steadily destroying not only the American family but also the nation. The pain and suffering substance abuse causes the American family is beyond measure in my opinion. Few American families are untouched by alcoholism and/or drug abuse and the many other problems that often accompany them: crime, violence, abuse, neglect, prostitution, poor health, accident, etc. And the number of victims, direct and indirect is mind-boggling. Lives and families are being virtually torn apart every day in every way.

Some professionals say at least one out of four families has been directly affected by either alcohol or substance abuse. Another estimate suggests that 28,600,000 Americans are children of alcoholics. About 6,600,000 of them are under eighteen years of age. Expressed another way, one in every eight Americans is a child of an alcoholic.

None is quite sure of the numbers of parents who are addicted to other substances. The numbers would be staggering I am sure. One thing is clear, drugs are everywhere and readily accessible to most who might want drugs. Drugs are being sold in the elementary school yard by elementary school children. An article by Ron Harris of the *Los Angeles Times* (appearing in the *Providence Sunday Journal* on May 26, 1991) makes a comparison between what a parent and his children experienced during their respective childhoods regarding exposure to drugs. Note the vast difference in then and now.

> Just about the time Bob was finishing high school in the late '60s, marijuana began to trickle onto campus. "It was really just a fringe crowd" that used it, Bob recalls. "You might go to a party and have a beer, but drugs weren't really socially acceptable."
> His daughter, Emily, can hardly recall a day when she wasn't aware of drugs. When she was 7, she was sent home after she took some marijuana that she had found in school. She has seen pills, cocaine, "just about everything," she says.
> Jarod and Michelle first saw drugs when they were 13. For Jarod, it was "guys on the street smoking crack" as he headed home from school. A classmate produced the first marijuana Michelle ever saw. Cocaine soon followed.

A substantial proportion of American families have direct experience with these destructive forces. My family is one of these victims.

Case study example:
At 22 years of age my brother was killed instantly in an automobile accident. He was a passenger. The driver was under the influence of drugs. I was in graduate school at the time. I often wondered how I ever managed to finish my graduate study. Weeks went by where I was unable to concentrate on my reading. I would read a paragraph and not remember one aspect about it. I periodically would notice tear drops on my book and would then realize I was crying in silence. I found myself occasionally loosing concentration while driving and this frightened me beyond description, especially since I was married and a father.

Family interactions were also disaffected. I recall my daughter shaking me and saying, "Daddy, I've been talking to you. Don't you hear me?" I was totally preoccupied with my thoughts and feelings and unaware of Veronica's attempt to converse with me. Being the insightful preschooler she was, she would typically say something like "You must be thinking of Ronald. I miss him too, daddy." We would commiserate with each other and then proceed to the topic of her conversation. I often felt fortunate during that period in my life that she was so insightful and understanding and able to not only articulate her own sense of loss but also appreciate mine.

I have seen so many other situations where family members were unable or not willing to talk about their thoughts and feelings. I also noticed how this inability or unwillingness hindered their resolution. When a family member is troubled by alcohol or drugs, this is a loss too. What is loss is the person who was and the person who could be. Interpersonal interaction often deteriorates and this is another manifestation of loss. There is a great emotional price that is paid by all family members.

Rhode Island has the unenviable distinction to invariably place in the top five among the fifty states on surveys which report the incidence of alcoholism. Over the years I have surveyed my classes by simply asking how many know directly beyond reasonable doubt that a member of their nuclear or extended families or a close friend is an alcohol troubled person. No matter what the size of the class, no one ever does not admit to this awareness. Even though this is not a scientific survey, I believe we must still be impressed by the response.

Interpersonal relationships are diminished by these insidious robbers of human sense and sensitivity. Drugs and alcohol make people slaves to insatiable appetites for excess. Excess in this case invariably spoils the person and his interpersonal relationships. Age and maturity level are no prerequisite. Adults, adolescents and children are diminished directly or indirectly by alcohol and drugs.

VIOLENCE
DOMESTIC AND SOCIETAL

American prominence in the world has eroded. We can no longer claim to be number one. By most reasonable criteria the American standard of living makes it best showing at about twelfth among industrialized nations. We no longer have the competitive, economical, and technological edge.

But there is still one area America and Americans excel in - violence. We demonstrate this in our homes, in our schools, in our shopping centers, in every niche of American society daily. And we unequivocally demonstrated our proclivity for violence as we heaped with pride and bravado our military weapons one upon the other in the Persian Gulf War. Is this the new world order? Do we really need to demonstrate before the entire world of nations how violent and destructive Americans really are.

In his book, *Twenty Years in Review*, James Hymes reports what he considers 1990's nastiest news:

> One-quarter of 1,000 Chicago inner-city middle school and high school students surveyed said that they had seen someone killed; 35% had witnessed a stabbing and 39% a shooting. While in New York City a company began marketing bullet-resistent vests for children. The demand: a rash of gunshot killings of young children. The price : $250 to $600. (p 412)

What has happened to America?

Violence Is Ubiquitous

It's everywhere! It is on TV, in movies, in magazines, in contemporary music, etc. But most depressing of all, violence is in our homes. Adults and children, young and old are victims. Wives are battered, husbands are battered, children are abused, and elderly family members are abused. No matter who is victimized and who is the victimizer, children live with and grow with domestic violence. The model they are given is clear: Yes, might is right! The solution to problems is force. When others don't submit willingly, beat them into submission.

Excessive Reliance
on Punishment

Even in non-violent homes, there is often excessive reliance on physical punishment in managing children. A slap, a spanking, a shake, a squeeze are long-standing, time-honored methods of discipline. Many parents were raised by such methods and they claim they "turned out alright." These are angry tactics. These are aggressive tactics. These are ineffective techniques that basically accomplish nothing more than to teach our children to use force rather than words and reason.

These harsh methods are violent and they weaken our relationship with our children and lessen our influence over them. And they teach our children many things parents do not intend to teach them: to fear their parents, to have contempt for their parents, to want vengeance and to be violent in their dealings with others. When these thoughts and feelings exist, the parent and child relationship has been diminished.

Case study example:
I recall a boy with whom I attended high school. Bobby was a quiet, gentle, good looking and generally well liked young man. He won the Golden Glove Award, which attested to his superiority in boxing. We occasionally spent time together and he was generous with his time and skill as he taught me how to better defend myself. It always amazed me how he could unleash such controlled power so quickly in a boxing match. Few were a match for him and he exuded a quiet, unspoken confidence.

During high school graduation week, Bobby murdered his father. As well as I thought I knew him, I had no idea of what was going on between Bobby and his father to precipitate such a violent and final act.

Bobby is like many, who remain silent, who do not tell others what is going on in their lives. It was only later that I learned that his father beat him almost daily. He was a man troubled by alcohol and failed aspirations. The violence he perpetrated on his son, flesh of his flesh, turned a gentle soul violent and was his own undoing. Some have speculated that this may have been the father's insidious plan. I don't know. But I do know that it is sad beyond all sadness.

Violence is mankind's "dark side." Its use represents a failure or lack of other more constructive, non-violent skills. It is often preceded by frustration and inadequacy and

114

often fueled by fear, false images or misunderstandings, and the need for power and control. The following example is a case in point.

Case study example:

At the time I was working with families where unemployment was the "presenting problem." George and Renee had been married several years. George had a poor history of employment. He had just been fired because he had assaulted his boss. My job was to assist George in getting employed. During the initial fact-finding visits I made to their home, I had noticed bruises on Renee's face, neck and arms. Nothing was said but it was apparent to me that George had difficulty managing his anger and was prone to violence. After I had gathered background data, I met with each individually and confronted each with my observations.

Each expressed "love" and "devotion" for one another but these were expressed more in terms of ownership: "He's all I have." She's my woman." They acknowledged that their relationship and general life circumstance could be better and in fact they both wanted a better life together. I made a judgement at that time that their relationship was more important than George's employment status. I offered my assistance in helping them work on their relationship. Renee was eager. George was reluctant.

But after much "nagging" from Renee, he agreed to meet just once to talk about their relationship and not his lack of employment. George had a long history of unemployment and under-employment. Therefore, my deemphasis on his employment status was somewhat baffling to him as he indicated that no social worker before me had ever wanted to talk about anything else but his getting a job. So he was somewhat suspicious. But agreement to meet for one marriage counseling session was eventually reached.

When I arrived for the first meeting I felt stressed because George had agreed to only one such meeting and I knew that if I "fouled up," my plan to get them to focus on their relationship would end with that meeting. I entered the kitchen and was greeted by Renee and at her invitation I sat at the kitchen table. George was not in the kitchen so I asked of his whereabouts. He was in the living room and Renee went to get him. He was still resisting and although I could not see their interaction it was apparent by what I heard that Renee was coercive and threatening. I overheard George question my motivation and ability to help. Speaking of me, Renee assured George that I was different.

After about fifteen minutes of sneering at each other and some physical prodding by Renee, George reluctantly accompanied Renee into the kitchen. Renee sat to my left at the table. George sat directly across from me and placed a hand gun on the table

immediately in front of him. My blood ran cold as I thought to myself "What in the hell am I doing here? I have a wife and child." I was beginning to have difficulty sorting these feelings and concerns from what should be my professional response. To be honest, I was terrified. Furthermore, I was never prepared for this type of situation professionally so I was operating on pure intuition.

I looked George straight in the eyes and said something of this sort: "George, if you do not want to meet and talk about what we had planned to talk about today, tell me so and ask me to leave. This is your home and I will not stay if I am not wanted. You agreed to just one meeting of this sort. Will you be a man of your word or not? If you tell me to stay, the gun must go!" George was silent for what seemed to me an eternity.

Renee began to prod and nag him. I turned to Renee and said, "Renee, please be quiet. This must be George's decision or the deal is off." She offered resistance but I was firm and uncompromising with her. She sat back in her chair and became silent. George watched my interaction with her very closely. "Stay!" George said. And so begun a long series of marital counseling sessions.

What I learned in the weeks that followed enlightened me. Each had learned the other's vulnerabilities and each used these to gain power and dominance over one another. As a child, Renee had an incestuous relationship with her father, who also beat her. Renee's father was a violent man who obtained what he wanted by force and intimidation of the less powerful. Outside of his home he seemed to be an inept and powerless white man with few skills and much bigotry and hatred, especially directed at black people. He would often feel guilt for his actions and Renee learned to use his guilt (his vulnerability) to get what she wanted. Her father showed her much favoritism and their relationship seemed to resemble a courtship in many ways.

George was born and raised in a southern black community where he learned as a black child that white people possessed the power and to never pursue a white female sexually because it was taboo and could kill you. As a child he observed many black males beaten for simply talking to a white female. Some black males were badly disfigured and some even killed for having sexual contact with white females. He was frequently warned by his mother against such behavior. White males raped black females and went without punishment. He lived a life of repression and oppression, especially by white people who prevented him from having what ever he wanted. As an adult, he relocated and eventually settled in Rhode Island.

When Renee and George met, their personal vulnerabilities meshed almost perfectly. Renee had learned to be a victim but was able to find what little power there was in her victimization. She used the underlying powerlessness and guilt of her victimizer (her father) as her source of power to get what she wanted. Her marrying a black man sent a powerful statement to her father: You no longer can dominate me. I am no longer your sexual property. I am now the sexual property of a black man. How does that make you feel?

These messages directed primarily at her father and her marriage to George terminated her relationship with her father. He lost his dominance and control as well as access to her sexually. She became free of her father's dominance and exploitation but the cost to her was the dominance and exploitation of another male. There was little gain for Renee and so her sense of entrapment and struggle for power and control was transferred to another arena - the marital relationship.

In marrying Renee, George obtained what he had been always told he could not have. She was his prize and he was afraid of losing her. This made him vulnerable. This vulnerability made him angry. Also he often felt manipulated by Renee and this added further to his vulnerability and sense of being controlled. Renee was acutely aware of the power and influence she possessed. What she did not realize initially was how similar this relationship was to what she had with her father. George had become a slave to what had been denied not only to him during his childhood but also to his slave ancestors. It seemed that George was trying to get even for all those generations of repression and oppression heaped upon blacks by misguided whites.

This case illustrates the powerful influence of childhood experiences, of patterns of interpersonal interaction that are established during childhood and that are perpetuated during adulthood, of the need for power and control, of false images, of the use of violence in place of more constructive, non-violent measures and more. It also shows how violence minimizes interpersonal relationships and family living.

SEPARATION AND DIVORCE

The potential negative impact of separation and divorce on children concerns most parents and child care professionals and rightly so. There is some good news to report however. The negative reactions that children initially show are usually short term. Children typically begin to accommodate to their sense of loss more quickly in fact than their parents. With proper support from parents and others, children from divorced homes are no less well adjusted than children from two-parent families. It seems that the structure of the home is less crucial than the behavior of the adults involved.

Adult Attitude and Behavior

A separated or divorced couple who are concerned for their child's well being and behave supportively to the child and remain positively connected to the him will help insure his eventual positive adjustment to the separation or divorce of his parents. A couple living together in disharmony and discord will do much to minimize the child's healthy growth and development. The structure of the home is not crucial. The important factor is the emotional climate of the home. If the home is happy, responsive to the child's needs, and not overburdened with other problems, the child will develop well. Sometimes separation and divorce help establish a better emotional climate by removing or reducing the stress and storm of a failing marital relationship.

Continuing Contact

Contact with both parents is usually important. But contact must be positive. If contact with the parent is negative and disruptive to the child and the family, then problems develop. Children who have established a sense of attachment or connection must be allowed to continue their contact and relationship with the parent. Even when children have been abused or neglected, they typically are still connected to the parent.

Contact with an abusive parent must be monitored closely to assure that abusiveness is not continued. Allowing contact with an abusive parent is certainly questioned by many. The child's attachment and desire to have contact with the parent must be considered and kept in mind. Furthermore, we must acknowledge that some child abuse is the consequence of frustration in the marital relationship and disappears under controlled conditions. When this occurs, the parent and child now have an opportunity to continue their relationship on more positive terms. Parents and child welfare professionals must support such constructive changes and opportunities.

Denying contact is easy but not necessarily in the child's best interest. Furthermore, denying a parent contact with the child may exacerbate the situation further. Many adult relationships remain hostile and injurious to the child because one parent may want to deny the other parent contact with the child. When children are used as pawns to fight old battles, children suffer and so do the parents. These counterproductive patterns must be given up and replaced by more constructive measures. The child may feel abandoned and unloved by the parent with whom he has minimal or no contact.

Adult Coping

Children have further problems when one or both parents are overwhelmed. Separation and divorce are matters of loss. Loss of contact with one or both parents, loss of contact with grandparents and other relatives, loss of domicile, loss of friends, loss of standard of living, etc. are some of the many losses that are part of separation and divorce. Losses need to be minimized as much as possible. When the children experience multiple loss, children have problems.

Faulty coping by the parent leads to problems in the child. These behaviors might include one parent being unfairly presented or portrayed by the other, the child being used as a pawn in a continuation of the marital struggle, the child being made to feel blame or guilt, or being compared unfavorably to the other parent. Children have problems when inappropriate demands are made of the child to meet the parent's emotional needs.

The Non-Custodial Parent

Reduced or curtailed contact may be a symptom of the non-custodial parent's inability to cope or may be changes that are forced as a consequence of separation and divorce. This parent may feel out of touch with events in the child's life and may be suffering from estrangement. This parent may have to invest more effort, energy and time to maintain the relationship with the child. This necessity may be threatening to the parent or simply difficult because of work and other demands.

The non-custodial parent may experience distress after visiting the child. The parent is reminded of the loss that has been suffered. Depression, anger, remorse, guilt, and other powerful feelings emerge. These feelings may actually serve as negative reinforcers to maintaining contact with the child. Not visiting the child as frequently helps to lessen the intensity and frequency of experiencing these feelings. Therefore the parent lessens the frequency of visitations.

The non-custodial parent may be the target of the child's anger and resentment concerning the divorce. The child's negative images of the parent, sometimes adversely shaped or influenced by the other parent, must be coped with. The parent may have fear of losing a place of importance in the child's life. This is further exacerbated by the fact that this parent's role may be defined by the other (custodial) parent. The other parent may limit the role or may expect more than the parent is able to give.

The non-custodial parent may also feel helpless in protecting the child from bad influences, threats, poor role models, etc. This is an especially sensitive area if the other parent enters into a relationship with another adult that this parent perceives as being detrimental to the child. Of course jealously enters into the picture also. If the child speaks of the other adult frequently and in favorable terms this parent may be threatened. If the child refers to this other person as "mother" or "father," this can be an explosive happening.

The non-custodial parent may lose the importance of being the child's main source of financial support. Support payments may be seen as supplemental or may even be lacking, thus lessening even further the parent's sense of importance. As a consequence, this parent may seek other ways of being important. These efforts may enhance the relationship but they may diminish it if the new means cause problems.

Visitation

Visitation times and location must be worked out. The visiting parent may have

117

difficulty finding a satisfactory place to visit with the child. Also the visiting parent may have to face the fact that the child may have other plans in place of the visit. This is especially common with adolescent children. When more than one child is involved, taking the children out together may present some problems. Age, gender and interest differences among the children are realities that must be addressed.

Work and personal schedules or routines may have to be adjusted in order to visit with the child. Visitation may require dealing with an ex-spouse who makes it inconvenient for the absent parent to visit. The visiting parent may feel an obligation to entertain during visits with the child and to be a "super" parent. This may cause special problems for all involved. The child may use this situation to win special favors, privileges, etc. The child may become excessively demanding and this may adversely affect parent and child interaction.

Both custodial and non-custodial parents may also have to face feelings of guilt, inadequacy, and lowered status in connection to parenting. Parents may feel even worse if the child seems to be doing better since the separation or divorce. It's ironic that the parent might feel disheartened by the fact that the child's situation has improved. But this underscores for some parents their lost status as a parent.

These are typical features and behavioral consequences of separation and divorce. These affect the child and parent in a variety of ways. How these are managed and accommodated to affect parent and child interaction, parent and parent interaction and sibling interaction. How parent and child emerge from separation or divorce and the long term consequences that follow are a function of many things.

But the overwhelming fact is that the child's adjustment to separation and divorce and the long term consequence for individual development are predominantly a function of parental behavior and adjustment. Parents who demonstrate predominantly positive behavior and healthy adjustment have children who show a similar pattern. Parents who show substantial negative behavior and maladjustment will have children who suffer greater and more long term negative consequences.

New Data

A major study of more than 20,000 children puts the impact of separation and divorce in proper perspective. Divorce per sé is not what triggers long-term problems in children. This study suggests that many of the problems children show preceded the actual separation and divorce and were more likely a consequence of living in a dysfunctional family. Marital discord and other problems are the most probable culprit. Children show an adverse reaction to these long before and long after the event of a divorce.

One of the researchers cautioned that this study "does not mean that there are no ill effects of divorce, it does not mean that divorce isn't difficult. It does mean that we have to be careful about attributing behavioral difficulties in children to the event of divorce rather than to other aspects of family relations." (*Science*, June 1991, reported in *The Providence Journal Bulletin*, 6/7/91)

In a substantial number of cases, children's attitude and behavior show improvement shortly following separation and divorce. This is especially so when the event brings about a substantial cessation or end to hostilities and other forms of family discord. Such data suggests that staying together for the sake of the children is ill-advised. A variety of sources suggest that marital fights and other forms of family discord hurt children more than divorce itself.

How are children affected in their adjustment and individual development. And what are the short and long term consequences for individual development. I shall use myself as just one example of the many possible outcomes.

Case study example:
I was nine years old when my father left the family unit. Contact with him was intermittent and brief following his official exit and persisted for less than a year. Since then I have had no contact with him except for one letter he wrote to me when my brother died. That letter nearly enraged me. I never responded but neither did I discard it. This was all I ever received from him since his departure.

Prior to foreclosure on our home, my mother attempted to work during the evenings while I watched my three-year-old sister and two-year old brother. The stress and anxiety of her children at home alone (child care facilities were nearly non-existent) and the insufficiency of what she was able to earn eventually forced her to apply for public assistance. That was the beginning of many significant changes in family life and living. Most changes were characterized by loss. Loss of relationships, home, economic comfort, dignity, etc. The family went from middle class to poverty in less than one year. My family had to move out of its home as my mother could not meet the monthly mortgage payments.

For me the greatest challenge was dealing with my feelings of abandonment and anger. Initially there were many things that I did not understand about what happened to us so quickly and unexpectedly. But my mother is a kind and gentle person and she took much time and effort to explain as much as she could to the extent that she understood it herself. Because of her good example, I adjusted to these changes and moved forward developmentally.

Although I consider myself to be a reasonably healthy person, I am not without some deficits as a consequence. The one thing that has remained a powerful force in my personality is my prevailing sense of abandonment. I vowed as a child that I would never abandon my children for I would never want them to have this same feeling. This feature of my personality has also made me a very devoted person to people, to issues, to causes, to justice, etc. I have had many friends over my life time. Some of whom have had major personality flaws and are very different from myself but I have never abandoned them.

This sense of devotion and long-standing feeling of abandonment and my vow (devotion in this connection) to not abandon my own children, kept me in a bad marriage long after I realized it was probably not going to work out. I am a diehard. I hate to give up on things. I have difficulty letting matters go if there is even a remote chance of success. Some people call this persistence. My point is that the same feature can be an asset or a liability depending on the circumstance. My other point is that even though I emerged from my parents' separation and divorce as a reasonably healthy person, some dimensions of my personality have been altered for all time, for better or for worse. And these alterations influence my behavior in concrete ways every day of my life. These characteristics have influenced my interpersonal relationships, my career choice, my task orientation, and more.

To conclude, children and adults are invariably influenced by separation and divorce. How well they adjust immediately and over the long term is a function of many things. The primary factor in children's development is how well their parents adjust. It therefore would behoove us as individuals and as a culture to be supportive to and assist parents (and their children) in their adjustment to separation and divorce. We must try to avoid adding to the loss that parents and children experience. We should try to minimize their losses. In so doing we shall minimize (not eliminate) the adverse effects of separation and divorce especially over the duration of the individual's development.

COMMUNITY RESOURCES AND SUPPORT SYSTEMS

The environment within which families live contribute directly to family life and living. Families show their intuitive understanding of this when purchasing a home. Notwithstanding financial and other constraints, families are interested in the immediate neighborhood and the quality of the schools their children will attend. Is the neighborhood safe with respect to such things as automobile traffic patterns and traffic signs and signals, incidence of crime, playground accessibility and security, police and fire services, etc.? These matters are of special concern to parents of young children.

Neighborhood

Families that reside in the inner cities where neighborhoods have suffered great deterioration often live under daily stress because of the risks that their children face daily and the lack of services that add to those risks. Playgrounds are absent or sparse. Those that exist are in considerable disrepair. Some of the problems: Equipment and landscape are damaged or more accurately vandalized. The areas are not adequately enclosed by fences. Transactions for drugs and sex take place there. There is no organized recreational program for the neighborhood youth. As a consequence, families try to restrict where their children go and play. Very often, yard space is limited or non-existent. Consequently parents and children find themselves engaged in a tug of war concerning with whom and where the children will play.

Families that reside in communities where there is an abundance of adequately maintained and wisely placed playgrounds enjoy a different kind of life style. In these neighborhoods, these areas are relatively safe along many dimensions, frequently patrolled by police, often frequented by families whose parents will employ a passive supervision and intervene if unacceptable behavior is observed. The families and community at large regard these areas as assets that are important to family life and worth maintenance and protection. In such neighborhoods, young children need not be restricted to their back yards and parents can relax in knowing that their children are close by and relatively safe. Consequently these parents and children enjoy a more relaxed family life.

Schools

Some neighborhoods and communities have schools that not only provide good basic education but also provide an interesting mix of extracurricular activities for children to participate in after school and occasionally on weekends. Children may remain at or return to the school setting after the normal school day to participate in such activities. Teachers and other adults offer leadership and supervision. Often this leadership is given on a volunteer basis. Such communities are very fortunate to have such wholesome adults.

Unfortunately, this society often takes the contribution of these adults for granted or minimizes its importance. A case in point: This culture shows its respect and appreciation for teachers, in particular, by rewarding them with the lowest of professional salaries. Of course some communities are attempting to address this issue by better compensation for teachers but we are very ambivalent as a society.

For example, during contract negotiations the very same community that has done much to raise teacher salaries points to the fact that a particular teacher group is among the highest paid in the state or nation as a ploy aimed to minimize the amount of the next teacher raise. Why this diatribe? Please understand, the quality of our educational system and the competence and commitment of teachers and other public servants directly affects the growth, development and behavior of our children and the quality of family life and living.

Other Human Services

Other human service organizations such as organized recreational programs, religious, civic, and special interest groups contribute much to the quality of life families enjoy. There should be something wholesome for everyone and every family. Communities that have such services and resources readily available and in abundance are better able to constructively occupy children's time and energy. Support services to children and families such as community mental health agencies, child guidance clinics, youth and family services, etc. play a vital role in maintaining family health and preventing manageable problems from becoming unmanageable ones. An ounce of prevention is indeed worth a pound of cure. A stitch in time often saves nine.

JOB OR CAREER

Job Related Absences

Job or career may have a positive or negative influence on family life and relationships. Some jobs result in extended separations from family members. People involved in sales, transportation, oil exploration, international trade, military service are examples of such work related absences. Of course there are also careers that allow for more family interaction and may contribute in a positive way to family relationships. Many women choose teaching careers so they may be at home with their children during school vacations and have a similar daily schedule as their school age children. Certainly many fathers have chosen careers or refused certain job opportunities out of concern for how family involvement might be affected if they were pursued.

Some jobs by their very nature involve unusually long or extended hours. The restaurant business is one that comes to mind immediately, especially if self-owned. Actually long work hours is rather characteristic of many self-employed individuals, especially if it is a newly established business.

Infringements

Home based work presents unique problems for both the work and the family. The work may interfere with the family. The family may interfere with the work.

Home based child care is a classic case. Long hours are common, a large portion of the home environment may be allocated for use during the work day, the equipment and materials needed to provide child care are interspersed among typical household furnishings. Non-family members are on the premises for long periods and develop a familiarity with the home environment that some family members resent. In her book, *Shared Spaces* (Consortium Publishing) Georgia Houle addresses the task of managing such problems.

Job Related Stress or Risks

Some jobs or careers are especially stressful or may even place the worker at real risk. Police work and fire fighting score high in both areas. The stress and risk is not confined to just the worker. Family members suffer.

A colleague of mine recalls that each time she heard the fire truck's siren when her husband was on active duty with the fire department, her heart would momentarily pound with great force. She would think to herself and repeat the phrase "I hope he is safe!" and anxiously await his telephone call which assured her he was in fact O.K. If her children had been attentive to the siren, they would inquire: "Did daddy call yet?" Her husband later suffered a heart attack which resulted in his early retirement. And although his ill health brought a new set of concerns and stresses, the sound of the siren no longer affected her viscerally as it once did.

Military Service

Military service must be mentioned because there are so many "military families." A husband or wife, mother or father, son or daughter, sister or brother who is serving in the military or has made the military a career impacts upon family life and living in profound ways. In recognition of this, the armed services have commissioned many, many studies in order to gain insight into the nature of this impact and how best to manage it in a constructive manner. Such studies have led to the armed services establishing a wide range of services and resources for military personnel and their families. These include educational and social service, religious services, child care services and more.

Disruption of Family Life and Living

The most common problem military families experience is the regular disruption of family life and living. There are many circumstances that cause these disruptions and there are many manifestations. All family members are affected. A common difficulty that exists is the regular and lengthily separation of family members and their reunification and the reintegration of the absent member.

Case study example:
Let's take the sailor who is at sea for a five or six month duration. Separation is lengthy and communication between families members is difficult. In the father's absence, the wife and children learn to manage well for themselves. Mother assumes all responsibilities that might be shared in a family where the couple assists one another. The children may even be encouraged to be more independent and self-sufficient and contribute to the care and maintenance of the home. The at home people work out a division of labor that they can live with happily.

Father returns to the home on leave from active duty for a month. He tries to reestablish his position as head of household. This means that his wife may have to relinquish some of her influence as well as responsibilities. It is frequently difficult for the wife to do this. Resentment and a struggle for power and control are characteristic. Even though the couple may recognize that this is happening and may want to avoid it, it still occurs.

Frustration and guilt are common as the couple is ambivalent about their respective feelings. The wife: "I should be happy he's home but I don't like his wanting to take over." The husband: "I am the head of this family but my wife and children seem to want me out of the picture."

Affectional matters have to be also addressed. Long periods of not being close sexually necessitates time and sensitivity in order to reestablish the sexual intimacy that has been shared in the past. One or both may show an insensitivity or lack of understanding of the necessity to allow each time and circumstance to recreate their past physical and emotional intimacy.

The children experience their unique challenges also. They must now take their "marching order" from someone who has been absent and who may be unfamiliar with how things have been done and why they are done this way and by whom. The children are confused and ambivalent also. They have missed their father but they have worked out a life style in his absence. His presence brings another adult to whom they must listen and he is competition for mother's attention. Father may be perceived as an intruder. They are angry for this intrusion and they also experience guilt for having these feelings.

Absence does not make the heart grow fonder. Any job or career which leads to regular and prolonged absence from the family unit will result in relationship problems of the kind mentioned herein. The incidence and degree of such problems will vary according to the duration of separation and the family members's capacity to manage the repeated separations and reunifications.

On the positive side, a job or career can contribute positively to a person's sense of value and accomplishment. And this may impact favorably on family life. Consider the mother who returns to work after being at home for several years. She is working at a job she enjoys and is experiencing many positive feelings about herself and her career. These positive feelings spill over into family life and enhance interpersonal interaction within the family unit.

Mother feels and acts revitalized by the challenges of her job. For her they are welcomed changes from the mundane job of housekeeping. Despite the changes her return to work has caused in their lives, her children have noticed a change in their mother's attitude and behavior, which they like. Her husband finds her more interesting and less preoccupied with matters which he did not consider very important. He is pleased that she is happy and satisfied with her work. Furthermore, his assumption of more child care responsibilities has brought him closer to his children. In the long term, mother's pursuit of her career has been a good thing for all.

EMPLOYMENT STATUS AND STATE OF THE ECONOMY

The employment status of family members may affect family relationships in a positive or negative manner. Many aspects contribute to which type of impact will be experienced. Both parents and children are included here as worker or non-worker and each is affected in different ways.

The Child's Employment Status

A child who is not attending school on a full time basis but is not gainfully employed may present certain frustrations for all involved. The state of the economy or the attitude or aspirations of the people involved may be complicating factors as well as the family's economic standing. A child who is a recent college graduate may simply be engaged in the job hunting process. This is new for the child and it may bring certain frustrations and disappointments, which may adversely affect family interaction. The child may be depressed and motivation to seek employment may be lessened. The parent may have to provide an extra measure of encouragement and support to the child during this period.

If the child has unrealistic expectations for his first job, the parent may be frustrated with the child's inability to view job offers as opportunities that will help the child eventually get that idealized position. Laziness on the child's part is yet another type of frustration that may result in much parent and child discord. The child may have many excuses for his lack of employment. And no matter how reasonable sounding they are, the parent eventually may tire of them.

On the positive side is the child who is not only gainfully employed and showing many signs of his new level of independence but also has a willingness to lessen the parent's share of supporting him and may now contribute concretely to the family's financial support. This does much to contribute to the parent's good feelings about the child and her success in parenting him. If all are reasonable in their expectations, family life and living is strengthened.

However, if all are not reasonable then there may be a weakening of family relationships. If the parent were to expect a disproportionate and unreasonable share of the child's earnings, problems would seem inevitable. If the parent's expectations were reasonable but perceived by the child as unnecessary and excessive, arguments would seem inevitable.

Although the family was not in financial need, I have known many families that have required their employed children to contribute to household finances. For these families it is a matter of principle and another lesson among many they want their children to learn. Some of these families have not used the money to meet household expenses. Rather they have established savings accounts unknown to the contributing child in the child's name, access to which may be given in the future.

Of course some children make their contribution with a good attitude. Others unfortunately come to feel that their contribution makes them shareholders in family assets or gives them equal or superior decision making authority regarding how family resources shall be used and allocated. I have known children who have demanded "their share" of the profit from the sale of the parent's home.

Some children come to the position that since they are now contributing to family finances, that they should no longer be expected to do certain household chores. The financial contribution may be regarded by the child as a substitute for services previously rendered by the child or as services the child should now be given in exchange for his financial contribution - a kind of payment for services. These misunderstandings and misconceptions must be confronted by the parent and reconciled by all involved to establish or reestablish a more sensible and healthy attitude.

Parent's Employment Status

Extended parental unemployment and underemployment is a very serious matter. My work with families where a parent was unemployed taught me many things about the importance of work to both adult health and family health. The self-concept, self-worth and self-esteem are quickly affected in a negative manner and continue to take a battering as unemployment continues. Depression often follows and family relationships invariably suffer to some degree.

Alcohol abuse is a common symptom and exacerbates the problem. Proud, strong, independent parents suffer the loss of their dignity and sometimes the respect of others inside and outside the family unit. The loss of self-respect is not far behind. The unemployed parent may be regarded by others as a malingerer, ner-do-well, etc. The unemployed parent may even come to accept these assessments himself. Further deterioration of the self-concept, self-worth, etc. follow such acceptance.

Failed expectations and a disruption of the status quo precipitate family discord. A wife who has been able to remain at home may now be forced to take employment. The couple's expectations for family living must now be adjusted. The husband may feel he has failed to uphold his end of their shared dream for family life. The wife may resent her having to work and exchanging roles with her husband. If they cannot reconcile these disruptions, discord is inevitable. Of course many couples successfully accommodate to such forced changes and reconcile their individual and shared disappointments.

Similar disruptions in family life take place even when they have been anticipated and planned for. A common occurrence in this regard happens when a wife and mother who has remained at home eventually ventures out of the home for employment or education.

Case study example:
    Consider a mother who has been trained as a teacher but has remained home while her children

were preschoolers. Now that the children are in school on a full time basis, the mother decides to begin or resume her teaching career.

When this change is implemented, it requires adjustment by all involved. The children have become accustomed to having their mother at home when they depart for and return from school. This may no longer be the case. They have also enjoyed a high degree of accessibility to mother and similar involvement with her. She has been attentive, encouraging, supportive, always available as a playmate, as a reliable service provider. This may change substantially as mother is no longer on the premises in waiting to respond to the children's needs and desires. The children may also be required to do things they may not have been required to do before, such as help prepare the evening meal, or assume other household chores. Children often find these changes disruptive and often resist when they are being asked to help.

The mother has her share of adjustments and ambivalences. She may have to give up her proficient management of the household. Letting go is not easy, especially when others may do things differently and not as expediently or proficiently. This may have been her sole domain and now it must be shared. She is ambivalent about this. She wants her family members to be self-sufficient and independent but she may still want them to need her. Part of her wants them to succeed and part of her wants them to have difficulty to demonstrate her worth or value to the family.

The job has its demands and she wants to do a good job. She may come home fatigued as extra time and energy often have to be allocated when beginning a new job. Her job may also require some preparatory work at home as lesson plans are developed, materials gathered, and student written work is evaluated. She welcomes these new challenges and revels in the excitement of thrusting herself into her career. But she also resents that this is taking her away from or depriving her of the family life she has come to know and enjoy. Husband and children may not be aware or understand these job demands and the ambivalences she is experiencing. She may be disappointed and even angry with them for their lack of understanding or insensitivity.

She may feel guilty when she has to refer the child to father so she may attend to what she is doing at the moment. It seems that so many things have an urgency now that did not have before she returned to her job or career.

Affectional expression may suffer. Even if her husband understands her fatigue and diminished interest in sexual intimacy, he may still show and feel his deprivation. He may wonder if his wife's return to work was such a good idea after all. And the children seem to be so much more needy now with so many more trivial concerns. He feels disappointment in

himself that he would consider that her return to work was not such a good idea in the first place and that his children would have trivial concerns in the second place. So much about family life has changed. Was this really a good idea at this time. He thought that they had thought it through carefully. Doubt is a common companion these days.

Similar changes and the accompanying thoughts and feelings are experienced by mothers who enter college or technical school to begin their education or update their knowledge base and skill repertoire in order to resume their careers. Children and husbands will sometimes make this process difficult. But on the other hand, children and husbands can also be wonderfully supportive and genuinely helpful to mothers as they venture beyond the home environment.

CIVIL RIGHTS AND OTHER LIBERATION MOVEMENTS

Along with the many changes in civil rights and the liberation of men, women and children from sex role stereotypes and other constraints, there have been commensurate changes in family life and living. These changes have not always been easy but they most often have been to the benefit of individuals, families and the culture in the long term.

Child care is a case in point. Day care services during President Richard Nixon's administration was cited as the biggest threat to the American family. In fact it was predicted that child care would actually bring about the demise of the American family if it were permitted to flourish. Nothing could be farther from the truth. The child care movement emerged out of need not as part of a plot to destroy family life. In fact, child care was a need resulting from changes already occurring in the American family. However, many misguided people would have us believe that it was day care that was creating such changes. The truth is that day care was helping to preserve and strengthen the American family not alter or weaken it.

Americans need to stop listening to the unaffected and begin listening to the parents for whom child care is either lacking or available. They tell a different story and their story is how it really is. Child care allows parents to keep their family together. Although some parents choose to work when they financially could manage without the employment, most parents need to work in order to keep their families financially solvent. But even among parents who must work, there is guilt and concern. Guilt about giving up their parental responsibilities for the child to another adult. Concern that the child will be harmed as a consequence. Guilt and concern are intertwined.

The unfortunate common view is that the parent is giving up her responsibility and that the children will be harmed. Public misunderstanding about this perpetuates this misunderstanding and keeps guilt and concern enmeshed. Many have attempted to show through systematic research that day care is harmful to children. What we have learned is this: Bad child care no matter where and by whom it is provided is harmful to children. Good child care no matter where and by whom it is provided is good for children. Child care in and of itself is neither harmful or beneficial to children. What is crucial is the quality of care that is provided.

So let's stop beating a dead horse and get on with it. Namely, let us as a nation provide the best child care we can to the children and families that need it. Namely, let us stop punishing families for their predicament and begin to help families improve their situation. Namely, let us stop blaming the victim. Let us attack the real culprits in American society: poverty, unemployment, prejudice and bigotry, alcohol and drugs, inadequate or absent family support services, and our own blindness to the real causes of the weakened American family.

The Feminist Movement

The feminist movement has focused on the status of women and has attempted to shed light on certain inequities in the American culture and improve women's status. But the feminist movement is not just about women. It is about men and women, boys and girls, adults and children, young and old. It is about people. Its issues are people issues.

In my opinion the feminist movement has done as much to advance the position of men and children as it has to advance the status of women. The feminist movement has helped free women to pursue interest and goals beyond children and families. This pursuit has been not in place of, not instead of, or in escape of, but in addition to. Certainly the feminist movement has forced certain issues that needed to be forced. Change does not come just because it is right or fair or needed. Change sometimes has to be forced down our resistant throats. History will ultimately show if I too am among the misguided or among the knowing.

Some Positive Changes

Consider some of the changes. Our children, both male and female, are beginning to see both men and women in a more enlightened manner. They are now more than ever before seeing their mothers and sisters as strong, competent people who have self-respect and interests and needs beyond caring for children. They see their mothers and sisters as doctors and lawyers, teachers and social workers, as athletes and achievers, as shakers and doers, as business owners and entrepreneurs, as laborers and thinkers, as maids and prime ministers, as activists and peace-makers.

Our children's view of men is changing as well. Our boys and girls are seeing their fathers and brothers as strong and gentle, manly and vulnerable, thoughtful and sensitive. They experience them as supportive and nurturing, involved and connected, and capable in and outside of the home. They observe their fathers and brothers as self-sufficient and proficient in household matters, capable of driving a nail and wiping a tear, partners not adversaries to women.

Men are also learning to accept and enjoy the changes that are occurring in their children and in their wives and sisters. Fathers are coming to appreciate that their daughters have drive and can be competitive, that they want to excel in all areas not just stereotypically prescribed areas. Men are learning that their daughters and sisters enjoy sports and closing a deal, advancing professionally and being recognized for what they know and can do.

Fathers are learning to accept the expression of feelings in their sons, and not negate or invalidate these feelings. Fathers are coming to realize that emotions do not make their boys less of a man, they make them more fully human. Men are coming to realize that boys and girls who are encouraged to play together and understand each other today will not feel estranged from and misunderstood by the other tomorrow.

Men are learning that their mothers, wives and sisters are not the enemy. Men are learning that they do not have to carry the responsibility for the family solely. They are learning that women can and want to share this responsibility. But they are also learning that with this shared responsibility they must share the rights or power for decision making. As a consequence of this new sharing of family responsibility, men are learning to live longer.

Men are also discovering that their wives and sisters are learning to share and give up the eminent domain of household and children. As this sharing takes place, men are beginning to experience and enjoy more meaningful relationships with their children and beginning to understand some of the mundane aspects of maintaining a home. Women's frustrations are becoming more clear and concrete. This leads to a new appreciation for the importance of such work and women's heretofore preoccupation with home and children. Men are coming to realize that their wives want to share their time in old age with them not spend their life insurance death benefit.

Women are making their own discoveries as they get what they have been pushing for. They are learning that having it all is easier said than done. But that having much of it is more possible and easier to the extent to which men will cooperate. Women are learning to make men equal partners not just good baby-sitters or house maids. Women too are learning an important relationship lesson: Men are better their partners than their adversaries.

Women are also learning that they must give up some things and share others especially with respect to their eminent domain. In the process, women are also learning that their husbands and children can manage for themselves. This is initially a disappointment for some but creative women have learned to turn a disappointment into a testimony to the wise choice they made in selecting a mate and the good job they have done in raising independent self-sufficient children.

The changes that have occurred in response to the feminist movement and similar pushes to equal the playing field and afford all equal opportunity have been many and varied and all people have been affected. Notwithstanding the difficult adjustments that have been required by all, I believe the net result is that the American family has been enhanced and strengthened by these changes to a far greater extent than it has been disadvantaged by them. In strengthening the American family we in turn help to strengthen the American society as a whole because the two are one and the same in many respects.

References

1. Berg, D. and Daugherty, G. *The Individual, Society, and Death: An Anthology of Readings.*

2. Grollman, E., Editor, *Explaining Death to Children* (Boston: Beacon Press, 1967).

3. Hymes, J. *Twenty Years In Review: A Look At 1971-1991*, (Washington, D.C.: National Association for the Education of Young Children, 1991).

Chapter 8

Child Rearing Approaches
Philosophy, Practices and Effects

Prologue

Before you read the chapters which follow concerning child rearing philosophy, practices, and their effects upon children and others, complete the questionnaires that follow immediately. If you read the chapters before completing these questionnaires, any choices made on the questionnaires will not be as valid, if at all, because the content of the chapters which follow shall bias your responses. This is why it is important to <u>complete the questionnaires before you continue your reading</u>.

These questionnaires may be used as a tool to help you gain insight into your parent's, your spouse's and your own approach to child rearing. They are not definitive but you may find them interesting and thought provoking. Depending where you are in terms of your own personal and professional development and parenting, the questionnaires may elicit different thoughts and feelings.

If you are a parent you will have many concrete experiences to refer to. Your children and your experiences in parenting them will serve as your frame of reference. These questionnaires may cause you to reminisce and think of how you have changed or might change your parenting views and behaviors.

If you are not a parent yet, they may cause you to look to the future and anticipate how things could be. Try to imagine how it might be and use what you already know about yourself as a person/professional in completing these questionnaires. Use whatever child rearing experience you have had and the children involved as your frame of reference. If you work with children, use this experience or similar child care experience as your frame of reference and as a concrete source of how you behave vis-a-vis real children. If you have had baby-sitting experience, or have had to care for siblings, use that as a frame of reference. Not being a parent, shall not exempt you from completing these questionnaires.

When you are completing these questionnaires from the perspective of trying to represent how your parent parented you and your siblings, you shall have to go back in time and recall when you and your siblings were young children. However, if you are still living with your parents, their approach to parenting may have or may have not changed much. Contrasting and comparing of the "then" and "now" may be a source of fruitful insights for you. If you have children, the way your parent interacts with them may also be of interest and a source of fascinating contrasts and comparisons.

In consideration of the above, *please complete the questionnaires before you continue your reading.*

Recommended Procedure for Completing Questionnaires

The following approach is recommended for completing the child rearing philosophy and practices questionnaires. Follow these steps as prescribed sequentially. If the person identified in a given step does not apply to you and your life situation, skip that step and proceed to the next step. Furthermore, I suggest that you use a different color ink for each person who is represented on the questionnaires as this will help you differentiate one from the other more easily.

First, complete the questionnaires for yourself. Be sure to use the proper designation (√). Upon completion, put the questionnaires aside in order to allow yourself time to clear your mind before returning to the questionnaires to predict someone else's response.

Second, if there is a spouse or special person, complete the questionnaires as you believe your spouse or special person might. This is your prediction of that person's response. Be sure to use the proper designation (s). When you have finished, put the questionnaires aside before you proceed. Allow youself sufficient time to clear your thoughts and feelings.

Third, complete the questionnaires as you think your mother would complete them. Be sure to use the proper designation (m). This is your prediction of your mother's responses. When done, put the questionnaires aside. Do something else to divert your attention before returning to the questionnaires.

Fourth, complete the questionnaires as you think your father might complete them. Be sure to use the proper designation (f). This is your prediction of your father's choices or responses.

Child Rearing Philosophy and Practices
Questionnaires

In using these three questionnaires, select the option in each category which best represents your view. When representing the view or predicting the response of others, note as accurately and as honestly as you can the view of others who may be involved in this exercise. Young children should be the frame of reference when using these questionnaires. Use the following designations when recording your choices or predictions. Place these designations on the line next to the option statement that represents your choice or preference.

√	=	your view or response
s	=	your prediction of your spouse or special person's view or response
sa	=	your spouse or special person's actual view or response
m	=	your prediction of your mother's view or response
ma	=	your mother's actual view or response
f	=	your prediction of your father's view or response
fa	=	you father's actual view or response

Questionnaire 1
Ideologies Concerning Family Structure and Roles

The following are some generalizations concerning family structure and roles. These characterize two basic and different views. These generalizations refer to certain factors which can be helpful indicators of a certain philosophical perspective. However, please keep in mind that they are generalizations and therefore may lack specificity or may not always be accurate in predicting attitude or behavior. Nevertheless, choose the option which best represents you view.

1. The family structure is
   _____ a. father as head and wife and children subservient to him.
   _____ b. authority is shared between husband and wife.

2. The roles of the husband and wife are
   _____ a. generally well defined and different.
   _____ b. often overlapping and interchangeable.

3. The marital relationship is based on
   _____ a. conformity to distinct, different and separate (sharply dichotomized) roles of husband and wife.
   _____ b. mutual respect, companionship and commonness of interest.

4. The husband's behavior should
   _____ a. conform to the masculine stereotype.
   _____ b. be flexible and may overlap those of the wife.

5. The husband's predominant personal traits are
   _____ a. ruggedness, determination, assertiveness and will power.
   _____ b. helpful, supportive, willingness to share the responsibility in family matters.

131

6. The wife's behavior should
_____ a. conform to the stereotype of femininity.
_____ b. be flexible and may overlap those of the husband.

7. The wife's predominant personal traits are
_____ a. sweetness, submissiveness, morally controlled who knows and keeps her place in the home.
_____ b. nurturing, helpful and supportive.

8. The parent's role
_____ a. emphasizes firm discipline and obedience to authority.
_____ b. emphasizes individual development.

9. In fulfilling the parental role, the parent
_____ a. attempts to suppress inappropriate sex role behavior.
_____ b. minimizes pressure for sex role conformity.

10. The parent tries
_____ a. to suppress behavior that does not conform to or fit in with conventional values.
_____ b. to minimizes pressure for conformity to conventional values.

Questionnaire 2
Basic Child Rearing Approaches in Terms of Parental Viewpoint

The following statements are some generalizations concerning the parent's point of view regarding various matters pertaining to child rearing. These characterize three basic and different approaches to child rearing. These generalizations refer to certain factors which may be helpful indicator's of the parent's viewpoint and approach to child rearing. However, please keep in mind that they are generalizations and therefore may not always be as accurate as we would prefer in predicting attitude and behavior. Furthermore, they may not be specific enough to permit making a classification that is as reliable as desired. Nevertheless, these responses may serve as helpful indicators of certain child rearing approaches in term of the parent's viewpoint.

1. The child's basic nature:
_____ a. The child has the tendency to develop bad habits that will get out of control.
_____ b. The child has the basic capacity to learn and mature without excessive pressure or protection.
_____ c. The child is constitutionally delicate, weak or extra vulnerable in some way.

2. Expectations for the child:
_____ a. The child is expected to conform to adult standards and behave in a manner pleasing to adults.
_____ b. The child is expected to behave according to his own age level.
_____ c. The child is expected to need a great deal of help and be unable to get along on his own.

3. The goals of child rearing are
_____ a. to produce a child who is socially acceptable to others and who fits the stereotype of masculine and feminine behavior.
_____ b. to help the child develop his own potential.
_____ c. to insure the child's physical survival.

132

4. The role of parent is
_____ a. to suppress the bad tendencies and/or push the child in the right direction.
_____ b. to provide guidance, encouragement and support.
_____ c. to protect the child from life's stresses.

5. The meaning of the child's behavior:
_____ a. The behavior is good or bad according to whether or not it violates some rule of conduct.
_____ b. The behavior is looked at in terms of the child's age level and other causes.
_____ c. The behavior is looked at in terms of constitutional factors that cannot be altered.

6. The meaning of discipline:
_____ a. Discipline is seen in terms of punishment for any disobedience to authority.
_____ b. Discipline is seen in terms of the child's need for limits or when behavior encroaches on the rights of others.
_____ c. Discipline is seen as something to be avoided because of the child's delicate condition.

7. Preferred or desirable methods for influencing the child's present behavior:
_____ a. Punish any behavior that doesn't conform to the parent's rules and regulations.
_____ b. Avoid setting unrealistic goals.
_____ c. Avoid setting any limits on behavior that encroaches on the rights of others.

8. Preferred or desirable methods for influencing the child's present behavior:
_____ a. Use corporal punishment or withdrawal of privilege.
_____ b. Learn what kinds of child behaviors are characteristic for each stage of development.
_____ c. Rely on coaxing, begging, pleading or offering material rewards to alter undesirable behavior.

9. Preferred or desirable methods for influencing the child's present behavior:
_____ a. Use timed restrictions of activity like requiring the child to stay in his room, in the house, in a chair, etc.
_____ b. Take the child's age into account when arranging household goods.
_____ c. Allow the child to disrupt home setting and routines.

10. Preferred or desirable methods for influencing the child's present behavior:
_____ a. Use verbal disapproval that devalues the child as a person: Shaming or ridiculing, comparing unfavorably with others, making moral judgements about the child are effective means.
_____ b. Gear expectations for the child's social and moral development to his developmental stage.
_____ c. Tolerate verbal and/or physical abuse no matter how bad it becomes.

11. Preferred or desirable methods for influencing the child's present behavior:

_____ a. The child is not allowed to explain things from his point of view.

_____ b. Expect some regressions and mistakes at each level or stage of development.

_____ c. Wait on the child and give in to his demands no matter how unreasonable.

12. Preferred or desirable methods for influencing the child's present behavior:

_____ a. Offer material rewards to alter behavior.

_____ b. Set limits on behavior that encroaches on the rights of others or endangers the child's own safety.

_____ c. Set limits on behavior that could conceivably expose the child to some kind of stress. This may require restricting the child's social contacts, keeping the child constantly in sight, giving up social contacts so the child won't have to be left with a baby-sitter, restricting the child's activity, taking the child to the doctor at the first sign of health change, delaying the child's assumption of responsibility for care of self and property.

13. Desirable methods for influencing the child's future behavior:

_____ a. Punish any behavior that does not conform to the parent's rules and regulations.

_____ b. Reason with and explain things to the child in order to increase his basic understanding.

_____ c. Avoid setting any limits on behavior that encroaches on the rights of others.

14. Desirable methods for influencing the child's future behavior:

_____ a. Use corporal punishment or withdrawal of privileges.

_____ b. Provide an example of tolerance and understanding for the child to identify with by using non-punitive measures when limits are necessary. Provide acceptable alternatives. Use verbal disapproval that does not attack the child as a person. Base restrictions of activity on the child's regaining of self-control rather than on arbitrary time limits. Limit physical interference to stopping undesirable activity or putting the child in his room without hurting the child.

_____ c. Rely on coaxing, begging, pleading or offering of material reward to alter behavior.

15. Desirable methods for influencing the child's future behavior:

_____ a. Use time restrictions of activity like requiring the child to stay in his room, in the house, in a chair, etc.

_____ b. Increase the child's desire to please and cooperate by spending time with the child and taking an interest in what he is doing, encouraging the child to participate in household activities, praising the child for behaviors that show increased maturity, and trying the understand the child's point of view.

_____ c. Allow the child to disrupt or abuse. Otherwise appease him.

Questionnaire 3
Parental Responses to Specific Child Behavior

The following choices illustrate three basic and different responses to specific child behavior. These responses may be helpful indicators of the parent's child rearing ideology and practices.

Although they are specific, they certainly do not account for every option. Nevertheless, try to identify those alternatives which are most characteristic of your behavior and others who may be involved. These specific responses may serve as a helpful indicator of basic child rearing practices.

Meal time behavior:

1. The child does not want to eat at the regular meal time.
   _____ a. The child is punished unless he complies with the parent's rule.
   _____ b. The child must adhere to family meal times but some delay is allowed.
   _____ c. The child is allowed to eat when he wants.

2. The child is not eating what the parent considers the correct amount or kind of food.
   _____ a. The child has to clean his plate or taste everything before being excused or given dessert.
   _____ b. The child is allowed to determine his own intake.
   _____ c. The child is begged, pleaded with or offered a reward for eating more.

3. The child accidentally spills or makes a mess while eating.
   _____ a. The child is punished or has to leave the table. Infants are not allowed to use their fingers.
   _____ b. The child is ignored or helped to clean up.
   _____ c. The child is ignored or the parent cleans up.

4. The child does not use proper table manners.
   _____ a. The child is punished or required to leave the table.
   _____ b. The child is ignored on some items but has some limits set on excessively silly behavior.
   _____ c. The child has no limits set.

Bedtime behavior:

5. The child does not want to go to bed.
   _____ a. Bedtime is set and deviation from parental rules is punished.
   _____ b. Bedtime is definite but leeway is allowed on occasion.
   _____ c. The child is allowed to set his own bedtime or the parent expects to stay in the room until the child falls asleep.

6. The child wants to sleep in the parent's bed or room.
   _____ a. This is not allowed.
   _____ b. This is allowed but not encouraged.
   _____ c. This is allowed and often encouraged.

Toilet training behavior:

7. The child does not go when put on the toilet.
   _____ a. The child is made to sit for a prolonged period (more than 15 minutes). The child is frequently put on the toilet throughout the day.
   _____ b. The child is allowed to get up and try again later.
   _____ c. The child is allowed to get up at the first sign of resistance.

8. The child resists sitting on the toilet.
   _____ a. The child is not allowed to get off and is punished.
   _____ b. The child is allowed to get up. Training may be stopped for a while.

9. The child has an accident after being mostly trained.
_____ a. The child is scolded and punished.
_____ b. The event is ignored.
_____ c. The event is ignored. The parent may express concern about the child's health.

Property oriented behavior:

10. The child touches or gets into things as a toddler.
_____ a. The child's hands are slapped or he is restricted. No parental preparation is made to avoid such incidents.
_____ b. The child is told "no." The house is baby-proofed. The child is removed physically. An alternative activity is provided.
_____ c. No limits are set on the child.

11. The child wants to leave his toys and clothes around the house.
_____ a. The child is made to put things away right after use and is punished for deviation.
_____ b. The child has several pick up times during the day. No physical punishment is used.
_____ c. No limits are set on the child.

12. The child wants to play in the living room: 1.) quietly with toys, or 2.) with messy toys, or 3.) "roughhouse."
_____ a. All three are not allowed. The child is punished for deviation.
_____ b. 1.) allowed, 2.) some limits are set, 3.) some limits are set.
_____ c. No limits are set.

13. The child breaks or damages something.
_____ a. The child is punished.
_____ b. Disapproval is expressed but the child is not punished. Breakable items are removed from the child's reach.
_____ c. No limits are set.

Aggressive behavior:

14. The child has a temper tantrum.
_____ a. The child is punished.
_____ b. The event is ignored.
_____ c. The parent gives in to avoid punishment.

15. The child gets angry at the parent, shouts and says angry things.
_____ a. The behavior is not tolerated. The child is punished.
_____ b. Behavior is tolerated unless excessive, then non-punitive limits are set.
_____ c. Behavior is tolerated and no limits are set.

16. The child gets angry at the parent and tries to hit the parent.
_____ a. This is not tolerated. The child is punished.
_____ b. Non-punitive limits are set like physical restriction or temporary isolation.
_____ c. Behavior is tolerated and no limits are set.

17. The child quarrels with siblings.
_____ a. The child is punished.
_____ b. The behavior is ignored or the child is helped to settle the dispute if it is getting out of hand.
_____ c. The sibling may be made to give in.

Behavior concerning obedience or respect:

18. The child disobeys.
_____ a. The child is punished.
_____ b. An explanation is given as to what is wanted; non-punitive limits are set if behavior persists.
_____ c. The behavior is tolerated. No limits are set.

19. The child acts sassy or impudent.
_____ a. The child is punished.
_____ b. Behavior is tolerated, but non-punitive limits are set if the behavior persists.
_____ c. Behavior is tolerated. No limits are set.

Sexual or moral behavior:

20. The child asks questions about sex.
_____ a. The child is told it's not nice or is ignored.
_____ b. Questions are answered matter-of-factly.
_____ c. Questions are ignored or evaded.

21. The child rubs or handles genitals.
_____ a. The child is told it is not nice or is punished.
_____ b. Behavior is ignored.
_____ c. The child is told it is not nice.

22. The child participates in sex play with other children.
_____ a. The child is punished.
_____ b. Some behavior is ignored. If continued, the child is told it is not socially acceptable. The child is provided with an alternative such as a book on the facts of life.
_____ c. The child is told it is not nice and will not be allowed to play with the other children again.

23. The child runs around the house without clothes on in front of others.
_____ a. The child is told it is not nice or is punished.
_____ b. Behavior is ignored.
_____ c. The child is told it is not nice.

24. The child uses bad language.
_____ a. The child is punished.
_____ b. Behavior is ignored.
_____ c. The child is told it is not nice.

25. The child tells a lie.
_____ a. The child is punished.
_____ b. The child is told why lying is not a good idea.
_____ c. The child is told it is not nice.

26. The child shows bad habits like thumb sucking, nose picking, etc.
_____ a. The parent tries to break the child of the habit.
_____ b. Behavior is ignored.
_____ c. The child is told it is not nice.

Dependent and independent behavior:

27. The child wants attention when the parent is busy.
    _____ a. The child is ignored or punished.
    _____ b. The child's desire is acknowledged and may be asked to wait.
    _____ c. The child is given attention. The parent stops what he/she is doing.

28. The child acts clingy or whiny.
    _____ a. The child receives an irritated reaction and is punished.
    _____ b. The child is comforted but limits are set if behavior persists.
    _____ c. The child is comforted and often held.

29. The child acts afraid.
    _____ a. The child is ignored or made to feel ashamed, especially if a boy.
    _____ b. The child is comforted.
    _____ c. The child is comforted. Parent expresses much concern and sympathy.

30. The child gets upset when his mother leaves.
    _____ a. The child is left anyway or is punished.
    _____ b. The child is comforted but the parent departs.
    _____ c. The child is comforted and the parent remains. The parent restricts
    his/her activity to avoid unpleasantness.

31. The child tries to perform routine tasks by himself.
    _____ a. The child is allowed to or the parent does it for expediency or
    efficiency.
    _____ b. The child is encouraged even if he is slow or makes mistakes.
    _____ c. The parent does routine tasks for the child.

32. The child wants to play out of sight.
    _____ a. The child is not allowed.
    _____ b. The child is allowed if it is safe to do so.
    _____ c. The child is usually not allowed. However, it may be allowed if the
    parent can actually keep the child in sight.

33. The child wants to play with other children.
    _____ a. The child is allowed.
    _____ b. The child is encouraged.
    _____ c. Censorship is placed on children who might be a bad influence.

34. The child wants to help with household chores.
    _____ a. This is expected. Chores may be excessive given the child's age.
    _____ b. The child is encouraged to help. Considerable leeway is permitted.
    _____ c. The child is not allowed.

35. The child wants to be waited on.
    _____ a. This is not tolerated. The child is punished.
    _____ b. Service is given but limits are set if unreasonable.
    _____ c. Child's demands are complied with even when unreasonable.

Key to Questionnaires

When you have completed the questionnaires as prescribed, you may resume your reading in this chapter or read the questionnaire answer key section in Appendix A. The key shall explain generally what each response suggests or indicates in terms of approach to the child rearing. Before you read this section, be sure you have completed the questionnaires by recording your responses and predicting the responses of your mother, father, and spouse or special person. You may even wish to postpone reading the answer key section until after you have completed reading Chapter 9. This is preferred and recommended.

If you have completed the questionnaires as prescribed, please resume your reading about child rearing philosophies, practices and their effects on the growth, development and behavior of children and parents. However, before you begin the substantive part of this exploration, there are some matters to consider beforehand. These matters are what have been identified herein as preliminary considerations.

PRELIMINARY CONSIDERATIONS

When one studies the different child rearing philosophies and practices, it becomes apparent that different approaches to child rearing seem to have different impacts upon the parents and the children involved. Furthermore, it seems that some forms of child rearing are more capable of producing certain effects relative to how children grow, develop and behave than other approaches.

Likewise, the different child rearing philosophies and practices necessitate and/or lead to differences in parent and child interaction. In effect, the various philosophies suggest different ways of behaving in order to accomplish certain things in relation to child rearing. Hence, these different philosophical and interactional variations account in large measure for the distinguishing effects a given approach to child rearing will have upon children in general. These distinguishing effects are recognizable and predictable.

Differences in child rearing philosophies and practices, in large measure (but not completely) account for the variations in young children's growth, development and behavior. It is important to keep in mind the following generalizations that emerge from a study of child rearing philosophies, practices and their respective effects upon children. These generalizations can help us understand or appreciate more concretely the nature of the child and his interactions. This understanding is essential to our actions with or on behalf of the child.

Children generally react differently to the various child rearing approaches. That is, there are certain predictable and distinguishable reactions to particular kinds of child rearing. Children raised autocratically will react to autocratic child rearing in predictable and distinguishable ways. Children raised democratically will respond to this approach in predictable and distinguishable ways. Children will individually show varying degrees or gradations of these effects but the general reaction will be predictable and distinguishable. Therefore, with respect to certain important dimensions of growth and development, children who are raised autocratically will be dissimilar from children who are raised democratically.

Additionally, different children will sometimes react differently to the same child rearing approach. This in part accounts for the striking variations that exist in children who come from the same family where the approach to child rearing has been relatively the same. Another way of expressing this notion is that a particular approach may have different consequences in terms of growth, development and behavior of children. A given approach may produce dissimilar effects. A particular approach to child rearing may have characteristically multiple effects upon children. Some children will manifest these different effects quite distinctly. Other children may show features that are characteristic of more than one variation of effects that result from a given approach.

Children react with varying intensity to the child rearing they receive. Some children are minimally affected while others are moderately affected in a positive or negative fashion. This fact partially accounts for the differences observed in children who come from basically the same child rearing environment. For example, let's consider an approach that is known for producing children of low self-esteem. In a given situation one child may emerge with extremely low self-esteem, whereas another child may show low self-esteem to a minimal degree.

How intensely or strongly a child reacts to the child rearing he receives is greatly influenced by, but not limited to, the following six important factors. These factors are variables, which the child brings to the interactions he has with the parent. They are either learned or inborn characteristics.

The Child

Temperament

The child's basic underlying temperament is important to how he shall respond to the child rearing he receives. Variations in response and the intensity of response are sometimes directly attributable to the child's temperament. From infancy, some children prefer a minimal amount of cuddling or holding. These children may perceive cuddling or holding as restrictive. This perception may be a function of central nervous system development (typically immaturity) and/or heightened sensitivity to touch.

These children will often react negatively to any child rearing approach that would be or seem to be restrictive in nature, especially those that employ physical restraint or constraint. In contrast, a child who is temperamentally more compliant might react very differently or less negatively to the same restrictive behavior of the parent.

Age and Developmental Level

The child's age and developmental level are important variables which influence how intensely the child will respond to the child rearing he receives. The needs of children change as they grow. Infants have a constellation of needs that are unique to infancy. The preschool child has his own set of unique needs. The infant by nature and circumstance is dependent. The preschool child by nature is striving to be independent. Infants enjoy having things done for them or to them. If they are developing well, preschoolers are very likely to resist adult efforts to do things for them. Often preschoolers insist on doing things for themselves. Consequently, at one stage in development the child accepts and enjoys certain services from the parent that at a later stage he shall not accept and not enjoy.

A child who is significantly developmentally delayed because of some handicapping condition or special need may not neatly fit into an "ages and stages" framework. A moderately retarded fifteen-year-old child will have some needs that are different from the typical fifteen-year-old. Consequently, his responses to child rearing may be significantly different than his "normal" agemate.

Physiological State

The child's physiological state or condition will effect his reaction to parental behavior. A child that is typically healthy, well rested, and well nourished will behave differently than when he is not physically healthy, not rested and not well nourished. A child who is at the beginning stages of an illness or in the process of recuperation will usually behave differently than when he is in a more healthful condition. Children who are fatigued may not be as attentive and consequently not as cooperative as they typically would be in a more rested condition. A child who has missed breakfast may be quite irritable by lunch time. The increased irritability may cause considerable changes in the child's behavior or response patterns. Lowered physiological status usually results in regressive or more "infantile" behavior in children. They become more dependent, less self-sufficient, more whiny, more demanding, less energetic, etc.

Psychological State

The child's psychological condition will affect his response pattern. A child who is momentarily feeling inadequate is less likely to

140

respond with enthusiasm or favorably to adult encouragement. A child who is angry and frustrated may resist an adult's effort to give comfort and assistance. These momentary shifts in emotional well-being are typical for children and account for some of the changes observed in children's behavior. For children who are acutely or chronically upset emotionally, the changes in behavior are often more dramatic and profound.

Interpersonal Relationships

The quality of the child's relationship to the child rearer shall significantly influence the child's responses. A parent who is loving and kind is more likely to help create a positive, constructive relationship than a parent who is non-loving and abusive. A parent who is clear and reasonable in terms of her expectations will be more effective than a parent who is unclear and unreasonable in her expectations of the child. Such aspects produce different interactions and result in qualitatively different relationships. In part, this notion explains why some children seem to behave so differently when in the care of different people. There is a qualitative difference in the relationships and these differences produce different behavioral reactions in children.

Interactional Patterns

The strength, tenacity and duration of certain interactional patterns that have been established between the child and the parent will influence how each will respond to the other. This is especially shown when parents attempt to change their approach to child rearing. The child will often resist the parent's efforts to change the nature of their interaction. Often matters get worse even when the parent is using a more appropriate or constructive approach. Sometimes the resistance to change from the child is so great that the parent "gives up" before more constructive interaction can be established. Hence, the child has managed to preserve the old ways even though the new ways would have been in the child's best interest.

By comparison, if the interactional pattern is not a long-standing or firmly established one (and it does not need to be long-standing to be firmly established), the child's reaction may

show less resistivity and a new pattern may be established that benefits both parent and child.

It is important to keep these factors in mind because the child's reactions and the intensity of these reactions are significantly influenced by these variables. An appreciation and understanding that such variables influence children's behavior is essential. They will appear to reside in the child and certainly characterize him and his behavior. However, they are more accurately a reflection of the interactional patterns that have been established and the roles that have been acquired as a consequence of those patterns having been established.

The Parent

As the child brings certain characteristics to his interactions with others, so does the parent. The following section will focus on some important features of the parent's attitudes and behaviors that directly influence the approach to child rearing that is chosen and employed by the parent.

Parental Understanding and Interpretation

A parent's state of understanding or misunderstanding, a parent's interpretation or misinterpretation of the meaning of the child's behavior can effect the interaction in either a positive or negative manner. When the parent properly understands or interprets the meaning of the child's behavior, she is in a better position to respond appropriately and have a positive influence on the child. When the parent misunderstands or misinterprets, she is less likely to respond appropriately and positively influence the child's behavior. This misunderstanding may lead the parent to behave in ways that make matters worse or intensify the child's negative reaction. Sometimes the parent may perpetuate an undesirable response, cause it to escalate and thereby contribute to the creation of a vicious cycle wherein matters continue to worsen by increasing degrees.

An example of such a scenario is when the child reaches a stage in his development when he insists on doing things himself. The parent

141

who misunderstands this change in behavior and perceives it as emerging obstinacy is likely to prevent the child from doing things himself. This may lead to anger and frustration in the child and his strong instance that he do things himself. This may result in a struggle for power and dominance between parent and child and further escalation of counterproductive interaction. Such a scenario could have been avoided if the parent had correctly understood the meaning of the change in the child's behavior and reacted appropriately to it.

Parental Behavior Counts

In the context of child rearing, parents recognize and appreciate the fact that what they do affects how the child grows, develops and behaves. When parents are dissatisfied with the effects, they often express this recognition and appreciation in the questions they ask: What should I do? What did I do wrong? The healthy parent seems to have a willingness to be held culpable to the extent that she is culpable.

Such questions also suggest that parents typically recognize that a change in their behavior may be necessary to effect a change in the child's behavior, even though they may not be fully aware of what else to do or how to make the change. Sometimes the changes that are needed are minimal. They represent slight variations or "fine tuning." Sometimes change involves using different practices or techniques. Such changes may require adjustments in underlying philosophy regarding child rearing. When changes in underlying philosophy are required, more time and energy are necessitated.

CONNECTION BETWEEN PHILOSOPHY AND PRACTICES

The relationship between what people say they believe about raising children (their philosophy) and what they do (their practices) and how they actually behave with respect to child rearing is highly correlated. Indeed, the correlation is significant but not complete.

From person to person the degree of correlation varies. For some of us, what we say we believe in is a fairly accurate reflection of how we live and what we do. For some, it is significantly less so.

Although there is a variation in degree of correlation between what people say they do and what they actually do, stated behavior is or can be a helpful indicator of actual practice. Encouraging people to talk about and describe their philosophy and practices can lead to insight and understanding. We need to often pay close attention to not only what people say but also how they say it. Word choice can be very significant and revealing.

Consider these two variations concerning the same matter. "I make him pick up and put away his toys before I bathe him." vs. "I encourage him to pick up and put away his toys before he takes his bath." The underlined portion of the first alternative may suggest control or power issues that are indicative of a particular approach to child rearing. The underlined portions of the second alternative suggest an attempt on the parent's part to foster control in the child rather than retain it for the parent. This may be indicative of a very different approach to child rearing.

Actual practice is far more important to children than what a parent describes as being done. Actual interaction is the more accurate reflection of a person's child rearing philosophy and practices. Therefore, it is helpful for the parent to become an objective observer of his or her own interactions with the child.

Likewise, it is beneficial for helping professionals to observe actual parent and child interaction in order to more accurately assess the quality of child rearing. This is one of the many reasons why early childhood professionals encourage parent participation in the classroom and make home visits. Similarly, social service professionals conduct interviews within the client's home at various critical times. However, in lieu of observing actual interaction between parent and child, it is helpful to encourage parents to describe in detail their interactions concerning specific child behavior.

Mixture and Degree

As we examine our own and the child rearing behavior of others, we come to realize that most parents do not behave exclusively in one way that is consistent with just one particular approach to child rearing. In fact, we shall often discover a mixture of philosophies and practices with many unique variations. These variations are a result of the incorporation of different philosophies and practices in varying degrees. The widest array of variations can be seen in societies, like the America culture, that are in transition and show relatively rapid changes in attitudes, values, life style, etc.

No one person is completely autocratic, or completely democratic, or completely indulgent, or completely protective. The significant differences that exist in child rearing philosophies and practices in the American society are a matter of degree. The extent to which the parent is autocratic or democratic or otherwise is what accounts for the differences in child rearing philosophies and practices and their dissimilar and distinguishable effects upon the recipient children.

Some parents behave more exclusively in one way than in another and this predominant mode characterizes a particular approach to child rearing. Other approaches may be employed but less exclusively. So although these other approaches influence the child's growth, development and behavior, their influence will be of lesser consequence.

Practical Applications

What is the benefit of studying the various child rearing approaches and their respective effects upon the growth, development and behavior of children? There are a variety of benefits that most importantly have implications for practice or practical application. That is, this knowledge can be used in a very practical way to change, improve and/or strengthen our child rearing practices and thereby promote more effectively the growth and development of our children.

Also to be gained are insight and awareness that will help us recognize the importance of certain behaviors in parents and children.

These behaviors can serve as indicators of particular kinds of child rearing philosophies and practices and their respective effects upon both parents and children. In short, these indicators can help us recognize behavior that is desirable (indicated) or undersirable (contraindicated).

Likewise, these indicators can help us identify the type of child rearing employed by the parent and help us understand the underlying reasons for the child's growth, development, and behavior. Being able to identify or classify the kind of child rearing that is being used can help us gain insight and understanding and help explain the nature of the child's behavior.

Similarly, these indicators can help us identify and classify the child's growth, development and behavior as being the possible or likely effect or outcome of a particular approach to child rearing. The child's behavior itself can provide us with some insight and clues to the parent's philosophy and practices. The child's behavior can help us gain insight and understanding and aid our prediction or identification of the child rearing approach being used by the parent.

Our ability to recognize certain behaviors, identify or classify certain child rearing philosophies and practices and their respective effects or consequences for children can provide us with some guidance as to which behaviors should be changed and improved and which behaviors may be retained and possibly even strengthened. We can learn which behaviors on the part of the parent produce the behaviors we desire in the child. We can learn which behaviors in the child are indicative of the actions we desire in the parent.

Conversely, we can learn which parental behaviors produce undesirable or inappropriate child behavior. Also we can learn which child behavior is indicative of undesirable or inappropriate parental behavior. Knowing such, we have a better sense of where to begin the process of constructive change and/or where to confirm or affirm the actions being employed. These practical applications can be employed in any and all child rearing environments. That is, they can be employed by parents in their homes, by teachers in their classrooms, by therapists in their helping settings, etc.

143

Chapter 9

Child Rearing Approaches
Philosophy and Practices

PHILOSOPHY AND PRACTICE

An ideology or philosophy can be said to be the expressed characteristic manner of thinking or a body of attitudes, values, beliefs and expectations concerning a particular matter. Child rearing ideology or philosophy refers to such an expression of thought or body of attitudes, values, beliefs and expectations regarding how children should be raised and how parents should interact with children. It can and often does include prescriptions for parent and parent interaction and child and child interaction. Some ideologies or philosophies incorporate certain devices for putting its ideas into action or operation. In this connection, such devices are referred to as child rearing practices and/or techniques.

There are many and varied approaches to child rearing. Each approach has its own unique ideology and accompanying set of practices and/or techniques. Also, each approach has its own unique impact upon the growth, development and behavior of children. Each child rearing ideology or philosophy represents a unique view of the child and the parent and what is considered desirable behavior for each and desirable methods for influencing the child's present and future behavior. Each child rearing approach also prescribes what the parent's responses should be to specific child behavior.

Additionally, each approach contains certain notions regarding family structure and roles. In this connection, each prescribes what the structure of the family should be; the roles of husband, wife, parent, and child; the basis for the marital relationship; desired behavior for husband and wife; and their respective predominant personal traits. Likewise, each approach contains certain philosophical ideas regarding the child's basic nature, child rearing goals, how the child is to be managed, and so forth. These philosophical notions form the foundation which guide or prescribe how the parent should respond to specific child behavior. These various notions and prescriptions shall be generalized and described in the following sections.

FOUR MAJOR APPROACHES TO CHILD REARING

Certain generalizations and specializations begin to emerge from a study of the various approaches to child rearing. These generalizations and specializations characterize each approach and enable us to identify or classify. If we compare and contrast the various child rearing approaches in terms of these generalizations and specializations as they relate to ideology, practices and their effects on the child, we come to realize that some approaches are quite similar, while others are quite dissimilar.

Based upon these similarities and dissimilarities, it is possible to group the various child rearing philosophies and practices and place them into one of four broad categories or classifications. The different approaches to child rearing shall be described employing this large categorical approach. The four major approaches to be described are the autocratic, democratic, indulgent, and protective approaches to child rearing.

Autocratic

One such category or classification shall be referred to as the autocratic approach to child rearing. This category includes a number of variations or types which have been labeled *autocratic, casual autocratic, rejectant, dictatorial, traditional, rigid, authoritarian*, and *non-permissive*. A review of the literature will show reference to these types and a close look will reveal that they have much in common.

Democratic

A second category or classification shall be labeled democratic. The democratic approach to child rearing includes such types or variations which have been named *democratic,*

developmental, equalitarian, optimal, cooperative and *permissive*. These variations have their unique characteristics; yet, they have very much in common.

Protective

The protective approach to child rearing is the third major classification to be used herein. This category includes approaches that have been labeled *protective* and *over-protective*. These two are basically the same except for degree.

Indulgent

The fourth major classification to be used is the indulgent approach to child rearing. This category includes *indulgent, over-indulgent, casual indulgent,* and *conciliatory*. These distinct approaches share many characteristics. These differences are basically a matter of degree also.

IDEOLOGIES CONCERNING FAMILY STRUCTURE AND ROLES

As indicated before, each approach to child rearing contains certain notions about family structure and roles within the context of the family unit. As a basis for comparison, some generalizations will be offered which characterize two basically different views. One view represents a more traditional view of the family; the other a more democratic or equalitarian perspective of family structure and roles. These generalizations refer to certain dimensions of family structure and roles which can serve as helpful indicators of a particular philosophical perspective. Some of these philosophical perspectives are often correlated with particular approaches to child rearing.

Historical Origin

Furthermore, I believe it is helpful to understand the historical origins of each. The traditional view is very European. Most American forbearers were of European origin.

Despite their search for new opportunities and a new way of life and living, they nevertheless brought with them a traditional view of family life and living. The democratic view is an attempt to put into practice the American experiment and apply it to family life and living. In comparison to the traditional European view, it is a new and maverick perspective.

The democratic view of the family has changed along with the changes in American culture. Yet both the democratic view of the family and American culture rely on and refer to their basic underlying democratic ideals and assumptions. The traditional view has also undergone what I refer to as its Americanization. Nevertheless, there are certain traditional notions of family life and living that remain basically unchanged.

The Traditional Ideology

The traditional view of the family regards the father as head and the wife and children as subservient to him. This view is often held and maintained even when in fact the wife possesses a disproportionate share of the leadership and decision-making authority.

The roles of the husband and wife are generally well defined and different. The wife cooks; the husband takes out the garbage. The wife has major responsibility for child rearing and the husband has major responsibility for supporting the family financially. These views concerning child rearing and financial support are clung to, even when the wife is employed on a full time basis and may in fact be the primary wage earner. The separation of the roles for husband and wife are often based upon gender. Men do certain things and assume certain roles. Likewise, women do certain things and assume certain roles.

In a similar fashion, the marital relationship is based on a conformity to distinct, different and separate roles for the husband and wife. The husband's behavior should conform to the masculine stereotype. The wife's behavior should conform to the stereotype of femininity. The husband's predominant personal traits are or should be characterized by ruggedness, determination, assertiveness, and will power. The wife's predominant traits are or should be

sweetness, submissiveness, morally controlled and knowing and keeping her place in the home.

Within the traditional view, the parent's role generally is to emphasize firm discipline and obedience to authority. In fulfilling the parental role, the parent tries to suppress behavior that does not conform to or fit in with conventional (traditional) values and also attempts to suppress inappropriate sex role behavior.

Such views are generally representative of a traditional ideology concerning family structure and roles.

The Democratic Ideology

The democratic view of the structure of the family maintains that authority is shared between the husband and wife in theory and in practice. There is a belief in and an attempt to put into practice a more equalitarian system of leadership and decision-making. Authority is often less concentrated even though one may assume or appear to have primary responsibility for leadership and decision-making.

As a consequence, the roles of husband and wife are often overlapping and interchangeable. The husband may cook more or less regularly. The wife may have the car serviced as part of her routine. Responsibility for child rearing is often shared to a greater degree. The family's financial status is not viewed solely as the responsibility of the husband even though he may be the sole wage earner during a particular stage in the family's development. The overlapping, interchanging and blending of roles is more possible because there is less adherence to gender sanctions and greater commitment to androgyny.

Consequently, the marital relationship is based on mutual respect, companionship and commonness of interest. The husband's behavior should be flexible and may overlap those of the wife. The wife's behavior should be flexible and may overlap those of the husband. The husband's predominant personal traits are or should be helpfulness, supportiveness and a willingness to share responsibility in family matters. The wife's predominant personal traits are or should be nurturing, helpful, and supportive.

Within the democratic view, the parent's role generally is to emphasize individual development of the child. In fulfilling the parental role, the parent attempts to minimize pressure for conformity to conventional values and tries to also minimize pressure for sex role conformity. Such views are generally representative of a democratic ideology concerning family structure and roles.

The traditional and democratic views described herein represent two basic and different views which shall be reflected in some fashion in the following discussion of the different approaches to child rearing as these views form the basis for particular types of child rearing philosophy and practices.

BASIC CHILD REARING IN TERMS OF THE PARENT'S VIEWPOINT (PHILOSOPHY)

This section shall describe four major approaches to child rearing in terms of the parent's point of view concerning some fundamental dimensions of raising children. Each descriptive section will contain some basic generalizations pertaining to the child's basic nature, expectations for the child, goals of child rearing, the role of the parent, the meaning of child behavior and discipline, and what is considered desirable methods for influencing the child's present and future behavior.

These viewpoints make these four approaches distinguishable. Therefore, familiarity with these different viewpoints will help us recognize and classify a particular approach to child rearing, enhance our understanding, and facilitate our actions as child rearers and helping professionals.

The Autocratic Viewpoint

Child's Basic Nature

The person who possesses an autocratic perspective regards the child's basic nature as being one where the child has a tendency to develop bad habits that will get out of control. Consequently, the parent believes that the child must be closely monitored and controlled so that the child's basic inclination does not take his behavior in undesirable directions. The parent has little trust of the child, particularly when he is unsupervised by an adult. Ongoing adult supervision is a way to keep the child from developing bad habits and getting into trouble.

Expectations for the Child

The child is expected to conform to adult standards and behave in a manner that is pleasing to adults. Children are often expected to be adults in miniature. Childlike behavior is often regarded as an annoyance and children are frequently advised to act like a big boy or a big girl, grow up, stop acting like a baby, etc. The parent views the child from predominantly an adult-oriented frame of reference where adult behavior is the standard. The parent has little interest in what is typical child behavior.

Goals of Child Rearing

In keeping with these expectations, the goals of child rearing are to produce a child that is socially acceptable to others and that fits the stereotype of masculine or feminine behavior. Once again, the frame of reference is adult-oriented. The child must be acceptable to other adults. The sooner his behavior approximates adult behavior the better.

Role of the Parent

The role of the parent in child rearing is to suppress the bad tendencies that are part of the child's basic nature and/or to push the child in the right direction. Behaviors that conform to adult standards, that are pleasing to adults, that are socially acceptable represent the right direction. Behaviors to the contrary represent the wrong direction.

Meaning of Child Behavior and Discipline

What meaning is attached to child behavior and the disciplining of children? The child's behavior is good or bad according to whether or not it violates some rule of conduct. These rules of conduct are often adult rules devised for adult convenience. Discipline is seen in terms of punishment for any disobedience to authority. Discipline is viewed in often a very limited way: Discipline is punishment. The child is not allowed to explain his behavior from his point of view.

Methods for Influencing Behavior

What methods does the autocratic parent regard as desirable for influencing the child's present and future behavior? The autocratic parent will often punish the child for any behavior that does not conform to the parent's rules and regulations. Timed restrictions of activity such as the child being required to stay in his room, in the house, or in a chair for a prescribed period of time are often employed.

Another method commonly used to influence child behavior is verbal disapproval that may devalue the child as a person. Such verbal disapproval may include shaming or ridiculing, comparing unfavorably with others, and making moral judgements about the child. Material rewards are also offered to alter a child's behavior.

These are the commonly held views for child rearing which are held by autocratic parents.

The Democratic Viewpoint

Child's Basic Nature

The democratic parent regards the child's basic nature as a reflection of the child's basic capacity to learn and mature without excessive pressure or protection. The child is viewed in a more positive way even though the parent recognizes that the child has the potential to develop both good and bad habits. Notwithstanding, there is a tendency on the part of the parent to view the child's basic inclination as benign. The parent feels a greater sense of trust and optimism about the child's potential and expresses this in overt and covert ways to the child and others.

Expectations for the Child

The child is expected to behave according to his own age level. Consequently, the democratic parent is often interested in finding out what behaviors are age-appropriate or what is typical for children of particular ages. Childlike behavior is regarded as appropriate for children. Adultlike behavior is regarded as a sign that children want to be mature and be like older significant others in their lives. Adultlike behavior is not required of children. Children are allowed to be children.

Goals of Child Rearing

The basic goal of child rearing is to help the child develop his own potential. There is an emphasis on individuality and discovering the individual child's strengths, gifts, interests, or inclinations so he can realize his potential whatever that might be. The frame of reference expressed by the democratic parent is child-oriented. The parent's goal is to help the child become what he (the child) wants to become not what the parent desires him (the child) to be.

Role of the Parent

The role of the democratic parent is to provide guidance and encouragement so the child may grow and develop in a positive manner and to be consistent with the basic goal of fostering the child's individuality. The democratic parent is often interested in learning which parental behaviors are growth promoting to the child. Helping the child learn how to balance his own inner needs and desires with those of the parent and the world at large is a substantial dimension of the parent's role.

Meaning of Child Behavior and Discipline

What meaning does the democratic parent attach to child behavior and discipline? Behavior is looked at in terms of the child's age level and other possible causes. The democratic parent will want to know if such behavior is typical for a child this age and

149

might there be other factors that are contributing to the child's behavior. A desire to understand and place the child's behavior in proper perspective is often apparent in the democratic parent.

Discipline is seen in terms of the child's need for limits or when the child's behavior encroaches on the rights of others. Discipline is not viewed in a limited way. Punishment and discipline are not equated. Rather, punishment is viewed as one of a variety of disciplinary techniques, which include guidance, support, encouragement, giving the child choices, etc. Children are not only allowed but also encouraged to explain their behavior from their perspective.

Methods for Influencing Behavior

What methods does the democratic parent regard as desirable for influencing the child's present and future behavior? The democratic parent tries to avoid setting unrealistic goals for the child and child rearing. Expectations for the child's social and moral behavior are geared to his developmental stage or level. In order to be realistic in this regard, the parent tries to learn what kinds of behaviors are characteristic for each stage of development. In educating herself, the parent comes to expect that some regressions occur and mistakes are made at each level where the child is concerned.

Similarly, the child's age is taken into account when arranging household goods and furnishings. The democratic parent is most likely to "child-proof" the house and put valuable breakable objects out of the child's reach until the child achieves a greater degree of maturity.

Limits are set on behavior that encroaches on the rights of others or endangers the child's own safety. Reasoning with and explaining things to the child is used to not only influence his present behavior but also to increase his basic understanding. The parent provides an example of tolerance and understanding for the child to identify with by using non-punitive limits when limits are necessary.

The techniques employed include providing alternatives, using verbal disapproval that does not attack the child as a person, basing the restriction of activity on the child's regaining self-control or acquiring the appropriate skill rather than time limits. Physical measures of control are limited to stopping an undesirable activity or putting the child in another location without actually hurting the child. Corporal punishment is avoided; but when used, it is used minimally or sparingly and often as a last resort.

Democratic parents attempt to increase the child's desire to please and cooperate with them by spending time with the child and taking an interest in what he is doing. Encouraging the child to participate in household activities, praising the child for behavior that shows increased maturity, and trying to understand the child's point of view are additional methods the democratic parent uses to motivate the child and solicit his cooperation.

These are views which characterize those held by persons who share a democratic perspective concerning child rearing.

Indulgent and Protective Viewpoints

The indulgent and protective approach to child rearing are distinct approaches to raising children from both philosophical and practical perspectives. The major distinction resides in the fundamental premise about the child and the parent's role vis-a-vis the child. The protective parent believes that the child needs a great deal of protection and that the parent's major efforts should be to provide that protection. To not provide protection is to fail as a parent and to place the child at risk. In contrast, the indulgent parent believes that children should be allowed to pursue their own purposes without parental restriction. To restrict the child would cause unnecessary frustration which may in effect stifle the child's basic tendencies and result in possible harm to the child.

Despite these fundamental differences, the indulgent and protective parent often share many views about the child and the kind of parenting the child shall require. Even when the underlying motives are different, their respective behaviors are highly similar and sometimes exactly the same. Because of this overwhelming similarity in parental behavior, these two approaches will be discussed together in this section.

Child's Basic Nature

The protective parent believes that the child is constitutionally delicate, weak or extra vulnerable in some way. Consequently the child may need an extra measure of protection and supervision by the parent.

For the indulgent parent, the child's basic nature is to become easily frustrated and possibly suffer from this frustration if the child's needs, desires, or inclinations are thwarted. Consequently, the indulgent parent has a tendency to acquiesce to the child's wants, desires, and demands often out of fear of placing too much stress on the child and thus causing him harm.

To some extent the indulgent parent shares a view similar to the protective parent that the child may be easily harmed or damaged if the child's basic inclinations are blocked or frustrated. In some measure this view is a philosophical perspective. In some measure it represents the parent's inability to set limits and adhere to them. And there are many underlying reasons that might explain the parent's inability to establish and maintain limits.

Expectations for the Child

Based on the premise that the child is delicate, weak or vulnerable, the child is expected to need a great amount of help and be unable to get along on his own. The indulgent and protective parents may often help the child where help is not really required or necessary. In many instances, the parent will do for the child what the child can or should do for himself. This kind of parental behavior has a tendency to limit the skill the child acquires because it lessens the opportunities the child has to practice certain behaviors and/or skills. Hence the parent's expectations become realities of his own making.

Goals of Child Rearing

In keeping with the parent's view of the child's basic nature and the expectations which evolve from that viewpoint, the protective parent's main goal of child rearing is to insure the child's physical safety and survival. This goal is achieved largely by parental behaviors which limit the child's actions and diminish his exposure to situations, which are perceived by the parent as threatening to the safety and physical well-being of the child.

The indulgent parent's main thrust is to prevent any unnecessary frustration from befalling the child. The parent's behaviors are then aimed at reducing frustrations, removing obstacles that block or make the child's aspirations difficult, and generally running interference for the child and clearing the way in the process. Anything or any person who hampers the child is regarded as an obstacle to be removed by the parent.

Role of the Parent

In keeping with these perspectives, the role of the parent is to protect the child from life stresses. At times the parent assumes a protective posture in order to fulfill this role and at other times the parent assumes an indulgent posture. In this regard, the indulgent and protective parents can be regarded as two sides of the same coin. Whether the parent's behaviors are indulgent or protective in nature, they are, nevertheless, engaged in to minimize the child's exposure to situations which may be stressful to the child or otherwise threaten his safety and well-being.

Meaning of Child Behavior and Discipline

What meaning is attached to child behavior and discipline? The indulgent and protective parent often look at the child's behavior in terms of constitutional factors that can not be altered in any way. If the child behaves unfavorably, the parent typically believes that this is just the way he is. After all, you can not change human nature! The role of learning or the notion of acquired characteristics is often not considered and when they are, their respective roles are greatly minimized by the indulgent and protective parent.

Since you can not change these constitutional factors, discipline has limited practical value. In fact, discipline is often regarded as something to be avoided because of the child's delicate condition or adverse response to it. Such responses would include frustration, anger, crying, crankiness, non-compliance, temper tantrums, and other negative reactions to the disciplinary measure employed. Hence, the use of discipline as a child rearing tool is of limited value to the indulgent or protective parent. Remember, the child's basic nature is set and most characteristics of importance can not be altered to any appreciable degree, if at all.

Methods for Influencing Behavior

What methods does the indulgent or protective parent regard as desirable for influencing the child's present and future behavior? Indulgent and protective parents often rely on coaxing, begging, pleading, or the offering of a material reward to alter undesirable behavior in children. Indulgent and protective parents will often delay letting the child assume any responsibility for care of himself and his personal property. The parent will often give up her own social activities so the child will not have to be left with a baby-sitter.

However, protective and indulgent parents do occasionally part company. It is in the area of limit setting that they do. Although protective parents show variation in their ability to set and maintain limits, even the least inclined typically far surpasses the indulgent parent in this regard. In fact, many protective parents are quite strong in this regard, especially when the child is young and still largely dependent upon the parent. The following addresses this fact.

The protective parent in particular will also set limits on any behavior that could conceivably expose the child to some kind of stress. Consequently, the protective parent often restricts the child's social contacts with other children because of fear of exposing the child to germs or bad moral influences. The child is constantly kept in parental sight and may sleep in the parent's bed or room at night, so the child can be more easily and conveniently monitored. The parent restricts the child's activities and is taken to the pediatrician at the first sign of a change in health status.

The indulgent parent characteristically avoids setting limits on behavior, even when that behavior encroaches on the rights of others. The indulgent parent often demonstrates an attitude that others should give in to the child also and let him do whatever he wants to do. The child is allowed to disrupt or abuse others and is often appeased in his demands by the parent. The parents will often take the child's side against the person who seems to be obstructing the child's inclinations. The child is also permitted to disrupt the home routine.

The indulgent parent will often wait on the the child and eventually give in to his demands no matter how unreasonable they may be. The parent provides a great amount of service to the child whether it is solicited or not. The indulgent parent will often tolerate verbal and/or physical abuse from the child no matter how bad it becomes.

These are the commonly held views of indulgent and/or protective parents.

PARENTAL RESPONSE TO SPECIFIC CHILD BEHAVIOR (PRACTICES)

This section shall describe how the autocratic, democratic, indulgent and protective parent respectively respond to specific child behavior. Each subsection shall describe how each parent type generally responds to specific child behavior in the following behavioral areas: meal time behavior, bedtime, toilet training, property oriented behavior, aggressiveness, behavior concerning obedience and respect, sexual and moral behavior, and dependence and independence.

These parental responses make these four parent types distinguishable. Therefore, familiarity with these characteristic responses to specific child behavior will help us to recognize and to classify a particular approach to child rearing, enhance our understanding and facilitate our actions as child rearers and helping professionals.

Autocratic Responses
To Specific Child Behavior

Meal Time Behavior

When the child does not want to eat at the regular meal time, he is punished by the autocratic parent unless he complies with the parent's requirement. If the child does not eat what the parent considers the correct amount and kind of food, the child is required to clean his plate or taste everything before he is excused or given dessert. When the child accidentally spills or makes a mess while eating, he is punished or has to leave the table. The autocratic parent does not let the infant child use his fingers to feed himself. When the child does not use the proper table manners, he is punished or required to leave the table.

Bedtime Behavior

What happens when the child does not want to go to bed? For the autocratic parent, bedtime is set and once it is established, deviation is not permitted. The child is punished for persistence in trying to change parental rules.

Toilet Training Behavior

When the child does not comply when put on the toilet, he is made to sit for a prolonged period of time (more than fifteen minutes). The child is frequently put on the toilet throughout the day. Should the child resist sitting on the toilet, he is not allowed to get off and is punished for his resisting. If the child has an "accident" after being mostly trained, he is scolded and punished by the autocratic parent.

Property Oriented Behavior

If a child of toddler age touches or gets into things, his hands are slapped and he is restricted. The parent makes no preparation to avoid such incidents. The strategy of "child-proofing" is not considered an option. The child must simply learn to not touch such things. The child is not allowed to leave toys and clothes around the house. The child must put things away right after use. The child is punished for deviation.

What happens when the child wants to play in the living room quietly with toys or with messy toys or roughhouse? The autocratic parent does not allow any of these behaviors or activities. The child is punished for deviation from these rules. If the child breaks or damages something, he is punished.

Aggressive Behavior

As a rule the autocratic parent does not tolerate aggressive behavior in children. The child is punished if he has a temper tantrum. If the child becomes angry and directs it at the parent, shouts or says angry things, he is punished. Anger directed at the parent is not tolerated. If the child is angry and tries to hit the parent, the child is punished. The physical expression of anger toward the parent is not allowed. The child is punished for quarrels and/or fighting with siblings.

Behavior Concerning
Obedience or Respect

The child is punished if he disobeys or shows intent to disobey. Sassy and impudent behaviors result in punishment. Any sign of disobedience or disrespect meets with the threat of punishment or actual punishment. The autocratic parent is inclined to regard most behaviors or attitudes that take opposition to the parent's view or way of thinking as being disobedient or disrespectful.

A child's effort to explain his behavior or point of view is generally regarded as disobedient and disrespectful. Such behavior is regarded as sassyness and impudence.

Sexual and Moral Behavior

If the child asks a question about sex, he is told it is not nice or he is punished. Likewise, the child is punished or told it is not nice if he or she rubs or handles his or her genitals. The autocratic parent will typically punish the child for participating in sex play with other children. If the child runs around the house naked in front of others, he is told it is not nice or is punished. The child is punished for using bad language or telling a lie. If the child shows bad habits like thumb sucking, nose picking, and so forth, the parent tries to break the habit.

Dependent and Independent Behavior

If the child wants attention when the autocratic parent is busy, the child is ignored or punished. When the child acts clingy or whiny, he receives an irritated reaction from the parent often followed by punishment. If the child acts afraid, the child is ignored or made to feel ashamed, especially if the child is male. Should the child become upset when the parent leaves, he is left anyway and may be punished or is punished.

The child is allowed to perform routine tasks by himself; however, the autocratic parent will sometimes do it for the child because the parent can do it faster or better. Expediency often influences the parent's behavior in this regard. The child is allowed to play out of sight of the parent, if it is safe in the parent's view. When the child wants to play with other children, he is allowed to do so.

The autocratic parent expects that the child will want to help with household chores. Household chores are often assigned and may be excessive. The child is punished if he wants to be waited on or expects other services the parent regards as intolerable.

You will note that the autocratic parent relies greatly on the use of punishment and that many childlike behaviors are simply not tolerated and often responded to punitively. These responses are characteristic of parents who possess a predominantly autocratic philosophy.

Democratic Responses To Specific Child Behavior

Meal Time Behavior

The democratic parent expects the child to adhere to family meal times but some delay is allowed should the child not want to eat at the regular meal time. The child is allowed to determine his own food intake, even if the child is not eating what the parent considers the correct amount or kind of food. When the child spills or makes a mess while eating, the action is ignored or the child is helped to clean up. If the child does not use proper table manners, the democratic parent may ignore some behaviors but sets limits on excessively silly behavior.

Bedtime Behavior

What happens when the child does not want to go to bed? For the democratic parent bedtime is definite but some leeway is allowed. Special circumstances and conditions merit consideration and bed time may be altered as a consequence of these considerations.

Toilet Training Behavior

The democratic parent allows the child to get up and try again later if the child is not able to toilet when placed on the potty. When the child resists sitting on the toilet, he is allowed to get up and the attempt is discontinued. The parent may perceive this as a sign of lack of readiness on the part of the child and the parent may stop training for a while. Accidents after being substantially trained are ignored as they are regarded as typical for young children.

Property Oriented Behavior

When the toddler touches or gets into things, the child is told no, may be removed physically and/or may be provided with an alternate activity. The democratic parent will "baby-proof" the house in an attempt to prevent the child from touching or getting into things that are either potentially harmful to the child or valued by the parent.

Should the child leave toys and clothes around the house, the parent will encourage the child to pick up several times during the day. The parent may even assist or participate in the pick up to support the child's efforts to do so. No physical punishment is employed. The child is allowed to play in the living room quietly with toys and some limits are set with messy toys and on roughhouse play. The democratic parent expresses disapproval when the child breaks or damages something but the child is not punished.

Aggressive Behavior

The democratic parent generally ignores

temper tantrums. If the child becomes angry at the parent, shouts and says angry things, this is tolerated unless it is excessive. Then non-punitive limits are set. Non-punitive limits may be in the form of physical restriction, or temporary isolation, should the child become angry and attempt to hit the parent. Quarrels between siblings are ignored or the children are helped to settle their dispute or disagreement if the matter gets out of hand.

Behavior Concerning Obedience and Respect

When the child disobeys, an explanation is given as to what is wanted by the parent. Non-punitive limits are set if behavior persists. Sassy or impudent behavior is tolerated but non-punitive limits are set when such behavior persists. The child's effort to explain his behavior or present his point of view is generally not regarded as sassy or impudence by the democratic parent. In fact, the democratic parent often encourages the child to express his thoughts and feelings in a socially acceptable manner.

Sexual and Moral Behavior

When the child asks questions about sex, his questions are answered matter-of-factly. The child's rubbing of the genitals is generally ignored especially if it does not occur in public. Regarding sex play with other children, some behavior is ignored. If the behavior continues, the child is told that it is not socially acceptable.

The child is provided with alternatives, such as a book concerning the facts of life, in an attempt on the part of the parent to meet the child's need or interest in a more acceptable fashion. Running around the house naked in front of others is generally ignored by the democratic parent. The use of bad language or exhibiting bad habits like thumb sucking, nose picking, etc. are generally ignored. When the child tells a lie, he is told why it is not a good idea to not tell the truth.

Dependent and Independent Behavior

The democratic parent recognizes the child's desire for attention when the parent is busy but the child may be asked to wait for

parental involvement. When the child acts clingy or whiny, he is comforted but limits are established if the behavior persists. The child is comforted when he acts afraid. If the child becomes upset when the parent leaves, he is comforted but the parent goes away after providing comfort to the child.

When the child tries to perform a routine task himself, he is encouraged for his efforts even if he is slow or makes mistakes. The child is allowed to play out of the parent's sight with other children, if the parent determines it is safe to do so. If the child wants to help with household chores, he is encouraged to help and considerable leeway is permitted. His desire to help is regarded as being more important than the degree of help realized. When the child wants to be waited on, limits are set if the child's expectations are unreasonable; otherwise the parent will occasionally cooperate and comply with the child's desire for service.

Such responses are common among parents who possess a democratic philosophy.

Indulgent and Protective Responses To Specific Child Behavior

Meal Time Behavior

If the child does not want to eat at the regular meal time, he is allowed to eat when he wants by both the indulgent and protective parent. When the child does not eat what the protective parent considers the correct amount or kind of food, the protective parent is inclined with some degree of persistence to beg, plea or offer a reward for eating more. The indulgent parent may employ the same strategies but will give them up as soon as the child shows any resisting or adverse response. Accidental spills or messes made by the child while eating are ignored or the parent cleans them up. The protective parent is less tolerant of messes than the indulgent parent and is therefore more inclined to act with dispatch in clean up. No limits are set on the child's use of improper table manners.

Bedtime Behavior

If the child does not want to go to bed, the indulgent parent is likely to allow the child to

155

set his own bedtime. The parent may also expect the child to stay in the parent's bedroom until the child falls asleep. Or the child may expect the parent to remain in the child's bedroom until the child falls asleep.

The protective parent would be more inclined to establish and maintain a bedtime for the child with the underlying belief that if the child were not to get adequate rest, he would be placed at risk. Consequently, there is less likelihood that the protective parent will allow the child to establish his own bedtime. However, the parent's physical presence and administration may follow a similar pattern as was noted for the indulgent parent.

Should the child want to sleep in the parent's bed or room, it would be allowed by both the indulgent and protective parent. The indulgent parent would be more inclined to actually encourage such practices, whereas the protective parent would typically not encourage this practice.

Toilet Training Behavior

Both the indulgent and the protective parent would generally allow the child to try again later if he does not go when placed on the toilet. The protective parent would be somewhat more inclined to have the child stay on the potty longer and try. The indulgent parent is least likely to insist that the child remain especially if the child shows any inclination of not wanting to sit any longer. Should the child actually resist sitting on the toilet, he is allowed to get up. Both types of parents may stop training for a while, if this behavior recurs. Accidents which happen after the child has been substantially trained are typically ignored by both the indulgent and protective parent.

Property Oriented Behavior

The indulgent parent sets no limits on the toddler who touches or gets into things. The protective parent is more inclined to set some limits for safety purposes and actually remove items which are perceived to be potentially injurious to the toddler. The indulgent parent sets no limits for toys and clothes left around the house. In contrast the protective parent may encourage the child to pick up or the

parent may pick up to minimize the potential of injury to the child if the child were to trip or fall upon an item. Safety and protection are ever present in the mind of the protective parent. Typically both parent types are inclined to pick up after the child but their underlying reasons are different.

What happens when the child wants to play in the living room quietly with toys or with messy toys or even roughhouse? Typically the indulgent parent will set no limits and allows the child to engage in these various activities. The parent will often have to clean up after the child and may even suffer the consequences of damaged or destroyed items as result of permitting such play.

The protective parent is likely not to set any limits on playing in the living room quietly or with messy toys. However, the protective parent may limit roughhouse play for fear the child may get hurt. If the child breaks or damages something the indulgent and protective parents will typically ignore the incident or generally not set any limits on behavior that might potentially result in damage or breakage. However, the protective parent is likely to become upset if there were a potential for injury. If this were the case, then the protective parent is more likely to establish a limit that would minimize such potential in the future.

Aggressive Behavior

The indulgent and protective parent typically give in to temper tantrums. The indulgent parent does so to avoid unpleasantness in parent and child interaction. The protective parent does so for fear the child may injure himself during the tantrum.

Sometimes the child may become angry at the parent and may shout and say angry things. Generally such behavior is tolerated and no limits are set. The indulgent and protective parents will behave the same way should the child become angry and try to hit the parent. When the child quarrels with siblings, often the parent may make the sibling, especially if older, give in to the child's position or request.

The indulgent parent is so inclined in order to avoid unpleasantness. The protective parent is so inclined in order to minimize any adverse effects to the child should he become upset or continue to be upset for a prolonged period of time.

Behavior Concerning Obedience or Respect

Child disobedience is tolerated by both the indulgent and protective parent and no limits are set. Sassy or impudent behaviors yield the same parental response by both parent types: it is tolerated and no limits are set.

Sexual and Moral Behavior

Questions the child asks about sex are ignored or evaded by the indulgent parent. The same is generally true for the protective parent, except if the parent determines that the child would be placed at risk if he were without this information. Such a determination might generally be forthcoming with an older child. Should the child rub his or her genitals, he or she is told it is not nice. If the child participates in sex play with other children, he is told that it is not nice by both the indulgent and protective parent. However, the protective parent generally goes a step further and will not allow the child to play with the other children again. The indulgent parent might make such a threat but typically will not be able to enforce it.

Both the indulgent and protective parent tell the child it is not nice to run around the house naked in front of others. The indulgent parent is least likely to be able to set any limits in this regard. In contrast, the protective parent is more inclined to set limits and adhere to them. The protective parent has another concern and it pertains to health. The child could become ill without adequate clothing on and this notion adds power to the parent's conviction that nakedness should generally not be allowed.

When the child uses bad language, tells a lie, or shows bad habits like thumb sucking or nose picking, the parent tells the child that it is not nice. The indulgent parent is likely to stop at this. The protective parent may set a limit on certain bad habits, especially if they could potentially place the child at risk. Behaviors such as nose picking would be habits to discourage and the protective parent would be more inclined to do so.

Dependent and Independent Behavior

If the child wants attention when the parent is busy, the child is given attention by both the indulgent and protective parents, who are inclined to stop what they are doing. Both would comfort and hold a child who acts clingy or whiny. Likewise both would comfort a child who appeared afraid. Should the child become upset when the parent leaves, the child will typically not be left. Both parent types will often restrict their own activity, the indulgent parent to avoid unpleasantness, the protective parent to minimize harm to the child.

Indulgent and protective parents do routine tasks for and provide services to the child even when the child shows an interest in doing these things for himself. Such parent service-giving persists even after the child has demonstrated ability in doing certain tasks himself. The child's demands to be waited on are typically complied with readily and expediently by the indulgent parent and eventually by the protective parent, especially if the child shows a degree of helplessness or ineptitude.

When the child wants to play outside of the sight of the parent, both the indulgent and protective parent make many attempts to keep the child in sight. Both may be apprehensive about such activities, especially the protective parent. The protective parent is more inclined to monitor the child's play and be persistent in this regard, even in the face of the child's protest. The indulgent parent is less likely to be persistent in this regard and more likely to curtail monitoring, especially if the child were to protest.

The protective parent is a stronger and more effective censor of the child's play with other children, who might be a bad influence. The indulgent parent is significantly less effective in this area and usually gives in to the child's protest and will typically cease and desist the censorship.

The child's desire to help with household chores is likely to be allowed by the indulgent parent in order to avoid unpleasantness. If chores are not completed to parental satisfaction, the indulgent parent is likely to do these over herself. With respect to the child performing certain chores, the protective parent is likely to discourage and not allow the child to

157

engage in many household chores, especially if there is even a remote chance that the child may get hurt. Should the child be allowed and subsequently suffers even the slightest discomfort, parental convictions are strengthened that the child should not have been allowed to perform the chore in the first place. Hence the protective parent is likely to prevent the child from doing so in the future.

These responses to child behavior characterize the indulgent or protective parent's behaviors. Their responses are often highly similar even though underlying reasons for them may be significantly different.

EPILOGUE

Having reviewed in general terms the four major approaches to child rearing and their philosophical and child rearing practice differences, let's complete this chapter by identifying some crucial child rearing phenomena. These phenomena involve the mixture of approaches, consistency or inconsistency, interactional patterns and roles, interactional shifts, and the use of different approaches with different children.

Child Rearing Mixtures

These various approaches have been described separate and apart from each other as though they were pure forms. In fact, we discover that parents typically do not show this purity in their interactions with their children. Indeed some parents may be so substantially inclined to one philosophical perspective and so predominantly employ the prescriptions of a particular philosophy that they may appear as "text book examples" of that particular persuasion.

However, in American society parents are more commonly observed showing various mixtures or blends of the different philosophies and practices associated with them. Consequently, we sometimes have to look very carefully to determine which approach is being employed in a given situation under a given set of circumstances. We must look for the parent's predominant mode or central tendency and how the parent departs from that to

adequately understand the parent's unique child rearing approach and the child's unique responses to the parent.

Consistency in Approach

Furthermore, we must realize that a parent may not consistently employ a given approach when interacting with the child each time. Some parents certainly do and are very predictable. But some do not. Therefore, we may observe that a parent may reflect one particular approach in her interaction with the child today and tomorrow may employ strategies that characterize another approach. Changes in approach confuse the child and he may reflect this in the form of erratic behavior. These changes also challenge our ability to understanding, our ability to accurately predict and most importantly our ability to help.

Interactional Patterns and Roles

Notwithstanding the occurrence of child rearing mixtures and fluctuations in consistency of approach, parents will usually establish a pattern in their child rearing interactions. As these patterns become established and strengthen, the parent begins to show a particular role that may characterize a particular approach or a common blend of approaches. If we learn what to look for, we can recognize these patterns. Recognition of these patterns can help us put the parent's child rearing into perspective and help us to understand the parent's behavior and the child's reaction to parental behavior.

Interactional Shifts

An additional caution involves the fact that some parents shift their approach to child rearing during the interaction with the child. For example, the parent may begin interaction with the child showing an autocratic posture. During interaction the child fights back or resists the parent's efforts to manage him. The child's reaction causes the parent to eventually give up. The child was not made to comply with the parent's original position and goes about his business as he wanted. The parent in effect, made an interactional child rearing shift from autocratic to indulgent. The child has not only experienced two different approaches to child rearing within the same interactional encounter but also has learned that if he fights or resists long enough, he can get his way.

Different Approaches Are Often Used For Different Children

Some parents may certainly employ the same approach with all their children. And they may do so very consistently and without showing any appreciable mixture of approaches or shifts in their interactions. They are highly consistent and highly predictable. However, some parents may not show such a high degree of consistency over time with each of their children. In fact, some parents actually show that they employ a significantly different approach from one child to another.

For example, we may find that a parent may raise one child by employing a predominantly protective approach and with another child use an autocratic approach. Consequently these two children receive very different parenting from the same parent. We can expect them to emerge from the child rearing they receive as very different individuals. This phenomenon explains how children can be so very different even when they come from the same family having been raised by the same parent.

The next chapter shall focus primarily on how children are effected by or respond to these four different child rearing philosophies and practices. Please be mindful of some of the phenomena immediately identified in this chapter as you read the content of the next chapter.

References

1. Chamberlin, R. "Approaches to Child Rearing: Their Identification and Classification." *Clinical Pediatrics*, 1965, **4**, p 150-159.

2. Chamberlin, R. "Approaches to Child Rearing II: Their Effects on Child Behavior." *Clinical Pediatrics*, 1966, **5**, p 688-698.

3. Chamberlin, R. "Early Recognition and Management of Vicious Circle Parent-child Relationships." *Clinical Pediatrics*, 1967, **6**, p 469-479.

4. Chamberlin, R. "A Study of an Interview Method for Identifying Family Authority Patterns." *Genetic Psychology Monographs*, 1969, **80**, p 129-148.

5. McCandless, B. *Children: Behavior and Development*, 2e (New York: Holt, Rinehart and Winston, Inc., 1967).

Chapter 10

Child Rearing Approaches
Effects on Children

Children show many common behaviors and characteristics by virtue of the fact that they are children and not adults. Children by nature are highly egocentric. This is a condition of their being children not of being parented in a particular manner. Children need love, care and nurturing. They need these because they are human first and children second. These needs are not a condition of the parenting approach that is being employed; they are a condition of being human.

However, certain approaches have a differential impact on these traits and how these needs are met and manifest themselves. One approach to child rearing clearly strengthens the child's basic egocentric nature. Another seems to help lessen it considerably. Similarly parents who employ a particular approach to child rearing often seem less able to adequately provide a full complement of love, care and nurturing. While other parents who prefer and use another approach seem generally more able to provide the full measure of love, care, and nurturing that children need to grow and develop well.

This chapter shall not focus on the many behaviors and characteristics that almost all children share. Rather, this chapter shall describe how children typically respond to the various child rearing approaches they encounter. Their behavioral responses will not only depict how they are being affected by the parenting they receive but also these responses will come to characterize them as individuals who have been parented in a particular way. This chapter shall focus on the behaviors and traits that distinguish children as having been raised either autocratically, protectively, indulgently or democratically.

These particular reactions to specific child rearing will influence the child's growth, development and behavior. Furthermore, these behaviors and characteristics will be those that have been incorporated into the child's personality structure. In time they come to characterize him as a person. They become his behavioral and personality signature. The child becomes what his response to parenting has been.

AUTOCRATIC CHILD REARING

The Autocratic Parent

The autocratic parent is typically the absolute ruler, a monarch who holds and exercises complete or substantial power and control over the child by right of parenthood. The autocratic parent does not perceive herself as subject to restrictions. She is in charge and the children are subservient and must obey without question. The children are not expected to question or challenge her authority and no explanations are owed to the child. The autocratic parent expects obedience and "adult-like" behavior from the child.

Children typically have to live with many restrictions and live up to adult standards and expectations. When children do not comply with these restrictions or live up to these expectations, they are punished. The autocratic parent relies extensively (sometimes almost exclusively) on the use of punishment when disciplining children. Children are typically managed with anger and hostility. Frequently there is verbal assault on the child's self-esteem, character, and personality that results in ego debasement. Often physical punishment is used. The child is spanked or required to remain in one position for an extended period of time, such as sitting still or kneeling in a corner.

Autocratic parents differ greatly in terms of the extent to which they employ these approaches. Some parents use these techniques to a limited degree. They are more autocratic in attitude than in their actual practices. Others apply these measures moderately. Their actual practices are a greater reflection of their underlying autocratic attitude.

Yet some autocratic parents employ punitive measures to a substantial degree and enter the realm of physical and verbal abuse. When parental behavior reaches this extreme degree, much damage - both physically and psychologically - can result to the child. Unfortunately, the extremely autocratic parent often does not perceive her behavior as extreme or abusive.

Two Common Reactions to Autocratic Parenting

Children generally respond to this type of parenting in one of two ways. Their reaction is a function of their basic nature. Some children will fight or resist the parent's autocratic ways. The child who responds this way is showing an aggressive response to the parenting he receives. Some children are more passive and submit to the parenting presented to them. The child who does not fight or resist, but rather submits to or acquiesces to parental behavior is showing a submissive response to parenting.

In either case there is generally an accumulation of anger and hostility in the child in response to the kind of management he receives. These feelings are often accompanied by resentfulness, revengefulness, contempt and hate. These feelings may or may not be expressed outwardly by the child. Their expression is a function of the child's basic nature and his experience in attempting to express these thoughts and feelings and what happens to him when he does so.

Notwithstanding their manner and degree of expression, these feelings manifest themselves in some fashion in the child's behavior. The child's anger, hostility, resentment, revenge may be directed outwardly toward people and things or they may be directed inwardly toward the self. Again, this inward or outward direction is a function of the child's basic nature and the consequences such expression has on parent and child interaction.

An Aggressive Response to Autocratic Parenting

Some children by nature will fight against or resist parental restrictiveness. These children "would rather fight than switch." The

162

more some parents insist, the more some children resist. If the parent hits, some children hit back. Some children run and invite a chase: "You can't catch me." Some stand their ground and enter into a power struggle: "That doesn't hurt me!" The parent intends to emerge triumphant...and so do some children.

The child who is more inclined to respond aggressively to autocratic parenting will show many if not all of the following common characteristics and/or responses. These behavioral responses are integrated into the child's personality and come to characterize his behavior and personhood in general.

Retaliation

This child returns like with like, kind with kind, an eye for an eye. He fights back powerfully and aggressively in a physical and/or verbal manner. He hits, bites, yells back, issues threats, and more. He typically does not yield or back down. He retaliates. He does not comply easily, if at all. He has learned to be powerful in the face of adversity. He has learned to fight in order to get what he wants or avoid doing what he does not want to do.

Resistance

To resist is to withstand parental action and strive against it or oppose it. This child will often refrain or abstain from parental demands or expectations. These behaviors are another manifestation of the child's tendency to fight back.

The child's resistance is an active or blatant form of resistance. He won't move. He becomes stiff. He stands his ground, nose to nose, fist to fist. He becomes a force in opposition to parental wishes. He can be wearisome to the parent, indeed.

Contrariness

The autocratically raised child often assumes a contrariwise position. He becomes diametrically opposed to the parent's position. He takes an opposite direction or view as the one prescribed by the parent. He may become contradictory, conflicting, and discordant.

These behaviors may not be limited to just his interactions with the autocratic parent. These behaviors often become integrated into the personality structure and then generalize to other people and settings. Hence, when the kindergarten teacher announces that it is time to put materials away and get ready for snack, the child counters that it is not time yet.

Negativism

The autocratic parent typically advises the child about what he cannot do, should not do, ought not do, and better not do. "You cannot do that." "I do not want you to go there." "It is not possible." "That is not correct." "You don't know how." "I will not allow it." The autocratic parent makes extensive use of "no" and other negatives.

The child assimilates this negative attitude. He expresses his refusal to do something. He does not consent to the parent's or the teacher's guidance. He takes a prohibitory stance as he exclaims a command or a negative order. His character becomes distinguished or marked by qualities or features, which lack a positive attitude or an optimistic view. His response to questions or situations is often marked by a negative statement, answer, word or gesture. He will take the side of the question which denies what the opposite side affirms. He often demonstrates a refusal to agree or admit the truth. He denies, contradicts, disapproves, pronounces against, counteracts, or veto's. He can be very negative in attitude and behavior.

Disagreeableness and Argumentativeness

These behaviors help establish a pattern of general disagreement and argumentativeness in the child. The parent and others come to expect such behavior. Their prophecy is frequently fulfilled. Each person is party to its perpetuation, complaints notwithstanding. Some parents and children even seem to enjoy the "fight;" some can't seem to help it. The pattern is strong and it influences the behavior of both the parent and the child.

Some examples:

The child will say "Yes" when the parent says "No."

163

The parent says to the child "I told you to pick up your toys." The child responds, "No, you didn't tell me to pick up."

The parent reminds the child, "It's almost bedtime." The child disagrees, "No, it's not time for bed yet."

Non-compliant

The child's negative posture influences other aspects of his interactions with the parent and others. For example, the autocratically raised child will often become generally non-compliant. He will not go along with or do what is requested or required. He generally fails or refuses to comply. He will typically not yield or yields uneasily to parental wishes, requests, commands, requirements, conditions, etc.

Uncooperative

Similarly, the autocratically raised child shows a considerable degree of uncooperativeness. He is not inclined to work or to act together or jointly with the parent or others or to unite in producing an effect or a result desired by the parent or others. As a consequence of this tendency, he has limited opportunities to learn cooperative behaviors. Therefore, he shows up lacking considerably in this social skill area. His typical uncooperative demeanor often alienates him from others. Sometimes estrangement results. Other children will not want him to play will them because he "doesn't play right."

The Submissive Response to Autocratic Parenting

While some children fight and resist the parent's autocratic behaviors, some children submit or acquiesce to the autocratic parenting they encounter. These children are by nature more passive, acquiescent, and submissive. Even children who may have initially offered resistance learned that the parent is too powerful, so they comply. In either case, these children "would rather switch than fight." Consequently, they show a very different profile in their general behavior and response to autocratic parenting. They are noted as having a submissive response. The following traits characterize the child who shows a more or less submissive response to autocratic parenting.

Reluctance to Act

The child who is inclined to show a submissive response to autocratic parenting often shows a reluctance, an unwillingness or a disinclination to act or take action on his own. In some respects the child seems somewhat immobilized. The child often is waiting for the parent, teacher or another authority figure to tell him what to do or to give him permission to proceed.

As a consequence of his interactions with the autocratic parent, the child has learned to wait for parental direction, sanction, or disinterest before proceeding. The child has learned that if he does what the parent prefers, he receives parental approval. If the child proceeds on his own and does the "wrong" thing, he meets with parental disapproval. To play it safe, the child has learned to wait for the parent's directive or sanction before initiating an action.

Consequently, the child seems to be reluctant to act on his own. Even when given the opportunity to act on his own, the child will often solicit guidance from the parent: "What should I do?" "Is this what you want?" "Do you think this is right?" Typically, the autocratically raised child has not been given many opportunities to decide for himself and initiate the action associated with the decision. Consequently, the child is often not a skilled decision maker and thus may require considerable input from others.

For some children this results in a "Catch 22" situation. If the parent decides that it is time for the child to make his own decisions and follow through on them, the parent may instruct the child to decide for himself. Since the child is lacking skill in this area he may be unable to proceed. The parent may then chastise the child for his inaction. If the child proceeds and makes a decision and implements a form of action to the displeasure of the parent, the child is admonished for making a bad choice and acting incorrectly. In a sense, the child is damned if he does, and damned if he does not. Consequently, many children take a safer course of action and do nothing.

Diminished Initiative

Closely associated with a reluctance to act is a general lack of initiative. Of course "lack" is an extreme condition. Indeed some children seem to be lacking or to be without any initiative. More typically however is the fact that children who show a submissive response to autocratic parenting often show diminished initiative. In comparison to their agemates, the autocratically raised child seems to have difficulty in beginning, starting, and originating thought and action.

The child seems to require an inordinate amount of prodding, encouragement, and motivation in order to get him started. Once started, he seems to require substantial support to continue. He may or may not solicit the encouragement and support. It is still needed if it is not solicited. Some children show their solicitation in the questions they ask: "Do you want me to help?" "Am I doing it right?" "Is this what you want?" Notice that the thrust of the child's questions is seeking approval from the authority figure. (A child who has grown in another child rearing environment might behave differently. For example: "May I help too?" "Look what a good job I am doing!" "You will like what I made.")

Diminished Assertiveness

Assertiveness means many things. When we are assertive, we state what we believe to be true, even in the face of adversity. We affirm ourselves, our beliefs, our position. We declare with conviction and if need be defend our perspective or point of view. We at times put ourselves forward boldly and insistently. We do this with conviction, not with anger or hostility. Assertiveness is not aggressiveness.

The autocratically raised child who shows a submissive response, sometimes lacks assertiveness, but most often shows diminished assertiveness. For it has often been the experience of the child that when he has asserted or attempted to assert himself, he has had "his hand slapped" or has been "cut down to size." Assertiveness vis-a-vis the autocratic parent has met with negative reinforcement. Consequently, the likelihood of assertiveness being incorporated into the personality structure and manifesting itself in the child's behavior has been diminished and in some instances

eliminated. (A child raised in another child rearing environment might show his assertiveness thusly: "I am going to help too." "I know I am doing a good job!." "I know you will love what I made.")

Withdrawal

The passive child is inclined to withdraw or "back down" from situations wherein he meets with resistance or receives a negative response. A very passive child will withdraw almost immediately. A less passive child may make some attempt to assert himself, but will eventually withdraw, especially if confronted with a powerful adverse response.

The autocratic parent will typically present a powerful profile. However some parents are moderately autocratic and some are minimally autocratic. These variations in the power or degree of parental autocratic behavior account for a substantial portion of the different responses we observe in children who have been raised in a predominantly autocratic manner. However, children who are more acquiescent by nature will be more easily intimidated than those that are less so. The net result is the same. The child withdraws. But also this has a significant effect upon how the child comes to see himself: a whimp, spineless, powerless, and the like.

Diminished Self-confidence

The characteristics that have already been discussed help to shape the child's view of himself and influence self-concept development, self-esteem, self-worth, and self-confidence. Confidence has to do with trust, a belief in trustworthiness, and the ability to rely on a person or thing, to be able to perform in a particular way, or live up to certain expectations. Self-confidence is placing that trust in the self.

The autocratically raised child in this instance, has learned that he cannot trust in his ability to act, initiate, assert, go forward, stand his ground, etc. He has met with too little success to trust in his own ability to do these things. He has learned that he cannot rely on himself. The result is that the child comes to lack or has a diminished sense of self-confidence.

165

Parental support is often lacking. Action on the part of the child is often discouraged by the autocratic parent. Feedback is typically negative. The messages given by the parent to the child diminish the development of self-confidence: "I don't think you should do that. The last time you made a mess." "This is not done correctly. Didn't you pay attention when I was showing you how to do it right?" "I can't rely on you. That's for sure." Of course these negative messages contribute to low self-esteem, low self-worth, and make a negative contribution to self-concept development in the child.

Compliant

By nature some children are prone to be more compliant. However, learning plays a powerful role here also. The autocratically raised child learns as a consequence of his interactions with the parent that compliance is what the parent wants. Furthermore, the autocratic parent is easier to live with when compliance is given. Hence, many children simply learn that it is safer, more expedient, less of a hassle to comply with parental wishes. When the child complies, the autocratic parent typically will give some form of positive feedback ("You're a good child.") or remove a negative reinforcement ("You are no longer grounded."). In either case, compliance has been strengthened. With repeated reinforcements of this type the child's tendency or inclination to be compliant has been greatly increased.

Acquiescence, Passivity and Submissiveness

This child initially shows a greater tendency to be acquiescent, passive, and submissive. Interactions with the parent and the reinforcements that are part of those interactions strengthen the acquiescent, passive, and submissive nature of the child. Consequently, it is a rather common profile for the autocratically raised child to show considerable acquiescence, passivity, and submissiveness. This tendency will also show itself more overtly vis-a-vis autocratic adults, other than the parent.

This tendency may be diminished somewhat in the presence of adults who have a non-autocratic or a more reasonable approach to parenting. We must be mindful of the fact that these children are highly sensitive to negative feedback of any sort. As soon as they perceive any reluctance or equivocation in the authority figure, they are inclined to retreat and then acquiesce or submit to what they perceive as the authority figure's preferred course of action or behavior. Consequently parents and teachers who are attempting to change this child's behavior must work diligently to minimize messages that might be construed as a negative sanction by the child. This is not easy work. It is often painstaking for adults who are trying to help children become less acquiescent, passive or submissive.

Shyness

This autocratically raised child prefers to not call attention to himself. He does not want to be in the spotlight. When you are in the foreground, rather than the background, there is greater risk that your shortcomings, errors, etc. will be noticed and result in negative feedback. To avoid having negative attention, the child withdraws to the background and tries to remain relatively inconspicuous. This is safer for the child. If your presence goes unnoticed, you don't get "clobbered." This strategy's manifestation is shyness or bashfulness. This characteristic is closely associated with poor self-concept, low self-esteem, low self-worth, and diminished self-confidence. Consequently these characteristics influence each other and contribute to the strengthening of attitudes and behaviors that are perceived by others as shyness.

Shame and Guilt Ridden

Shame and guilt are very similar. One is simply the public manifestation of the other. If I get caught with my pants down in public, I am embarrassed and I feel shame. There I am in public to be seen by all. If I am naked in the privacy of my home with no one present, I might feel guilty about doing something I may have been taught is wrong. In this instance I feel guilt not shame, because there is no one to see me. The feelings are very similar. Guilt I experience in private. Shame I feel in public.

Autocratically raised children are often shame and guilt ridden. This is so because the

166

autocratic parent makes extensive use of shame and guilt to influence the child's behavior. The parent's techniques are very apparent: "Shame on you for saying that." "You ought to be ashamed of yourself." "Aren't you the least bit embarrassed? You should be!" "I can tell that you are lying. You look guilty. I always know when you are lying." "You are driving me crazy. A good child would feel guilty about that." "It's your fault I am so upset."

These parental strategies promote a tremendous and unnecessary amount of shame and guilt in children. Many autocratically raised children show a large amount of shame and guilt as a consequence. Some even become shame and guilt ridden. Some children feel shame and guilt for things that they are not directly responsible for.

Some children even confess to things they have not actually done in order to purge themselves of the shame and guilt they feel. When such confessions are followed by punishment, and they usually are, the child experiences a sense of relief. In essence the punishment exonerates the child and he can now go forward free of guilt. Such a pattern has serious implications for personality development. Some professionals believe that such a pattern is a precursor to masochistic behavior patterns.

We must be mindful that many of these children are going to be made to feel unnecessarily uncomfortable and negative about themselves if we employ such strategies. Furthermore, we must realize that all confessions are not valid. Police personnel recognize this and do not necessarily close a case following a confession unless they are sure that the confession is valid. Parents, teachers and others who work with children must employ a similar policy.

Furthermore, we must employ means other than punishment to avoid strengthening in the child a need for punishment. This is a peculiar situation indeed! But it is one we must understand. Punishment in this instance serves to strengthen the feelings of shame and guilt and the inclination to confess to acts that have not been actually committed.

Prevailing Feelings and Attitudes of Autocratically Raised Children

There are many feelings and attitudes that are associated with being raised autocratically. The more common ones shall be identified herein.

Whatever the individual child's response to being raised autocratically, the child is very likely to feel one or more of the following emotions or possess one or more of the following attitudes. These are often closely associated feelings and attitudes. Therefore we frequently observe many if not all of these attitudes and feelings in children that have been raised autocratically. We also may observe such feelings and attitudes in children that have been raised in another manner, as they are rather common human emotions and attitudes. The difference is not one of absence or presence but rather one of degree. The autocratically raised child often possesses these feelings and attitudes in a substantial and significant degree in comparison to children raised differently.

Anger and Hostility

As indicated previously there is a substantial build up or accumulation of angry and hostile feelings. This is often the consequence of the frustration the child often feels in being restricted or forced to conform, or in trying to meet expectations that are beyond his ability at the present time. It is a well established principle that frustration leads to aggression. Anger and hostility are manifestations of aggression. These feelings also manifest themselves in the form of anxiety, tension, stress, and depression.

How anger and hostility are expressed is a matter of the child's basic nature and his experiences in being parented and attempting to express his feelings. These emotions are shown overtly and/or covertly. They are express, suppressed or repressed. These emotions may be directed outwardly at other people or things or they may be directed inwardly at the self.

Feeling Controlled

Autocratically raised children often feel controlled. The autocratic parent can be powerfully controlling and may force, if necessary, the child to conform to parental expectations. The child is often dependent upon the parent for permission to think, feel and behave in certain ways. Even the child who fights the parent at every encounter, and often manages to do what he (the child) wants still feels controlled. The child's fight response is dependant upon the parent's posture. Another parent might not elicit the fight response in this child.

Self-determination is at issue. Exercising self-control is part of the autonomy strivings that emerge in all children. The autocratic parent does not want self-determination in the child. The autocratic parent wants compliance. The autocratic parent wants control.

Feeling Dependent

Closely associated with self-control, autonomy, and will power is independence. Independence is typically not encouraged and reinforced by the autocratic parent, especially at a time when it should be. Later the parent may want and expect the child to behave more independently, exercise greater self-control and self-direction. However, by this time, dependent behavior has been substantially strengthened so that it may have become strongly integrated into the child's personality structure. Even punishment for dependent behavior strengthens dependent behavior rather than weakens it. A very perplexing phenomenon indeed!

Furthermore, the parent may have been very deliberate about reinforcing dependent behavior in the child at an earlier stage in the child's development. The messages were many and strong: "Ask me first!" "Did I say you could do that?" "Do what I tell you to do. You are too young to decide for yourself." At a time when the parent should be encouraging independence, the autocratic parent is discouraging it. At a time when the parent should be attempting to minimize the child's dependency, the autocratic parent is maximizing it. And later when the parent should be ignoring dependent behavior, the autocratic parent meters out punishments for it.

As a consequence of these misguided actions, the parent fosters feelings of dependence in the child.

Feeling Blame, Shame and Guilt

Autocratically raised children carry much blame, shame, and guilt inside of them. The autocratic parent has used these as a means of managing the child. The child unfortunately assimilates a large measure of the blame, shame, and guilt despite the fact that almost all are unjustified. The parent's misguided practices weave the design of blame, shame and guilt into the fabric of the child's personality.

Feeling Exploited and Deprived

Parental behavior and expectations often result in the autocratically raised child feeling exploited, abused, and victimized. An older child may be required to care for younger siblings. Some children are given excessive household chores to perform on a regular basis. Such requirements may limit the child's opportunities with playmates. As a consequence, the child may feel exploited in having to be responsible for child care and/or household maintenance. The child may also feel deprived of desired and preferred contact with peers. The child may feel "robbed of his childhood." Feelings of exploitation and deprivation set in and often become affixed to the personality structure.

Feeling Abused and Victimized

The circumstances that lead to feelings of exploitation and deprivation also contribute to the child's feelings of being misused, abused, and victimized. But what actually reinforces these feelings is the harsh measures that are employed by some (not all) autocratic parents. In some instances, the autocratic parent is clearly abusive either verbally or physically or both. In such cases the child is certainly abused and victimized.

The extensive reliance on punishment exacerbates this condition. Even parents that are minimally autocratic, often rely on the use of punishment to influence, control and manage the child's behavior. Repeated punishments contribute to the child developing a victim mentality and feeling abused. Such feelings are justified, because non-punitive means are much more effective in managing child behavior. Unfortunately for the child, the autocratic parent does not regard these other measures as viable techniques.

Moral Indignation

Autocratically raised children are often moved by a feeling of wrath which is mingled with scorn or contempt, especially in instances which they perceive as wrong, unjust or unfair. This in essense is moral indignation. The wrath, scorn, or contempt the child feels toward the parent may generalize to other parent figures and parent figure institutions. Hence, such feelings may generalize to the teacher, the school, the church, society, etc. Along a similar vein, the autocratically raised child is easily morally outraged and often righteous, upright and godly.

These are all manifestations of residual anger. For some these are impediments or handicaps. For others they are put to good use and turned into "assets." Of particular note here is the fact that autocratically raised children often become very powerful advocates for the downtrodden, disadvantaged, exploited and abused. Some of the most capable human service workers and activists that I have known or are familiar with have come from autocratic child rearing environments. They seem to have committed themselves to righting the wrongs and freeing the oppressed. This is something they may have been unable to do for themselves as children; but now that they are adults, a new chapter shall be written in their life story.

The Autocratically Raised Child's View of the Parent and Others

Children who are raised autocratically often perceive the parent and other authority figures as punishers; yet they also view them as sources of power. Because of this view, the child may align himself with the parent or model himself after the parent. In Freudian psychoanalytic terms this is known as "identification with the aggressor." In order to get or share the power of the parent, the child

may become like the autocratic parent, protest notwithstanding.

Of course, some children may reject what the parent is and may work diligently at not being like the parent. It is common for autocratically raised children to vow "I will never treat my children like I have been treated." Some are able to be faithful to this commitment. Others may have a very difficult time doing so because the interactional patterns of autocratic child rearing have been assimilated and integrated into the personality of the child to some degree. This is especially the case if the child has had no or limited exposure to other parenting approaches.

Alternate Parenting Models

The difficulty or ease with which the child can "break away" from the autocratic parenting he has experienced is greatly influenced by the availability of alternate role models. An alternate role model is someone who exhibits more positive parenting behaviors that can be copied and who provide the child with positive experiences. Another parent or teacher or therapist may serve as this more positive parent role model and may serve as another person with whom to identify. For identification purposes, the child needs an alternate role model, one who is more positive, more constructive, more growth enhancing.

The alternate role model may be real or imagined, factual or hypothetical. Another parent, teacher, or therapist are real models. They can play a significant role in liberating children from less preferred parenting models. They provide not only a prototype for better parenting but also the nurturing, guidance, etc. that the child needs in the here and now. Teachers may play a very significant role in this regard, especially with young children during their formative years. Passing the National Teacher Exam is nearly not enough. Teachers must also be able to parent well and provide a good model with which children can identify. Likewise, therapists must know how to parent well also because often they serve as parents within the therapeutic relationship.

Children who have limited exposure or access to other parenting approaches will sometimes imagine what another approach to parenting might be like. These children use their creative faculties to imagine other ways they might be treated or how they might treat their own children. These options often come out of the child's real life frustrations. For example, the child who is not allowed to express his thoughts and feelings, might imagine his doing so and having the parent respond in a more accepting manner. Likewise the child may imagine himself as a parent and encouraging his child to express himself without chastisement or punishment.

People seize what is readily available and make use of it to the extent that they require or can. Sometime these models are not readily available to us in terms of direct interaction; yet, we have knowledge of them through other means. I recall Carla, a former student of mine. She is a case in point.

Case study example:
Carla's mother died when she was a very young child. She was raised primarily by her father who had done a fairly good job of parenting, despite his moderately autocratic manner. She loved and respected her father. Nevertheless, Carla longed for a mother figure and fantasized often of herself having a mother and being a mother herself. She became pregnant during her later adolescence at about the same time Sophia Loren, the actress, became pregnant.

Carla read every magazine and newspaper article having to do with Sophia Loren. She imagined that Sophia was her mother and vowed to be a good mother just like Sophia appeared to be. In these media articles, Sophia spoke of the importance of good nutrition, exercise and good prenatal care in general. Carla followed Sophia's advice closely. When Sophia's child was born, Sophia was depicted in the media as being an outstanding mother, who spent much quality time with her child and seemed to be well informed about child development and parenting.

Carla was determined to follow Sophia's model. Among other things, she enrolled in a parent and child relations course that I was teaching and this was how I came to know Carla. From my contact with Carla, she appeared to be determined to learn more effective ways of parenting. She asked questions and participated fully in class discussions. She was energetic and candid and it was apparent that she was working very industriously to change the "script" of autocratic parenting inside her. And she was making considerable progress in doing so. Sophia Loren had served as her guide and source of inspiration.

Theoretical or Hypothetical Models

Some of our models are theoretical or hypothetical. Such models exist in text books, parenting guides, and as part of the curriculum of human service professional preparation. Teacher preparation programs, social service training, pediatric nursing, etc. are examples of the latter. These sources offer us models that have been applied within various professions with success and thus represent preferred ways of behaving. As part of professional preparation, teachers, social workers, etc. take courses in child development, parent and child relations, and human behavior in general. The purpose of such exposure is to help the developing professional gain insight and understanding. The practical benefits in terms of parenting knowledge and skills are apparent.

PROTECTIVE CHILD REARING

The Protective Parent

The protective parent is typically inclined to employ a variety of measures intended to protect the child from adverse experiences and generally keep him safe both physically and psychologically. These measures vary in degree. Some measures would be considered normal behavior for any parent. After all, every parent has a responsibility to keep the child safe and healthy. In this regard, all parents employ measures to protect their child. The distinction to be made here is that the protective parent often seems to be excessive in these measures. And of course there is also the parent who over does even these excessive measures and may be regarded as over-protective. A normal degree of protectiveness is necessary to keep children out of harm's way and generally safe. Protective child rearing employs these measures in excess and often unnecessarily.

Two Common Reactions

In order for the protective parent to adequately protect the child to her satisfaction, the parent must limit or restrict a considerable portion of the child's actions and interactions with people and the physical environment. Children respond to these limitations and restrictions in characteristically two different ways. Some children fight against the parent and this reaction is regarded as an aggressive response to parental protectiveness. Some children simply acquiesce or submit to the parent's protectiveness. This response is regarded as a submissive response. In either case, there may be a build up of angry or hostile feelings in the child if the child feels too restricted or too hindered by the parent's protective behavior.

An Aggressive Reaction to Protective Parenting

Some children will resist the parent's attempt to restrict or limit the child's behavior. This child in essence fights against the parent's efforts to protect him. He is inclined to reject the parent's endeavors at protection. A struggle for power may ensue depending on how strongly either one is willing to engage the other in this struggle.

There are certain traits or characteristics that distinguish children who are showing an aggressive response to protective child rearing. Children who are raised protectively may show some of these, most of these, or all of these traits. They may exhibit these in varying degrees because the intensity of their reactions vary. Some children will show a substantially intense or aggressive reaction. By comparison, other children may show a less intense reaction but are nonetheless still showing an aggressive response. Similarly a particular child may exhibit some traits in a very pronounced or even exaggerated fashion and other common traits will be mild by comparison. Hence, the variety and intensity of these traits not only may vary from child to child but also may vary within a particular child.

Resistance

Generally children who respond this way would "rather fight than switch." This inclination to protest against parental protectiveness may take on different forms. Regardless of its manifestations, very often a pattern of resistance in the child is established

and this comes to characterize the child and his interactions with the parent. Should these patterns or characteristics become firmly established, and they often do, they tend to generalize beyond interaction with the parent and beyond the home setting. That is, children often take these patterns and characteristics to their interactions with other people and to other settings, such as the teacher and the school.

Defiance

Defiance may show itself in both attitude and behavior. The child may show his defiance by challenging the parent's efforts to protect him. He may resist these efforts boldly and openly. For example, the parent advises, "Put this coat on. It's cold outside." The child responds by saying, "I don't want to. It's not cold."

There are other manifestations of defiance. The child may show his defiant character by doing something deemed impossible by the parent. The parent forewarns: "You won't be able to stay outside long. It's too cold." The child accepts the challenge: "Oh yes I can. See..." (And the child demonstrates that he has endurance in cold weather without the coat the parent recommended.) Of course it is not uncommon that protective parents under estimate or over estimate the conditions. In this case it is temperature. The temperature may in fact be mild enough so the child can manage comfortably without a coat. This discovery on the child's part tends to discredit the parent's judgement and/or authoritativeness. More will be said of this later.

The child may register his defiance in the form of combat or contest. The parent attempts to put the coat on the child and the child puts up a struggle in open combat or resistance. Likewise, the parent may instruct the child to put on the coat. He may respond with a challenge or contest: "You can't make me!" or "I won't keep it on." or "You can't catch me. Ha, Ha."

This child and the protective parent are often in disagreement. The parent says something and the child takes issue. The parent makes a statement and the child contradicts the parent. The parent forewarns and the child attempts to prove the parent wrong. The parent says "Yes" and the child says "No."

These challenging, resisting, and combative attitudes and behaviors are often perceived by the parent as defiance. Often the child is label as such or some facsimile. Often the protective parent will see the source of the problem in the child: "He has a defiant nature." "He is such a brat! What am I to do with him?" Typically the protective parent does not perceive her approach to child rearing as the precipitator or cause of such behavior in the child.

Non-attentiveness

The child who shows an aggressive response to protective parenting may come to reject parental authority. He simply may not listen or attend to what the parent has to say. It may appear like an "attention deficit" but this inattentiveness or disregard is learned behavior. Let's go back to a preceding example where the child discovers that the temperature outside is quite mild and he can manage comfortably without a coat. The child has learned in this incident that the parent is not a good judge of outside temperature and what is needed in terms of clothing. He is beginning to learn not to pay attention to the parent's concerns. When similar incidents are repeated, the child comes to eventually learn to disregard or not pay attention to what the parent says.

Disregard of Parental Authority

If similar incidents occur on a regular basis, and they often do with protective parents because they commonly over or under estimate conditions, then the child learns to discount or disregard parental input or advice. The parent forewarns: "You'll get hurt." The child does not. "You will catch a cold." He does not. "Those children are too old. They won't want to play with you." And they do. The parent's doomsaying or predictions are not reliable and the child discovers this soon and learns to not only not pay attention to parental anticipations but also to disregard parental input.

When this attitude and behavior become strongly integrated into the child's personality structure, they become his "signature." The parent may lament, "He doesn't listen to a word I say. He tells me I don't know what I

am talking about." These attitudes and behaviors often generalize to other people and settings. The teacher describes him in frustration: "He does not pay attention. If he were more attentive, his grades would be better. I know he is capable of doing the work. If he would only listen..."

Mischievousness and Boldness

The protectively raised child often becomes a mischief-maker, one who makes mischief, one who stirs up discord. The child is accustomed to fighting the parent's protectiveness and often behaves with that mindset. Depending on the child's unique nature and his life experience, his mischief-making may take on one or both profiles. One profile is that the child may be or seem intentionally hurtful or injurious or malicious. Another profile is that the child may be playfully annoying or roguish or teasing in word, deed, and mannerism.

The aggressive child is not hesitant in the face of actual or possible danger or rebuff. He has faced this many times vis-a-vis the protective parent, who is especially restrictive. He is not hesitant to breach the rules. He may even call for a dare, as in the instance where the child issues a challenge to the parent: "You can't stop me!" This child will often overstep usuals bounds or conventions.

Bravado

Such audacious inclinations in behavior characterize the child as bold, brazen, forward, and presumptuous. These "demonstrations" of boldness in behavior are in part intended to over come the protective restrictiveness of the parent and others who are inclined to be protective. This is bravado, which is a showy bravery, a facade of bravery, or false bravery. Unfortunately the child has internalized the many apprehensions and warnings of danger. So the child develops bravado also to combat these internalized apprehensions or anxieties.

Risk-taking

To further combat these feelings of apprehension or anxiety concerning the dangers around him, the child challenges these head on.

172

In the process he may become a risk-taker. Thus the child may expose himself to the chance of injury or loss. He engages in risk-taking behavior, on the one hand to defy the protective parent and on the other hand to prove that these dangers are not as they are predicted to be by the parent.

If the child frequently engages in risk-taking, the tension associated when facing a risk and the relief which follows when the child has survived the risk become integrated into the personality as excitement or thrill. The child then may develop an excitement-seeking, thrill-seeking personality that may lead to more and more risk-taking, greater and greater defiance, and more and more disregard of authority.

A Submissive Reaction to Protective Parenting

Children who by nature or temperament are more passive or acquiescent will show what is regarded as a submissive response to protective parental behavior. In this profile, the child accepts parental protectiveness and becomes a passive recipient of parental behaviors that are intended to protect the child. The degree of acquiescence may vary but generally the child goes along with parental protectiveness.

Anxiety Bound

Children that accept parental protectiveness and the restraints that accompany it often become anxious about many things. They often show considerable apprehension, worrisomeness, and even fear about many things and situations. The child has assimilated and incorporated the parent's many warnings and concerns about the many dangers that exist.

The protective parent expresses her own worries, anxieties, apprehensions, and fears repeatedly to the child: "You'll get hurt." "I am afraid you'll get lost! Stay close to me and hold my hand tightly." "You'll catch a cold." "Those children are too rough. They'll hurt you."

The child internalizes these messages and often repeats them himself: "I'll get hurt!" "I am afraid I'll get lost. Hold my hand." "Those

children have runny noses. I don't want to play with them." "They play too rough. They will hurt me."

Insecurity

Because the child often hears from the parent of the many bad things that can happen and because he may assimilate many of the anxieties, worries, apprehensions, and concerns that are associated with these, his sense of security is seriously compromised. Hence the child will feel insecure. His insecurity will manifest itself in many and often subtle ways. He may not want to slide down the slide. He may be reluctant to join a group of children in play. He may be reluctant to use a scissor, or finger paint, or play in the sand and water table.

The child who shows a submissive reaction to protective parenting may require considerably more encouragement than his agemates to try new or different activities. He may cling tenaciously to a parent or sibling or teacher. These behaviors may or may not be accompanied by the child's words. When the child does speak, he often echoes the words of the protective parent: "I'll get hurt." "I am afraid. I don't want to..." These are a few of the many manifestations of an insecure child.

Inferiority and Inadequacy

The child who accepts parental protection and assimilates the many messages conveyed about his need for protection, often develops strong feelings of inadequacy, incapability and inferiority. What are the messages the child receives that leads to his developing such feelings? The child is reminded often and in many ways that he is inadequate, incapable, and inferior. It is not the parent's intent to make the child feel inadequate, incapable or inferior; but, the parent's words lead the child to conclude that he is inadequate, incapable or inferior.

He hears and assimilates her words: "You are too small." "You can't do that." "What a mess you make. I knew I should have done it myself." "You are not ready for that yet." "It is easier if I do it for you. You take too long." "You'll get hurt."

173

Few parents intend to promote these feelings in the child. These are the unintentional by-products of too much misguided parenting. The parent wants to protect, to keep the child out of harm's way. These are noble and appropriate intentions. The method or approach and its accompanying messages are the source of the problem for the child. The child's interpretation is that what he does is not good enough, that he is a baby, that he is less than adequate.

Diminished Skill and Competence

In comparison to his agemates, the protectively raised child is often limited in terms of skill development. He is not able or can not do as well many of the things his agemates are able to do. This is primarily the consequence of having been deprived of or given limited opportunities to develop the skills that many children of comparable age have been afforded. Skill development leads to feelings of competence. Lack of skill or diminished skill leads to feelings of incompetence and inferiority.

Skill development plays an important role in the child's development of competence and his believing that he is capable. The protected child is often limited in or deprived of skill-building opportunities by the parent. The protective parent may often prevent the child from engaging in certain activities or simply do too many things for the child. Giving too much service to the child limits or prevents the child from developing the skills that will contribute to feelings of competence and help him overcome feelings of incompetence.

Despite the limited opportunities afforded by the protective parent to the child for skill development, some children nevertheless develop a degree of capability. This is especially so when another parent, or sibling or teacher encourages and supports the child's efforts at skill-building. Such opportunities may help the child develop a level of skill that places him within the normal range of his agemates. Sometimes protective parents are surprised at what their children are able to do: "I didn't know you knew how to do that. Where did you learn to do it?" As a consequence of such exposure and opportunities, some protectively raised children

learn to overcome their feelings of incompetence and inferiority.

Unfortunately, some have developed a very tenacious image of themselves and their capabilities, and continue to perceive themselves as less skilled than others even when objectively this is not the case. This is one of the damaging results of prolonged protectiveness of children. Some children, because of their submissive nature, simply acquiesce and subscribe to the previously developed image of the self as being unskilled, incapable and inferior.

Low Self-esteem

Skill development also plays an important role in the development of a positive self-concept, high self-esteem and genuine self-worth. Lack of skill or diminished skill, feelings of incompetence and inadequacy lead to poor self-concept development, lowered self-esteem and diminished self-worth. Children who show a submissive response to protective parenting often show poor self-concept development, lowered self-esteem and diminished self-worth.

Helplessness and Dependence

Parental protectiveness, especially when accompanied by too much service-giving and too few opportunities for skill-development, contribute to the child developing feelings of helplessness and dependency. The messages heard by or given to the child by the protective parent are crucial in this regard: "You can't do that yourself. I need to do it for you." "Tell me what you need. I will give it to you." "He needs me. He depends on me for everything." "No one cares for and loves him the way I do." "I don't know how he will get by in kindergarten without me."

Strivings toward independence, self-sufficiency, self-care, and autonomy in general are natural drives in young children. Protective parents typically resist, thwart or attempt to delay these natural strivings in children. When the parent is successful in this regard, dependency is strengthened.

Dependence interferes with the emergence and

174

development of autonomy. When autonomy is limited, shame, doubt, and diminished self-control and diminished will power are strengthened. These traits often characterize children who have submitted to or acquiesced to protective parenting.

Protectively Raised Child's Prevailing Attitudes Toward Others

Certain attitudes develop in the child as a result of his being raised protectively. Depending on whether their reaction is an aggressive one or a submissive one, children will show one of the following two common views.

The Aggressive Child's Prevailing Attitude

The child who responds with aggression or resists or fights parental protectiveness often regards the parent and other authority figures as being restrictive or as obstacles to go around or to be ignored or to be discounted. This prevailing attitude reflects many of the child's characteristics that are his signature or indicative of his response to protectiveness.

The Submissive Child's Prevailing Attitude

The child who responds submissively or simply accepts parental protectiveness often views the parent and other authority figures as protectors or someone who will take care of the child or the situation. Protectively raised children often expect "someone" to take care of them or things or "fix" matters. This prevailing attitude mirrors many of this child's characteristic traits, especially dependence.

INDULGENT CHILD REARING

The Indulgent Parent

How does the indulgent parent typically behave toward the child? The meaning of the word "indulge" provides some insight.

Indulge means to allow one his way, to gratify, to yield to or be compliant in relation to another. The indulgent parent gives in to or indulges the child. The indulgent parent often goes along with what the child wants whether that be an outright demand or subtle manipulation by the child.

The indulgent parent often seems unable to set limits at all. If limits are established, the parent may be unable to stick with them or enforce those that were established. Also some indulgent parents even seem unwilling to set limits for the child. In the final analysis, the child gets his way or what he wants. In many respects the parent becomes subservient to the child. Sometimes it is not clear or evident who is in charge. Sometimes the child appears to be.

Two Common Reactions to Indulgent Parenting

Children exhibit two common reactions to being parented in a predominantly indulgent fashion. The difference in reaction is largely a function of the nature of the child.

An Aggressively Opportunistic Response

Some children respond to the parent's tendency to indulge the child in an opportunistic manner. That is, some children make active use of the parent's inclination to be indulgent. They actively take advantage of this tendency, or actively use it to their advantage, or actively accept and welcome it, sometimes to the extent of soliciting it or even demanding it. Often the child clearly controls the parent to get what he wants. The child is aggressively opportunistic. These and similar behaviors and attitudes characterize the child as having an aggressive response to indulgent parenting.

A Passively Accepting Response

Some children are not as actively opportunistic in their response to indulgent practices. Some children by nature are much more passive. They are inclined to simply acquiesce to or passively accept the parent's indulgent practices. However, some children are more active in their response even though they fit into this category. Such children would be regarded as being passively controlling. Whatever their degree of passiveness, or whatever elements of actively taking advantage of the parent's inclination, these children are regarded as being predominantly passive. They demonstrate a characteristically passive response to being raised indulgently.

An Aggressive Response to Indulgent Parenting

Children who show a predominantly aggressive response to indulgent child rearing may possess one or more or all of the following characteristics or behavioral traits. A child may possess these traits in varying degrees but they manifest themselves to some extent in the child's attitudes and behaviors. These become characteristic features of the child's personhood.

Demanding

Children who have been raised indulgently are often seen as being demanding. The demanding child will ask for things with authority, sometimes with forceful authority. He may claim that he has a right to what he wants and insists on having it, even if someone else possesses it at the moment. The indulged child may insist that the other person relinquish the item to him. Indulgent parents often support this claim or right and demand that the other child give the item to their child and find something else to play with. Siblings are often required by the indulgent parent to relinquish to the child what he wants.

Some children show this demanding attitude in somewhat less direct ways. The child may express a certain urgency or state a pressing requirement regarding what he wants: "I need it now!" "Do you want me to starve to death?" "I don't feel well. I think I am going to be sick. I would feel better if I had..."

Some children employ a bartering technique or offer a trade in conjunction with their demands: "I won't like you if..." "I'll be quiet if..." "I'll tell my mother on you if..." Elements of a threat can sometimes be seen in this approach. Also the child may predict impending doom: "You're in big trouble now!" "But I won't tell if..."

This demanding attitude and behavior also shows itself in the form of dogged insistence, pestering, nagging, and the like.

Self-centered

Children who are raised indulgently and are aggressively opportunistic in their response, often are seen as being very self-centered. Egocentricity is a common characteristic of young children. The indulgently raised child is typically much more egocentric than his agemates who have been raised in other ways. The indulged child is less likely to see a perspective other than his own. Quite simply, this child has not been encouraged to consider another point of view or has not been required to do so. What he sees, he wants. What he wants, he typically gets. The child often expresses the attitude that what he wants, he wants now. Indulgently raised children are typically not required to wait very long, if at all for anything. They are accustomed to immediate gratification from the parent.

Bully

The indulgently raised child who is aggressive in his response is frequently a blustering, quarrelsome, overbearing person who brow beats smaller or weaker people. Sometimes those weaker people are adults who kowtow or succumb to the child's bullish behavior. The child may be loudly arrogant in his overbearance. This is a ploy often used in the presence of others or in public places. Obstinacy and stubbornness are other forms of bullishness.

Socially Abrasive

The indulged child is often socially abrasive. He often causes tension or heat in his interactions with others. The social arts of compromise and diplomacy have not been learned. Typically there has been little effort to teach or no requirement for the child to learn any social interaction skills. The indulged child simply pushes, shoves, and grinds his way through life.

Interestingly enough, we sometimes see these same characteristics in the indulgent parent. But it is not simply a matter of role models. The child's abrasive behaviors have frequently helped him get what he wants. These results have reinforced the child's abrasiveness. Some indulgent parents are as equally appalled by this trait as others are.

Inconsiderate or Unaware

The indulged child is often inconsiderate or simply unaware of other people's thoughts feelings, and needs. He is often inconsiderate or unaware of their circumstance or situation. The child typically considers one perspective only - his own. To some extent this is a manifestation of his self-centered or very egocentric nature. To some extent it is the consequence of not having been required to take into consideration another person's thoughts, feelings, needs or circumstances.

The indulgent parent often fails to provide adequate teaching or attention to these aspects. The parent often does not take the time to bring these aspects into the child's consciousness or stream of thought. The child's inconsiderate attitude and behaviors may be deliberate, but they may also be the result of the fact that he is simply unaware.

The "Prima Dona" Type

The indulged child often behaves like a prince or princess, king or queen. The child will demand, boss, bully and otherwise behave as though he reins supreme. The indulgent parent has been excessively subservient to the child and the child has come to expect similar behavior from others. The child has typically received what he wants, regardless of the means he has had to employ to obtain it. Consequently he behaves like a "spoiled brat" or despot. He will often meter out orders, demands, proclamations, etc. that he expects others to respond to with dispatch.

When others do not respond as expected, more negative behavior is usually forthcoming. The notion is that if he behaves badly enough, others will eventually give in to him. He gets

what he wants through misbehavior. In esense, parental behavior teaches the child how to misbehave rather than behave in more acceptable ways.

Manipulativeness

This indulgently raised child is often seen as manipulative by others. The parent sometimes shares this view with others. The degree and style of manipulativeness may vary. However, it is usually of an active variety and sometimes even aggressive in nature. The child's skill or ability may vary but the intent is the same - to get others to give in or indulge the child. Toward this end, the child will employ different strategies to manage, handle or maneuver another person's thoughts, feelings, and behavior. With some children it is an artful skill. The recipient often feels used or duped. The child often ends up advantaged and the other person often ends up disadvantaged or compromised.

Expectation of Service

The indulged child is given very much service by the parent. The parent often expects that others will or should provide a similar level or kind of service to the child. As a consequence the child comes to expect that the parent and others will and should provide this service. The child may issue orders, directives, commands, demands to both adults and playmates: "Get me a drink." "I need that block. Give it to me." "It's my turn to play with the doll carriage." "I will tell the teacher if..."

Sense of Entitlement

If the child generally gets what he wants, regardless of the strategies he has had to employ, he may develop a "sense of entitlement." That is, the child develops the attitude that he is entitled to whatever he needs, wants, or desires: "I want that!" "I need one too." "I must have one!" "I have to have it!" When the child does not get the response from others that he anticipates, his behavior may worsen or he may feel "short-changed," deprived or even victimized.

Jealousy

The indulged child often wants what others have. The indulged child wants to be loved best, wants all or most of the attention, wants to be first on the swing. This excessiveness of need or desire is often a manifestation of jealousy. Necessity is not an issue here as a rule. Someone else has it and I want it. That sense of entitlement begins to influence the child's perception of what he needs. If he does not get it, he feels deprived. If others do not attempt to get it for him, they are perceived as conspirators or even victimizers.

The indulged child often regards it as the parent's or the teacher's duty to get for him what he wants or needs. With indulged children, a want or desire quickly become a necessity or need, which must be satisfied with dispatch. Typically when given what he wants, the child soon loses interest. This is another manifestation of jealousy.

Difficulty with Sharing

This sense of entitlement and feelings of jealousy often lead to difficulty in sharing or taking turns. The indulged child has not learned to wait. His needs have been typically met with dispatch, often at the expense or inconvenience of others. Typically the indulged child has not had to share, wait for another to finish with something, or take turns.

The indulged child is often given his own way or another person is required to relinquish to the child what he wants. He often will insist on having it all rather than a portion thereof. As a consequence the child has not acquired skill in the ability to share and take turns.

In sum, these attitudes or behavioral traits often characterize the child who assumes an aggressively opportunistic stance relative to the parent's inclination to indulge the child. He may possess some, or most or all of these characteristics. Certainly he will exhibit them to a significantly greater degree than children who are raised differently.

A Submissive Response to Indulgent Parenting

In contrast to the aggressively opportunistic child, there is the submissive child who simply goes along with the parent's indulgent attitude and behavior. This child shows acquiescence or passive acceptance of the parent's indulgent practices. Sometimes the child may show some manipulativeness but it is of a passive type.

Submissiveness

This child is typically by nature submissive. He simply allows the parent to indulge him. He passively accepts the services provided to him by the parent. Sometimes the child learns to use his submissiveness to passively control the parent's behavior or influence the outcome to his advantage. This is a form of passive manipulation or passive control.

Shyness

The submissive child who is raised indulgently often shows a considerable amount of shyness. Young children are shy by their social inexperience. The indulged child who is submissive shows a significantly greater degree of shyness. The shy child is bashful or retiring. He may be timid or easily frightened away. There is an inclination in some to draw back or move away from new people or activities. The shy child may also show suspiciousness or distrust depending on the intensity of his shyness.

Notwithstanding these variations, the shy child is typically reluctant or wary. This child's behavior may often show discomfort or lack of confidence in association with others or unfamiliar activities. Shyness implies a tendency to shrink from contact or close association with others. This is often accompanied by a wish to escape notice or recognition.

178

Bashfulness suggests timidity about meeting others and trepidation and awkward behavior when brought into prominence or notice. Diffident emphasizes self-distrust, fear of censure or failure and a hesitant, tentative manner as a consequence. Lack of self-confidence comes to mind. All these words describe to some degree the child who responds submissively to indulgent parenting.

Coyness

Coy is similar to shy. It suggests being shy, modest, bashful, diffident, and demure. It is often associated with girls but not limited to girls. Most importantly, coyness may also be a pretending to be shy. It is in this sense that we recognize the passive manipulativeness of this child.

This passive manipulativeness characterizes the child who shows shyness to gain our attention and service. The child who bats his eyelashes or strikes a charming pose to engage us is a child who has learned the artful skill of passive manipulation and has learned to use his charm or attractiveness to his advantage.

Passive Manipulation

Some children learn to use their "cuteness," smallness, shyness, helplessness, etc. to engage others and solicit service or whatever else they desire. Some children manage this with little or no talking. They simply look helpless, intimidated, fearful, or nod affirmatively or negatively at our guesses. The child is getting what he wants and is passively controlling or influencing the outcome he desires. Adults often feel great sympathy for this child and wish they could do more to "help" the child.

Passively Demanding

Some indulged children become passively demanding. This child does not have the power of the more aggressive child, consequently his demands are of a more passive nature. They manifest themselves in whining, pouting, huffing, sighing, and the like. This child may use his learned helplessness, dependency, inferiority to demand that his needs be satisfied immediately

in the manner he prefers. For example, the child may employ tears or more precisely, "crocodile tears" to get his subtle demands met. This is certainly manipulative; however, it is often not recognized as such soon enough because sympathy often overrides adult response to the child and his behavior.

Coquettishness

One who behaves coquettishly is one who tries to gain the admiration and affection of others for mere self-gratification. This word is more or less exclusively used to describe female behavior, but males can and do employ the same strategies. Both males and females can be flirtatious and engage in frivolity to gain advantage, service, or to simply get what they want from another. Some indulgently raised children develop this skill to a fine art and figuratively "wrap others around their fingers."

Service Recipients

Indulgently raised children are prone to get and receive a great deal of service from their parents. Some children solicit this service through manipulation, projected helplessness, dependence, etc. Some are merely the passive, compliant recipients of this service. Because the child receives a great deal of services from others, he does little for himself. Because others are prone to provide service, the child often has limited opportunities to learn to be self-sufficient and develop the knowledge, skill, and personal attributes that accompany self-sufficiency. This is a "Catch 22" for the child. The child often pays a substantial price in terms of his personal development. The following characteristics address the cost to the child.

Expectation of Service

Because the child often receives a great deal of service, he comes to expect to receive services not only from those that have provided such service but also from others. Those that are willing to provide this service do not pose a problem for the child. However, those that are unwilling to provide the same level of service do present a social interactional problem for the child. The child may perceive these reluctant service providers as uncaring, unhelpful, or

179

mean. The child may perceive their lack of service as an indication that they do not like the child.

Notice how this child's perception is highly egocentric, that is, everything focuses on the child. The indulged child does not consider that the other person might be involved in something else or is too busy at the moment to attend to what the child wants. The indulged child expects the other person to simply stop what she is doing and attend to him immediately. All others must wait. The child perceives himself as most important and in greatest need. Even the passive child will often have this attitude. However, he may not be as blatant in his manifestation of it.

Helplessness

The indulged child may feel or be helpless. This is a consequence of doing too little for himself or of his solicitation of help from others. This helplessness is not the natural helplessness of infants and very young children, who must rely on the service or caregiving of others. This helplessness is learned as a consequence of the child's continued interactions with a parent who provides too much service or limits too much the child's opportunities to become helpful to himself. Remember the saying, "God helps those who help themselves." This is not a concept that is practiced or utilized by the indulgent parent or the indulged child.

Frequently, the indulged child is intentionally helpless. He will insist that he needs help with things that he has been observed doing himself quite adequately. Subtle manipulations may be employed by the child. For example: "I make such a mess with this. Could you do it for me? You are so good at this. I am such a klutz." When these thoughts are repeated often, the child comes to believe them to some degree, manipulation notwithstanding. The indulgent parent comes to believe them as well.

Dependent

The passive child who is indulged often becomes dependent. He is dependent upon the parent and others for service. The natural state of dependency of children is prolonged unnecessarily in this case. For proper development to proceed, the child must be encouraged and supported in his natural drive to become independent. The indulgent parent is less inclined to provide sufficient encouragement and support in this regard.

Should the parent attempt to be encouraging and supportive, the passive child's dependent behavior is perceived as his being not ready. The indulgent parent gives in or allows the child to continue in his dependent behavior. Consequently, dependent behavior is strengthened and independent behavior is weakened by the parent's response. The child's dependency shapes his image of himself as being dependent.

Feeling Inferior and Incompetent

Competence is the result of skill development, self-sufficiency and many other closely allied matters. The indulged child frequently has limited opportunities for skill development and self-sufficiency. In comparison to his agemates, this child often seems inept or developmentally delayed. The child may be told by the parent and others that he can not do it yet or that he does not do it well.

The child's playmates may give him similar messages: "Give that to me!. You don't know how." The child may observe by comparing his actions with those of others that he is incapable, thus inferior. Such messages from others and such conclusions on the child's part may cause him to integrate feelings of inferiority and incompetence into his self-concept. This is rather common among indulged children who are basically submissive.

Skill development plays a crucial role in self-concept development. Skills help make the self-concept more concrete and specific and give the child real reasons for feeling good about himself. Compare the child who proudly and enthusiastically says "I can reach the third shelf now!" with the child who says "I can't do anything well." Self-esteem and self-worth are significantly different in these two children. The child who passively accepts the indulgent behaviors of the parent often suffers from feelings of inferiority, incompetence, poor self-

180

concept development and lowered self-esteem and self-worth.

Sense of Entitlement

What has been said of the more aggressive child can substantially be said of the more passive child who has been indulged. Because the child has been indulged and has been given what he wants, he becomes accustomed to getting his way, being given into, gratified, and having another yield to his position or want. Out of this expectation of service and indulgence develops a sense of entitlement. The child comes to believe that he is entitled to what he wants or is entitled to what others have and he does not. The latter leads in some instances to jealously.

Jealously

When the indulged child observes that someone else has something that he regards as desirable, he wants and expects to have it. If his desire is thwarted, he becomes envious or jealous. The child's sense of entitlement leads him to a position that he must have that which another has. The other person must surrender it or the indulged child must be given one of his own.

A portion of this stance and the thoughts and feelings that are associated are influenced by the child's sense of inferiority, low self-esteem and self-worth. The child becomes somebody of value because he possesses valued items. The child's worth is measured by his possessions not by his character or behavior. Feelings of jealously are common among people who have low self-esteem and self-worth. Jealousy is a rather common characteristic of indulged children.

Prevailing Attitudes and Feelings of Indulged Children

Certain attitudes develop in the child as a result of his being raised indulgently. The more common ones follow.

Indulged Child's View of the Parent

As a consequence of his interactions with the indulgent parent and others that may be somewhat indulgent, the child develops certain attitudes regarding the parent in particular and other adults in general. For both the child who shows an aggressive response and the child who shows a submissive response to being indulged, the prevailing attitude that emerges is quite similar. Indulged children tend to perceive the parent and other adults and authority figures as sources of power and gratification, who are capable of giving the child what he wants.

Sometimes the parent and other authority figures are seen as fools to be used to the child's own advantage. This attitude is more obvious among children who show a more aggressive response. It is more subtle and more camouflaged among children who are more submissive; but it exists nonetheless in many indulged children. The passive child employs more subtle manipulations. In contrast, the aggressive child is more blatant in his maneuvers.

Insensitivity to Others

For both the aggressive and submissive child there is a significant degree of insensitivity to the thoughts and feelings and circumstances of others. This degree of insensitivity is greater than what we would customarily expect of children in general of the same age. So what accounts for this significant difference? It is explained quite simply. The indulged child is rarely required to consider someone else's thoughts, feelings or circumstances. Indulgent parents typically fail to explain how others may think, feel or provide information regarding their circumstance or situation. The indulgent parent typically fails to encourage the child to consider such aspects.

The child's needs or wants are gratified without any consideration of the impact to or of the role of others. The child is not taught to be attentive to the thoughts, feelings, and circumstance of others. The result is a child who is highly egocentric or self-centered. This manifests itself in an apparent insensitivity to others. In Eriksonian terms, this attitude often leads to self-absorption and eventual stagnation of the personality.

DEMOCRATIC CHILD REARING

The Democratic Parent

The democratic parent is guided by democratic principles and the belief that the child has the capacity to respond favorably to parenting if treated with reasonableness and informed guidance. The democratic parent is typically an informed parent, who has taken the time to educate herself about what is reasonable to expect of children at different ages and stages. Children are encouraged to pursue their own goals, even when they may not necessarily match what the parent prefers, as long as they do not place the child at risk or infringe upon the rights of others.

Democratic parents do not have to be right or to be the boss. Children are encouraged to express their thoughts and feelings and have these considered when the parent is attempting to make an adjustment in parenting. What is in the child's best interest is often of paramount concern and serves as a guiding consideration when the parent is trying to determine which course of action to pursue in relation to the child or in relation to others on behalf of the child.

The democratic parent considers her role of child advocate to be especially important until such time as the child can advocate effectively for himself. In this regard the parent will help the child develop the awareness, knowledge and skill he needs to act in his own behalf. This is viewed as a gradual process which involves much parental encouragement, support, and direct teaching. To be effective in this area, the child is helped to develop social interaction skills, as the parent believes such skills will equip the child well for life in general. Being aware and attentive to the thoughts and feelings of others is a key ingredient here and the democratic parent attempts through modeling, interpretation, explanation, and other means to help the child grow in his awareness and attentiveness. People are important and the child is helped to learn this early in life.

Child's Response to Democratic Parenting

The child who is raised democratically does not show the typical schism or bifurcation of response that has been described for the other approaches to parenting. That is why we do not see the characteristic aggressive or submissive reaction to being parented democratically. Of course some children by nature will appear more aggressive while others will seem more submissive. These variations will be manifested in differences in degree not in kind.

Children who are raised democratically typically show one response with minor variation in intensity or degree. Likewise the behaviors which characterize children's reaction to democratic parenting become integrated into the personality structure once again with minor variations in degree rather than in kind Such variations certainly are a function of differences in the child's basic nature and are also the consequence of the normal variations typically found in democratic parenting or among democratic parents.

Positive or Benign Feelings

In contrast to the autocratic and the protective approach, we do not see an accumulation of angry or hostile feelings in the child who has been raised democratically. The democratically raised child shows a general attitude of positive or benign feelings. This is the case because angry and hostile feelings are allowed to be expressed in socially acceptable ways. Such expression helps to dissipate the child's frustrations. Consequently there is typically no repression, suppression, and accumulation of these feelings.

Furthermore this expression contributes to the child's perception that his thoughts and feelings count and that they shall be addressed in some fashion by the parent. This contributes to his perception that he is being treated fairly and that he is important. Since the child is typically treated in a positive and caring manner

182

by the parent, who is attentive to his needs and concerns, the democratically raised child often shows a preponderance of positive feelings toward his parent, himself and others.

Childhood is full of frustrations, feeling small and inadequate, being dependent, etc. The democratic parent makes a conscientious effort to minimize these to the extent that she can. But because these are part of the life experience, the democratic parent attempts to help the child cope and manage these inevitable feelings. Such efforts by the parent contribute to the growing sense in the child that the parent is on his side. Hence the child is inclined to view the parent in a positive manner.

Cooperative and Helpful

Democratic parents stress cooperativeness and helpfulness. These are concepts and words that are a regular part of parent and child interaction. When the child expresses a need, the parent cooperates to the extent possible to satisfy that need. When the child is in need of help, the democratic parent offers it in word and deed. When the child makes an effort to help the parent, the intent and effort is graciously received and praised.

Further reinforcement of this helpful attitude is achieved as the child overhears the parent telling others of the child's helpfulness and cooperativeness. These are valued behaviors and they are strengthened in many ways by the democratic parent. Hence democratically raised children typically behave in a helpful and cooperative manner. And they learn to take pride in their helpfulness and cooperativeness.

Cooperation is often so highly stressed that it influences the way democratically raised children challenge what is being asked of them. The child may challenge but his challenge is intended to gain understanding or to be provided with a reason as to why his cooperation is needed in this particular matter. The challenge is not to resist but to gain information, justification, or clarification. Democratically raised children are accustomed to being provided with reasons and explanations, consequently these are sought when they are not clear to the child, or implied by the parent or occasionally not given.

If the request is perceived as unfair or unjustified by the child after an explanation is provided, the child may register a protest or express his disagreement. However, he typically will cooperate, partially because he has learned the value of cooperation and helpfulness and partially because of his trust and respect for the parent.

Assertiveness

The democratically raised child is generally assertive. He is inclined to declare his position strongly and defend his perspective by reasoned argument. He is self-confidently affirmative. He is not hostile or aggressive; but rather he is assertive. The child is able to assert or present his thoughts and feelings in a constructive, non-hostile manner.

The democratic parent typically spends much time helping the child become socially aware and diplomatic in his interactions with others. The parent has encouraged such expression and articulation and the child has learned to be confident in this regard. He is not inhibited or intimidated in matters of self-expression and self-affirmation. He has been given much parental encouragement and support in this aspect.

The democratically raised child may resist or challenge when it is appropriate to do so, that is if his rights or privileges are being infringed upon or when another's rights or privileges are being infringed upon. Note that the child's reaction to such infringements is not limited solely to self-interest.

Awareness and Concern for Others

The democratically raised child is typically characterized by a strong awareness of and concern for the thoughts and feelings of others. He is in vivid contrast to the indulged child who shows a significant degree of unawareness and insensitivity in such matters. The democratically raised child is outstanding in this regard because the parent has invested considerable time and energy raising the child's level of consciousness concerning others.

Democratic parents typically do this by the information they provide to the child and the questions they ask of him: "Grandma is not feeling well today. Her arthritis is causing her much pain. That is why she seems cranky. Try to be understanding and helpful today." "I am sorry I snapped at you, dear. I have many things on my mind and I know I was not being kind to you. What do you need?" "How do you feel when someone takes a toy from you?" "Jennifer is angry because I prevented her from leaving the yard. Do you remember when you were younger and wanted to do the same thing?"

Mindful of Rights and Privileges

Democratically raised children are greatly aware of their rights and privileges and those of others also. They will assert these rights and privileges with determination and self-confidence: "I am playing with this now! It is my turn. You may have it when I am finished. We can take turns." "May I play too?" "No hitting! Hitting is not allowed here." "The teacher gave me permission to wash this table." "Teacher, you said yesterday that Joey could wash the tables too."

Democratic parents inform children about their rights and privileges. It is part of their typical interaction as they attend to daily matters: "No one has the right to hit you. Do not allow others to hit you. Mommy and daddy do not hit you. No one else is to hit you either." "What did we agree to yesterday about hitting? You are to use words to get what you need. You are not to hit. Can we agree on this again? Good. Now tell me what you need and I will help you." Notice how the parent's dialogue with the child is extended and how it depends on cooperation and help to be achieved. Democratic parents are inclined to be more verbal in their interactions with their children and stress certain values like cooperation and help.

Case example:
I recall an incident with my son, who was just under three years old at the time. We were having a difference of opinion. I was attempting to get him to do something that he did not want to do at the time. I was making little progress in my effort to persuade him and probably showing some frustration as a consequence. He was strongly refusing to cooperate. To make his position clear to me that it was not his intention to

cooperate under any conditions, despite whatever arguments I might make or strategy I might employ. he said, "You can't make me. And you can't hit me either. That's child abuse and I'll report you to DCF." (DCF is the agency in Rhode Island to which abuse of children is reported.)

The point is not to demonstrate my ineffectiveness as a parent but to illustrate that children that are raised in democratic households are made aware of their rights and privileges, often at an early age. Even parents must respect these boundaries. Democratic parents attempt to teach these principles to their children even at the risk of having such understandings used by the child to assert his position in opposition to the parent. There are more important issues of concern here than parental dominance.

To bring the example to conclusion, the episode continued as follows. I responded to my son John by acknowledging that it was not my intention to hit him in order to get him to cooperate. "You know I do not believe that children should be hit. Hitting children can be abusive and your parents are not abusive. I understand you do not want to cooperate now, but you will eventually have to do what I am requesting you to do. You decide when you are ready to cooperate. If you need help I will help you." I discontinued interaction and left the room.

Approximately five minutes later John came to me and said everything was put away except for two things that he needed help with. "Can you help me?" he asked. We each proceeded to put away one of the two remaining items. "Can we eat now?" John asked. I informed John "Now that the dinner table is cleared, I'll need your help to set the table and then we can eat supper." "OK" he responded as he proceeded to help set the table for supper.

Note by this example that democratically raised children are not "perfect" children. They do not always do what is expected of them at the moment the expectation is made known. But also note that when parental patience is exercised and children are given an opportunity to decide for themselves (autonomy), they typically cooperate, in part or fully.

Also note that parent and child interactions are more complex and occur over a longer time duration. Democratic parenting is much more time and labor intensive. Most things that are worthwhile are so.

Independence

Democratically raised children often show considerable independence in their actions and interactions with people. Democratic parents attempt to foster autonomy, independence, self-sufficiency, and the like. Children are given an opportunity to express their emerging autonomy, to decide for themselves, to take care of themselves, etc. Children are encouraged and supported in their autonomy strivings. Children receive much positive reinforcement when the child demonstrates these behaviors and attitudes. Consequently, democratically raised children emerge from their interactions with their parents with a well-established sense of autonomy.

Although these children show substantial independence, they seem to be comfortable with their relative dependence. This is so because the child is not punished for dependent behavior. It is accepted. It is allowed. Yet, dependent behavior is not intentionally reinforced by the parent. Consequently dependent behavior is not strengthened in the child. It is also important to note that when children are punished for dependent behavior, their tendency to be dependent is strengthened. This is perplexing indeed. Democratic parents generally avoid the use of punishment and other punitive measures.

Self-confidence

Self-confidence is substantially the by-product of independence, self-sufficiency, making and doing, and deciding for oneself. The democratic parent guides the child in these endeavors and manages the environment and situation in an effort to insure that the child's efforts turn out well. The parent tries to insure the child's success and minimize his failures. It is within this child rearing environment that the child acquires skill in doing for himself, deciding for himself, etc. Success and skill leads to the development of confidence in the self. The child learns to trust in his ability or capacity to be independent, self-sufficient, etc. This is self-confidence.

Responsible

Also closely associated with greater independence and self-confidence is an emerging sense of responsibility. As the child cares for himself he becomes responsible for himself. As the child makes decisions and exercises choices that affect him, he becomes responsible for his decisions and choices. When these efforts, guided by the parent, turn out well, the child learns the rewards of responsible behavior. Responsible behaviors receive parental acknowledgement and reinforcement. Hence responsible behavior in the child is strengthened and becomes integrated into the child's personality structure and eventually comes to characterize him.

The parent accepts the child's efforts in these areas and reinforces them. When the child offers to help set the table, the messages he is given by the parent strengthen his inclination to assume such responsibility: "I certainly can use your help. This is a very important job. I am pleased that you want to be responsible for setting the table." The child's efforts receive similar positive reinforcement: "You are being very helpful. You are doing a good job and being very responsible. I am proud of you." The parent shares with other the good deed the child has assumed responsibility for: "Jenny has assumed responsibility for setting the table. She did a great job. We are so fortunate to have such a helpful and responsible child!"

Notice that the words "helpful" and "responsible" are repeated often by the parent. This is a deliberate attempt on the parent's part to shape the child's behavior and attitudes and inculcate certain behaviors, attitudes and values such as helpfulness and responsibility. Such interactions with the parent foster the development of responsible behavior in the democratically raised child.

Friendly and Socially Oriented

Friendly and socially oriented are often descriptive of the democratically raised child. Although shyness and timidness generally characterize most young children, these traits are diminished or relatively uncommon among children that are raised democratically. The democratic parent encourages and supports friendly and socially oriented behaviors. The parent offers guidance as to how children should approach people or how to behave when approached by others: "Go to that child and ask him if he would like to play with you.

185

It's OK. I'll be watching from this bench." "I think this child wants to be your friend. Say hello and tell her your name."

Democratically raised children are thus helped to develop the social interaction skills that will help them be perceived as friendly and safe by other children and adults. The child's awareness and sensitivity to others helps make him a desired playmate. He typically has many friends or playmates and is a sought after person. He is usually willing to take turns and share what he has. Language is the primary way he gets what he wants and communicates his thoughts and feelings. Physical means have been discouraged by the democratic parent and so the child typically does not use physical force to get what he wants or to make his thoughts and feelings known to others.

Optimistic

The democratically raised child is typically optimistic about his ability to change things or get what he wants. He has learned at an early age to approach others in a friendly and non-threatening manner. His acquired social skills play an important role in the attitude or demeanor he presents. Past successes have contributed to his sense of self-confidence. That trust and faith in himself and the belief that things will turn out well (hope) contribute greatly to his sense of optimism and his optimistic attitude. Nothing succeeds like success. The child expresses this attitude in word and deed: "That looks like fun. I know I can do that!" as he races to be among those who will climb aboard the fire engine.

Democratic parents foster an optimistic attitude in the child in their interactions with the child. They express their own faith and sense of optimism regarding the child's potential to do certain things: "I believe you will enjoy sliding down the slide. It's fun. I know you can do it. Try the small slide first so you can build your self-confidence." Notice not only the expressed faith in the child's ability but also the parent's guiding the child to choose the small slide in order to maximize the child's chance for success.

Democratically Raised Child's Prevailing Attitudes and Feelings Toward Parents and Other Adults

Given the typical kind of interactions the child has with the democratic parent, certain attitudes toward the parent begin to emerge and solidify in the child's frame of reference. These attitudes tend to transfer easily to other adults such as the nursery school teacher or kindergarten teacher.

The democratically raised child's general attitude toward the parent is that he is inclined to regard the parent as helpful, cooperative, benevolent, kind, and caring. The parent is typically viewed as capable of providing guidance, support and encouragement. And this is sought from the parent and eventually from other significant adults.

The child perceives other adults in general as valued individuals who have knowledge and skill that they are willing to share. They are regarded as resources and mentors. Adults are seen as people to be trusted or relied upon. This is what the child has experienced in his interaction with his parent and this is what he continues to expect from the parent and comes to expect from other significant adults.

IS THERE A PREFERRED APPROACH TO PARENTING?

Based upon the effects that these different approaches have upon the growth, development and behavior of children, I will ask the question. Is there a preferred way to raise children? I believe there is. But my answer is influenced by my values and what I believe is in the child's best interest. Likewise, your answer shall be influenced by your values and what you believe is in the child's best interest.

Rudolf Dreikurs, a student of Alfred Adler and founder of the American Adlerian Psychology Movement and also founder of the

Family Education Centers in Chicago settled in the USA after escaping Nazi Germany during World War II. Based upon his professional work with children and parents, he has made some important observations and come to some important conclusions about child rearing. He has surmised that "what is wrong with American families" is that parents too often try to raise children autocratically when they should be employing democratic measures. We live in a democracy and we should be helping our children to learn how to live successfully in a democratic society. The autocratic ways of parenting do not prepare children well for democratic living. In fact, the autocratic approach stifles them and sets them up to have problems.

This is Rudolph Dreikurs' conclusion. I happen to agree with him fully. I believe that the best way to raise children is to employ predominantly democratic measures. The other approaches employ too many practices and attitudes that are not in the child's best interest. There is no one singular, perfect approach to parenting. But in my informed view, the democratic approach is as close as one singular approach can be to being most friendly and supportive to promoting healthy growth and development in children. Of course parents who choose the democratic approach and try to employ its philosophy and practices fully are not perfect either. Therefore, any shortcomings that result from democratic parenting are more often the shortcomings of the person rather than of the approach.

What do you believe? Which approach do you prefer after you have been exposed to the data presented herein?

To conclude, this chapter has focused primarily on how children respond to and are affected in terms of their growth, development and behavior by the child rearing they receive. The following chapter shall focus on how parents, siblings, teachers, and others are affected by the child's response. It shall also describe how the parent's behavior is affected by the approach to parenting that has been employed. A review of the research literature shall also be included to exemplify these various reactions and effects.

References

1. Chamberlin, R. "Approaches to Child Rearing: Their Identification and Classification." *Clinical Pediatrics*, 1965, **4**, p 150-159.

2. Chamberlin, R. "Approaches to Child Rearing II: Their Effects on Child Behavior." *Clinical Pediatrics*, 1966, **5**, p 688-698.

3. Chamberlin, R. "Early Recognition and Management of Vicious Circle Parent-child Relationships." *Clinical Pediatrics*, 1967, **6**, p 469-479.

4. Chamberlin, R. "A Study of an Interview Method for Identifying Family Authority Patterns." *Genetic Psychology Monographs*, 1969, **80**, p 129-148.

5. Driekurs. R. with Soltz, V. *Children: The Challenge* (New York: Hawthorne Books, Inc., 1964).

6. McCandless, B. *Children: Behavior and Development*, 2e (New York: Holt, Rinehart and Winston, Inc., 1967)

Chapter 11

Child Rearing Approaches
Effects Upon Parents and Others

The previous chapter has focused primarily on how children respond to and are affected in terms of their growth, development and behavior by the child rearing they receive. But it must be recognized that parents are also affected by the approach to parenting they employ. Likewise others who have contact with the child are also influenced in their interactions with the child by the child rearing the child has received.

Also, as others interact with children, they employ various child rearing strategies themselves to a greater or lesser degree depending on the age of the children involved and the setting wherein interaction takes place. For example, teachers of young children engage in a substantial portion of parenting as they attempt to educate the child and provide care to him. Professionals who enter more therapeutic relationships with children may also employ various parenting strategies. In fact, a major approach to psychotherapy is know as the "parenting technique."

This chapter shall focus on how parents and others are affected by the child's response to the parenting he receives. It shall also describe how the parent's behavior is affected by the approach to parenting that has been employed. A review of the research literature shall also be included to exemplify and substantiate these various reactions and effects.

EFFECTS UPON THE PARENT AND OTHERS

By virtue of the approach they have chosen, parents will encounter certain responses from the child. The child's response shall influence the parent's perception of the child, the parent's sense of success or failure with respect to parenting and the parent's view of parenthood in general.

189

Autocratic Parent's Response

View of the Child

The autocratic parent's response to the child is in large measure influenced by the nature of the child's response. A child who shows the characteristically aggressive response will most likely have a parent whose reaction to the child will be substantially different than if the child were to show the characteristically submissive response.

The Autocratic Parent's View of the Aggressive Child

The autocratic parent is most likely to view the aggressively responding child as "difficult." The child fights, resists, is contrary, negative and uncooperative. He is regarded as a "bad" child. The child does not do what he is supposed to do when he is supposed to do it, at least not without a struggle. He often is seen as misbehaving. Everything is perceived as a fight, a struggle, a challenge with this child. The child does not comply as he is expected to by the parent.

Interaction is difficult and often unpleasant. Interaction is often imbued with anger, hostility, and resentment. The autocratic parent often develops an expectancy of difficulty when approaching or being approached by the child. Of course this expectancy contributes to the tension the parent and child often experience in their interactions with one another. (The child often develops a similar expectancy.) The child often finds himself in disfavor.

The Autocratic Parent's View of the Submissive Child

The autocratic parent's view of the submissive child is in stark contrast to her view of the aggressive child. The submissive child is regarded as "easy." This child submits or acquiesces to parental wishes. The child does what he is supposed to do when he is supposed to do it. This child is perceived as compliant, dutiful, cooperative and "good." He behaves himself.

The autocratic parent typically has more positive feelings for the submissive child than she has for the aggressive child. Consequently, when the parent approaches or is approached by the submissive child, the parent's expectancy is to anticipate acceptable behavior from the child. Interaction has not been colored with frustration, anger and hostility, at least for the parent. Interaction, by comparison, is much more positive and easy. The submissive child is often "favored" by the autocratic parent. This child behaves as he should from the parent's perspective.

Autocratic Parent's View of Parenthood

The parent's view of parenthood is significantly shaped by the child's response. The parent of an aggressively responding child may come to regard parenting as difficult, relatively unrewarding, and much more labor intensive than was anticipated. Generally, the parent develops many negative thoughts and feelings about parenting and parenthood. The parent may even come to regret having become a parent and may even express this openly in the child's presence. The child may come to be viewed as the primary source of the parent's dissatisfaction with parenting and possibly family life in general: "If only I didn't have children..." "My child has driven me crazy!" "Who in her right mind would want to become a parent?"

In contrast, the parent of a submissive child will typically develop another view. Parenting is regarded as "easy." You simply meter out commands and children comply. Parenting is a "snap." The parent may come to regard children in general as "no trouble at all." It is a matter of simply letting children know who is boss. Once that is established, children "fall in line."

The autocratic parent of a submissive child may not appreciate nor understand the frustration that other parents speak of. Unless of course the autocratic parent has a child who shows an aggressive response. In this case the aggressively responding child is likely to be viewed in a more negative fashion. Most typically, the child is at fault or to blame for his negative response. After all, just look at how well behaved the submissive child is. Why can't the aggressive child be more like the submissive child? What is wrong with him anyway?

Autocratically Raised Sibling Response

When children in the same household respond differently, they often show interesting reactions themselves to these differences and toward one another. An aggressive child may view the submissive sibling as a whimp: "What is wrong with him? Why doesn't he fight back?" This child may perceive the sibling as someone he can "push around" too. Thus the aggressive child may take advantage of the sibling's submissive nature.

On the other hand, the aggressive child may encourage the submissive sibling to fight back, stand his ground, etc. Or the aggressive child may take on the protector role toward the submissive sibling. This may give the child the feeling of power and righteousness.

Another common likelihood is that the aggressive child develops animosity for the submissive sibling because the aggressive child is made to "look bad" by comparison. As a consequence, the submissive sibling may be the recipient of the aggressive child's scorn, ridicule, and verbal and/or physical abuse, in the parent's absence usually.

The submissive child may develop different views of the more aggressive sibling. The submissive child may be baffled by the aggressive sibling's response: "Why does he behave that way? Doesn't he realize he could avoid so much unpleasantness if he just did what is expected? Is he a glutton for punishment?"

On the other hand the submissive child may look toward the aggressive sibling with envy and admiration and a source of vicarious pleasure or satisfaction: "I wish I were more like him." "I feel so good inside when he stands his ground and doesn't give in." "Some day I will..."

Another possibility is that the submissive child may align himself with the parent and the parent's view and come to regard the aggressive sibling as a "bad" child also. Such a conclusion would be even more likely if the

aggressive sibling were to take advantage of the child's submissive nature. Alliance with the parent might also give the submissive child a feeling of power that is otherwise unattainable with the autocratic parent.

Protective Parent's Response

View of the Child

The protective parent's response is also influenced by the nature of the child's reaction to protective parenting. These responses will align themselves along the two major ways children respond to protective parenting: aggressive and submissive.

The Protective Parent's View of the Aggressive Child

The child who responds to protective parenting by resisting or fighting is likely to be viewed as a difficult child. The parent may regard him as defiant, not listening to parental cautions and generally ignoring much of what the parent tells the child. The child may be perceived as a "brat", as bold, mischievous and engaging in the very same behaviors the parent advises the child against thus placing himself (the child) at risk.

The parent comes to anticipate "brattiness" and a considerable amount of behavior that causes considerable parental frustration, anxiety, and worry. Parenting this child is a "full time job" and "you must anticipate the worst." The parent concludes that the child must be watched constantly because he seems to lack the good sense or judgement to not do those things which will place him at risk and get him in trouble. Indeed, he is constantly in trouble.

The Protective Parent's View of the Submissive Child

Because the submissive child accepts the parent's protectiveness and is more compliant to the parent's efforts to keep the child safe and secure, the parent has an easier time of parenting this child. When the child is told to stay in the yard, he stays in the yard. When the child is told not to play with certain children, he complies: "My daddy said I cannot play with you."

Despite the child's greater compliance and ease of parenting, the indulgent parent often expresses concern and frustration about certain child characteristics. The parent perceives the child as apprehensive, worrisome, even fearful at times. The child is seen as showing insecurity, inadequacy, and is often less capable than his agemates. Sometimes the child's helplessness and dependence is seen as a source of frustration and as a burden. Sometimes the parent feels anger and resentment toward the child especially in relation to his dependent behavior and lack of self-sufficiency. The protective parent sometimes wonders: "Will he ever be able to take care of himself?" "Am I ever going to have time for myself?" "When does parenting end?"

Protective Parent's View of Parenthood

The parent of the child who fights parental protectiveness comes to regard parenting as exhausting. It requires constant vigilance, and still that is not enough. Parenthood is marked by too many frustrations, anxieties, and worries. It is a wonder that the child survives childhood at all! It is a wonder that the parent survives the child's childhood! "Never again" the protective parent often concludes. Parenthood is filled with too much stress.

The parent of the submissive child also regards parenting as exhausting and a "full time job." Children certainly do require constant supervision. However, this parent shows less frustration in actual parenting because the child is simply more cooperative with the parent's efforts to keep the child safe. The protective parent has anxieties and worries but experiences these to a somewhat lesser degree because the child adheres to parental limits or restrictions. Parenting the submissive child is relatively less exhausting and frustrating but nonetheless, a "full time job."

Regardless of the child's response, protective parenthood is viewed as a commitment to service-giving and to the protection of the child. A "good" parent is one who "does" for the child, who "puts herself out" for the child, who places parenting as the "top priority;" nothing is more important. A "good" parent is one who keeps the child safe and insures his survival. A parent who allows the child to get hurt or ill is perceived as a "bad" parent.

Protectively Raised Sibling Response

The protectively raised aggressive child has difficulty understanding why the submissive child is so passive and accepting of the parent's restrictions. The aggressive child may try to convince the submissive sibling that the parent does not know what she is talking about and that he need not be so reluctant to act: "Did I fall off the fence and get hurt? No! I told you I wouldn't. Don't listen to mama. Come up here and see for yourself. Don't be afraid. You won't get hurt." If the aggressive child is unable to convince the submissive sibling to venture and take the risk, he may belittle the sibling: "You're a big baby! You'll never have any fun."

The submissive child may hold the sibling in awe and envy his daring nature. In fact, the submissive child may "live through" the more venturesome sibling and derive vicarious satisfaction from his bold, risk-taking accomplishments. Ideas and encouragement may be offered for adventures they share in very different ways: "I'll bet you can't walk along the fence backwards. Try it. Let me know what it is like." The audacious sibling accepts the dare and the two share in the performance, one directly, the other indirectly. Each enjoys a level of excitement each can manage.

The submissive sibling commonly shares many of the parent's concerns. Consequently, the submissive sibling may mimic the parent's warnings, concerns, etc. vis-a-vis the more daring sibling: "Don't do that, you'll get hurt." "The reason you are always in trouble is because you don't listen to daddy." "Remember what happened the last time when you left the yard!"

The submissive sibling may even assume many parental roles in relation to the brother or sister like fretting, worrying, nagging, admonishing, etc. This assumption serves to escalate the submissive child's level of apprehension.

However, in some cases, when this child sees that many of the concerns are not realized, the child may come to trust his own judgement about things less or venture forward with a little more daring himself.

Indulgent Parent's Response

View of the Child

The indulgent parent may also be faced with two very different reaction profiles depending on the nature of the child's reaction to being raised indulgently. The variation in parental response will then be a function of the variation shown by the children who are raised indulgently by the parent.

The Indulgent Parent's View of the Aggressive Child

Although it is the parent's inclination to indulge the child, the parent may frequently feel taken advantage of: "I am so good to him. I've devoted my whole life to him. But he doesn't seem to appreciate anything I do for him." The parent may recognize in the child certain traits that typically characterize the indulgently raised child, but they are often dismissed as features that can not be changed and therefore must be taken in stride: "He is such a brat and so demanding. That's just the way he is." "It's her temperament. What can you do?" "Maybe she'll outgrow her selfishness. I hope so. I don't know what to do about it."

Indulgent parents tyypically and often express exasperation at how difficult, selfish, jealous, or demanding the child can be at times: "He expects me to wait on him hand and foot. He's like a child king, spoiled by all he has. Sometimes I feel I am his slave." Despite this high degree of revelation and honesty about the child, indulgent parents frequently do not recognize that their own behavior has contributed to the conditions and traits about which they lament. When they do recognize the connection, they often feel powerless to do anything about changing matters.

The Indulgent Parent's View of the Submissive Child

The indulgent parent often feels greater satisfaction with the submissive child. The child willingly accepts the services the parent provides. The submissive child is not demanding, abrasive or aggressively manipulative like the aggressive child. The submissive child is easier, despite his greater dependence, helplessness, shyness, passiveness, etc.

Because the submissive child typically has diminished skill and is not assertive, the parent is often kept busy doing things for the child, advocating for the child, and generally providing services to the child. And although the parent may occasionally feel some resentment regarding this preoccupation with service-giving, the parent typically believes the child needs this in order to manage well. Also the submissive child often appears more appreciative of services rendered. This leaves the parent with a greater sense of satisfaction and appreciation.

However, the parent is not without concern about the future well-being of the child; for the parent recognizes many characteristics that may be perceived as possible shortcomings in the future. The submissive child's dependence, helplessness, passiveness, inferiority, lack of skill and low self-esteem concern the indulgent parent. The hope is often expressed that the child will outgrow these traits or that someone will take care of the child when the parent is no longer able to do so.

That someone else may be a teacher, sibling, friend or spouse. The child is typically not seen as realistically being able to change much himself and so greater hope is invested in the someone else who will "take care of my baby." For some indulgent parent and child relationships, this concern and hope for another service provider may continue long into the child's adulthood.

Indulgent Parent's View of Parenthood

Not withstanding the child's response, the indulgent parent is likely to view parenthood as a committment to service-giving. With either child, parenting is demanding and requires a great deal of self-sacrifice. Anyone who does not feel this way is shirking parental responsibilities. Parents who are not inclined to give an extensive amount of service to the child nor make the many sacrifices that indulgent parenting requires, are perceived by the indulgent parent as selfish or not concerned about or devoted to their children: "Why did they become parents anyway?" "How can they be so selfish and so mean to their own children?"

The degree of satisfaction in parenting is influenced by the child's response. The indulgent parent of an aggressive child is likely to feel less satisfaction than might be felt in relation to parenting a submissive child. Aggressive children simply seem less appreciative; submissive children seem more appreciative. In contrast, parenthood has relatively fewer worries and concerns for the future regarding the aggressive child and more for the submissive child. The aggressive child seems better able to take care of himself or get others to take care of him than the submissive child.

The indulgent parent often views parenthood as a form of martyrdom. The parent has devoted a substantial portion of the self to parenting and in the process has made many sacrifices. This devotion and self-sacrifice may not be rewarded in the parent's lifetime. Death is sometimes the martyr's reward. The more optimistic indulgent parent may be rewarded when someone else assumes responsibility for and takes care of the child.

Indulgently Raised Sibling Response

The indulgently raised aggressive child is likely to regard a submissive sibling as a fool for not taking greater advantage of the parent's indulgent tendencies. Furthermore, since the submissive sibling is likely to use tears, pouting and other passive, manipulative measures to obtain parental service, the aggressive child is likely to regard the sibling as a baby.

In fact, he may tease, goad and otherwise move his sibling to tears. This behavior may bring some form of negative feedback from the parent: "Don't be so mean to your sister. You are making her cry. You are such a brat." Such negative feedback from the parent may cause the aggressive child to feel resentment toward the sibling and hold her responsible for his problem with the parent. This is the classic case of the aggressive child "blaming the victim," his passive sibling.

The submissive child may wish he were able to be more demanding at times; however, he seems to manage quite well most of the time. Unless of course he is competing with an aggressive sibling for parental attention or service. The aggressive child will typically dominate the interaction, with negative behavior if necessary. The passive child is easily and often pushed aside by a more aggressive sibling. The submissive child develops resentment toward the aggressive sibling along with feelings of being abused or victimized by him.

The submissive child may draw conclusions about the aggressive sibling that are similar to those made by the parent. An alliance of parent and submissive child may develop as they share agreement about the various undesirable traits possessed by the aggressive child. Some comfort giving may be shared between parent and submissive child as they commiserate. When this occurs, the aggressive child may feel jealous, possibly even estranged. He may force himself on the parent, push the submissive sibling aside, and even strike at his passive sibling. The passive child is once again abused by the aggressive sibling.

There is much jealousy and difficulty in sharing among indulged children. Sharing involves the parent and the parent's time, energies, and services. The parent is often torn between the two and often told to choose between them. These are not conditions that promote family solidarity.

Democratic Parent's Response

The democratic parent's response is typically more realistic and reasonable with respect to the child, parenting and parenthood. Problems in these areas are recognized for what they are: simply matters that require adjustments or changes so that one may proceed with the business of life and living in a more normalized fashion. Frustrations and satisfactions are involved of course. But all things considered, the assets outweigh the liabilities.

The Democratic Parent's View of the Child

The democratic parent is not faced with the extremes in child behavior that are noted among the other approaches to parenting. Certainly there are differences in child behavior: between children and within the same child. But these differences are viewed as the individual expression of children's unique nature. They are not viewed as problems or as extremes that are troublesome. Consequently the parent exhibits a more reasonable and positive view of children in general.

Of course the parent's view of the child is concretely influenced by the interactions the parent and child share and the attitudes and behaviors the child exhibits. Thus the parents's view of the child mirrors the child's generally positive behavior. Consequently, the parent regards the child as basically good with primarily positive feelings about himself and others. The child is perceived as helpful, cooperative, and an asset to have around usually.

The child is seen as developing socially and exhibiting greater and greater social awareness, sensitivity and understanding of himself and others. He is regarded as typically kind and thoughtful of others. The child is seen as showing increasing autonomy, becoming more responsible and reliable, and showing positive features and satisfaction with himself as a learner and doer and person. The parent notices that the child is expressing his self-confidence, is learning how to express himself in positive and constructive ways and is relying increasingly on words and less on physical measures to achieve his goals.

The parent observes that the child is generally responding well to parenting and seems to be showing many signs that the parent's efforts are "paying off." The parent is generally satisfied with how the child is progressing. Generally the child is regarded as a source of pleasure and satisfaction to the parent as the parent monitors the child's course of increasing maturity.

Democratic Parent's View of Parenthood

The democratic parent typically expresses much satisfaction with parenting and parenthood. This general sense of satisfaction is tempered with a highly realistic attitude and a reality based frame of reference. The democratic parent acknowledges that parenting has had some frustrations, and problems, and occasional challenges; but when put in perspective they seem less important than they were at the time they presented themselves. Having lived through and adjusted to these, both parent and child are the better for them.

Parenting is an endeavor that requires much time, commitment, and energy. But it is something that has paid off: "I know this for sure when I see the wonderfully good person my child has become!" The democratic parent often speaks of how being a parent has contributed greatly to his or her own development as a person: "I am a better person today because of the parenting I've done and the child I have helped and guided. I am proud of myself and the job I have done as a parent. I hope my child will feel the same way when he is a parent. I hope that I have helped him eventually become a better parent than I."

Democratically Raised Sibling Response

Democratically raised siblings are usually characterized by their closeness and commitment to one another. They share many positive or benign attitudes and feelings and typically look upon their childhood with favorable, fond memories. They are encouraging and supportive to one another. Their qualities of helpfulness, cooperation and reliability are generously shared with one another.

They have learned to rely on one another for assistance but have not become dependent upon one another. They strive to reinforce each other's sense of independence and self-reliance. During adulthood they frequently serve as cheer leaders for one another and one another's children. Their own children often show very close attachment to their brothers and sisters (the children's aunts and uncles) and to the children of their siblings (the children's cousins).

The interactions of democratically raised siblings are characterized by friendliness, playfulness and positive feelings toward each other. They do not always agree but they respect one another's opinion and the right to pursue one's own individual interests and goals. They freely express their opinions in agreement or in opposition emphasizing reason and justification not what others "should" or "must" do. Their relationships with one another are not perfect. There are occasional disputes and jealousies but these are few and far between. Generally their interactions are positive and constructive.

REVIEW OF RESEARCH

There is a considerable amount of research concerning child rearing philosophies, practices and their effects upon the growth, development and behavior of children. A sampling of these shall be provided herein to illustrate how these findings generally support the descriptions presented in this and related chapters and the conclusions drawn from these.

These examples are considered to be representative of what the student would find if he or she were to make a review of the child development research literature. Certainly I would encourage the student to undertake such a review for personal edification or for purposes of verification or term paper writing.

The studies reported herein will be grouped into one of four classifications:
1.) family studies,
2.) classroom teaching studies,
3.) youth group and adult leadership style studies and
4.) psychotherapy studies.

Family Studies

One grouping is termed family studies because the children are viewed primarily within the context of the family environment or the child's behavior within the family is the primary frame of reference for other comparisons. In these studies an assessment is typically made of the parent's child rearing approach. Also the behavior of children is assessed. Correlations are then made between parental approach and child behavior and characteristics.

Classroom Teaching Studies

The second grouping is termed classroom teaching studies. These studies focus on children's classroom behavior. In these studies an assessment is made of the approach the teacher uses in managing the children within the classroom setting in addition to the parent's approach. These classifications are very similar to those made of parents. These similarities exist because much of good teaching, especially with young children, is in large measure good parenting. Correlations are then made with reference to the child.

Youth Groups and Adult Leadership Studies

The third grouping is termed youth groups and adult leadership styles. In these studies children's behavior is studied within the context of youth groups like the Boy Scouts, Girl Scouts, 4H groups, Boys and Girls Clubs, YMCA groups, and the like. The children's behavior is measured against the leadership style employed by the adult group leader. Classifications of leadership style are very similar to classifications made of parenting and teaching style.

Psychotherapy Studies

The fourth group is termed psychotherapy studies. In these studies the characteristics and behavior of those seeking help are assessed in relation to the approached to psychotherapy employed by the helping professional. Some approaches to psychotherapy can be classified as being autocratic or democratic in approach. Once the classification is accurately and justifiably made, the responses of the client within the context of the therapeutic relationship can be observed along with other aspects of the therapeutic experience. From these assessments, conclusions can be drawn and correlations made.

Family Studies

Study 1

In one longitudinal study, fifty children from birth to three years were studied over a period of time. The researchers interviewed parents at various intervals. The parents talked about their children and their parenting. They discussed their problems and concerns regarding children and parenting with the researchers whom they came to know well. The researchers noted and subsequently classified parental expressed concerns into two main types of problem areas. One problem area categorized the difficulties the children were having as being aggressive in nature. The other problem area involved problems of a submissive nature.

The type of problems that were listed in the aggressive category involved the child resisting eating, resisting going to bed, resisting toilet training, and generally being negativistic. Problems that were classified as being submissive included the child constantly wanting to be fed by the mother, wanting to sleep in the mother's bed, not wanting to play out of the mother's sight, and showing excess fear of strangers.

These reactions were more frequently reported by mothers who were "rigid" (autocratic) or "over-indulgent" or "over-protective." These reactions were less likely to be reported by mothers who were using a more cooperative or democratic approach. Not only was the incidence of these problems low among cooperative and democratic parents but also they often did not regard these behaviors as problems. Such behaviors were often regarded as normal child behavior not problem behavior.

Study 2

In a series of separate studies the parent's approach to child rearing was identified and also children's behavior in a nursery school setting was noted. The assessments made of parental behavior and child behavior were made separate and independent of each other by different evaluators. This of course was done to eliminate evaluator bias or what is otherwise known as the *Hawthorne Effect.*

Children from cooperative (democratic) homes were described as being more active, more outgoing, more assertive <u>and</u> more cooperative with peers.

Children from autocratic homes showed two distinct reactions. Children from autocratic homes were described as being more hostile, power assertive towards others, resistive to others, and having very little consideration for others. (These behaviors reflect what has been referred to repeatedly as an aggressive or hostile response to parenting. It certainly is in stark contrast to the reaction of children from more cooperative child rearing environments.)

Some children from autocratic homes were described as being more quiet; more well behaved; non-resistive; socially non-aggressive; and more restricted in curiosity, originality and fancifulness. (These behaviors are consistent with what has been referred to as a submissive response.)

Study 3

This study took a look specifically at maternal over-protectiveness and found two basic reactions to this form of child rearing. The researchers described these reactions as being either submissive in nature or to some extent, aggressive in nature.

The children from one group were described as shy, dependent, obedient, and submissive. The other group of children were described as impudent, demanding, disobedient, and disrespectful (the aggressive response).

The differences noted in the two groups were primarily attributed to the parent's ability or inability to set limits and exert controls. The children who responded in a more submissive fashion had parents that were typically better able to set limits and exercise control. The more aggressive children generally had parents who were significantly less able to set limits and exert controls.

Study 4

This study assessed children from two different types of child rearing environments: children coming from a strict or autocratic home and children coming from a permissive or cooperative (democratic) home. In this study various projective techniques were used to assess the child's development and responses. The Rorschach test , MMPI (Minnesota Multiphasic Personality Inventory) and other projective tools were used to develop a personality profile for each child.

After these projective tests were administered separately and by different researchers, assessments of each child were compared. There was much overlap found but some differences were noted between the two groups of children that proved to be statistically significant. Those differences follow.

Strictly or autocratically raised children were found to be more dependent upon the examiner, reacted to the testing situation with either over-compliance or negativism. In the testing situation some children were either extremely persistent or gave up very early with little effort expended. This group of children showed less originality in their responses and less creativeness during free play. They typically showed more hostile feelings toward others.

Permissively raised children were found to be less dependent upon the examiner and more cooperative with them. In the testing situation, they were more persistent in trying to solve problems that were too difficult for them. These children showed more originality and creativeness during free play. They expressed more positive feelings towards others. (Please recall that the permissive approach to child rearing is grouped among other "democratic" approaches.)

Study 5

This study examined some of the long term effects. It studied a group of adolescents over a seven year period. At the end of the study period, each adolescent was classified according to his or her dominant character type. This classification was then correlated with the

assessment made of the home environment.

The adolescents who developed the most mature ways of relating to people came from cooperative (democratic) homes.

The adolescents who tended to be either overly conforming to authority or overly rigid in applying their internalized rules of right and wrong came from autocratic homes.

The adolescents who related to people in a self-centered, manipulating way came from indulgent or over-protective homes. This was especially so where there was a noted inability on the part of the indulgent or protective parent to set limits.

Classroom Teaching Studies

There have been many studies which have assessed and categorized the classroom setting into categories that are similar to the designations used to describe parenting approach. Teachers' child rearing philosophies and practices not only influence the strategies they employ to teach and manage but also the classroom emotional climate they create.

Study 6

This study observed the behavior of children in cooperative (democratic) classroom settings. It found that the primary grade school children in these settings were more spontaneous, showed more initiative, were less easily distracted from their school work, and were less submissive and less resistive to their teachers.

Study 7

This study examined the behavior of children in classroom settings that were identified as being strongly democratic in demeanor and practices. The children in these classrooms were found to hold more positive attitudes about their teachers and their school work. They showed significantly less anxiety in relation to their school work and in their interactions with their teachers and classmates.

Study 8

This study looked at college students in cooperative and competitive classroom settings. The students from the cooperative settings generally showed more friendly contacts with other students, and showed less aggressive behavior of a negative and obstructive nature. They exhibited greater student participation and attentiveness in class, and showed fewer misunderstandings and less of a need for repetition.

The opposite was indicative of the students in the competitive classrooms. They showed less friendly contacts with other students, and showed more aggressive behavior of a negative and obstructive nature. They exhibited less student participation and attentiveness in class, and showed more misunderstandings and a greater need for repetition.

However, there were no differences in the learning achieved by the students and each group preferred its own system or type of classroom at the end of the study. (In my view, this observation shows that older students are better able to separate themselves from the impact of the classroom environment. In contrast young children are less able to separate themselves from the impact of the environment and actually prefer settings that are more democratic in nature. It seems that young children are "smarter" in that they recognize what is in their best interest and prefer a "kinder and gentler" classroom setting.)

Youth Groups and Adult Leadership Styles

Study 9

In this study boys were placed in groups with different adult leadership styles: autocratic, democratic, and laissez-faire. The one variation of note is the use of the term "laissez-faire." This approach frequently employs the policy of non-interference and the attitude of "live and let live." This approach is for all intent and purposes equivalent to the indulgent classification. These different leadership types had different effects on the boys in their respective groups.

Autocratic Leaders

The general reactions of the boys in the groups with autocratic adult leaders were as follows: The boys were generally submissive with lessened interpersonal interaction. This group had the least intermember aggression in the presence of the leader. There was little spontaneous, friendly, cooperative behavior and less conversation of all kinds. The boys in this group asked more for help from the group leader and competed for the group leader's attention and praise.

Work production was the highest when the leader was present; however, when the leader left, production dropped more rapidly than in other groups under leader absence. The end result was moderate output and low satisfaction. Aggressive behavior increased when the leader was absent. There was generally greater dependency on the leader's directions; yet, greater tendency to deliberately ignore or disobey the leader's remarks.

Democratic Leaders

The boys grouped with democratic leaders showed the following characteristic behaviors: They exhibited a moderate amount of aggression between members which was balanced off by the largest amount of friendly, cooperative behavior. Fewer demands for attention and praise from the leader were noted as there was a greater reliance on the self or other group members. There were fewer instances of ignoring or disobeying the leader's remarks.

Conversations of a more spontaneous kind were observed between group members and the leader. The boys showed greater identification with the group: A greater incidence of "We" vs. "I" remarks were noted. There was little activity loss when the leader was gone from the group. As a consequence production remained relatively constant and substantial. Satisfaction with one's own work was the highest in this group.

Laissez-faire Leaders

Laissez-faire leadership provided a setting

with much freedom but very little guidance from the leader and no clear limits. Consequently group member behavior under these conditions showed great disorganization, much less work done where the quality of work was relatively poor.

There was much frustration due to interference between members. There was much "horse play" or outright loafing. The lack of help from the leader led to efforts that were half-hearted or hurried, disorganized and ineffective. Production was at it poorest in these groups.

Leadership Preferences

The boys that were exposed to all three leadership forms preferred the democratic form. These groups of youths seem to exercise better judgement than the college students previously cited. The youths' preference once again shows that children are less able to free themselves of the influence of the environment of which they are a part. But when they have a choice, they seem to know what is in their best interest.

Studies establishing similar conditions with groups of adults show results very similar to those cited for this study. That is, the individual and group behavior of adults is very similar to that observed in youth studies and this adult response is a function of leadership style.

Psychotherapy Studies

In these studies, the approach to psychotherapy employed by the therapist was classified as being predominantly autocratic or democratic. The impression of colleagues, supervisors and the reactions and progress of the clients were studied and correlations were subsequently made between therapist approach and these client variables.

Study 10

This study found that therapists who were regarded as highly skilled by their colleagues were more likely to fit into the democratic designation.

Study 11

Counselors in training who were judged by their supervisors to be more effective often matched the democratic profile.

Study 12

This study found that schizophrenic patients responded better to therapists who were democratic in their approach to working with their clients.

Study 13

Hospital settings were examined in this study. It found the greater benefit to patients was observed in more democratic settings. The least benefit was found in autocratic hospital settings.

To conclude: These examples are my baker's dozen. They were intended to provide the student with a flavor for the research data and to support some of the generalizations made in this and associated chapters. The sampling of family, classroom, youth groups and psychotherapy studies was to illustrate the consistency and importance of these observations relative to how children, parents and others behave and are influenced by different child rearing environments.

Such consistency and importance across these very different settings or environments is especially noteworthy in my opinion. I believe that these lend considerable support to the observations that have been made relative to the impact that the various approaches to child rearing have on the growth, development and behavior of children.

Is There a Preferred Approach?

Based on the data presented herein, I shall ask the question once again. Is there a preferred way to raising children? Is there one that maximizes the child's growth, development and behavior on the one hand and the parent's potential for successful parenting on the other? Which one do you believe accomplishes these broad goals best?

Chapter 12

Patterns of Interpersonal Interaction

The interactions we have with others become to some degree characteristic of how we interact with particular people in given situations and circumstances. Likewise these same interactions also influence how we generally interact with others in a wide array of situations, circumstances and settings. We know people who are typically helpful, or optimistic, or supportive. We know others that are typically contrary, or argumentative, or pessimistic. We come to know these people by the kinds of interactions we have with them and by our observation of them interacting with others. These interactions come to characterize these people and the type of interactions we come to expect from them. Thus these expectations prime us to have particular kinds of interactions with particular people. These expectations are strong and influential because these anticipated interactions are patterned modes of interaction that are the insignia of certain people under certain circumstances in particular settings or situations.

PATTERNS OF INTERACTION

A pattern is a model, example or guide. A pattern also refers to that which is repeated or replicated over time and space. There are certain features of a pattern that are important, especially with respect to interpersonal interaction. There is a certain regularity and predictability to patterns. With respect to learning, it is easier to learn something that has a pattern because of its inherent regularity and predictability. In contrast, it is more difficult to learn something which is irregular and unpredictable or non-patterned.

For example: It is easier to learn the fox trot which is a patterned dance step and to dance with another individual who has learned the proper dance steps and pattern. However, modern jazz dance is typically improvisational, unstructured and non-patterned. Therefore, partners

203

performing a jazz dance must provide or impose a pattern so that the performance will proceed smoothly.

People seem to prefer and be more comfortable with patterns because of their inherent regularity and predictability. This is the case especially with respect to interpersonal interaction even when those patterns are undesirable. This explains in part why change is often difficult to make and why people remain in unproductive relationships for long periods of time.

We know existing patterns and can anticipate certain reactions to them. To change a relationship pattern introduces an element of the unknown, which may not be easily anticipated or planned for. People become comfortable with existing patterns, even when they leave something to be desired. People are generally uncomfortable with change and the anticipated unknown it may bring. This explains, in part, why people generally resist change, even when it might be in their best interest. People seem to not prefer and be less comfortable with things that are irregular and unpredictable or non-patterned. This also explains in part why change is often difficult.

Establishment of Patterns

Patterns of interpersonal interaction are established as two or more people interact with each other in more or less the same way over a period of time. Because people have a propensity towards patterns, they are established often very quickly. Parents have often scratched their heads wondering how they and their children became involved in certain routines or rituals. This is so especially when the pattern that is established was not by design of the parent. It seems they just "fell into it."

Reinforcement of Patterns

As the participants of the interaction repeatedly behave in certain regular predictable ways with each other within a given context or situation, the pattern becomes strengthened and firmly established. Although the participants of the interaction determine the type of pattern which is established by how each behaves in relation to each other under a given set of circumstances, *the pattern itself eventually becomes a powerful determiner of behavior.* This is an important phenomenon!

Patterns Influence Behavior

The pattern of interpersonal interaction that is created by people acquires the power to influence or determine their behavior. In some respects the pattern itself becomes a stimulus for what might be regarded as a conditioned behavior. As people come to learn the pattern well, they are capable of recognizing a pattern early in its interactional sequence. Consequently, not much actual interaction necessarily needs to take place before the participants begin to assume their respective roles within the interactional pattern. In effect, people become sensitive to certain cues that are used to identify on the one hand and precipitate on the other hand certain interactional behaviors of those involved. These cues may be very apparent or they may be, in some ways, subliminal. Nevertheless, people begin to respond to these very quickly and predictably.

The pattern may influence people's behavior. The ability to identify and respond to these cues accounts for why some people will leave the room when another enters. Others will "fly off the handle." In a given situation, one will "pucker-up" in anticipation of a kiss and another will step backwards to avoid it before interaction is actually initiated. Most of us have had experiences wherein the moment a particular person enters the room we can tell if there is going to be a good or bad encounter. Our perception of the cues and our anticipation of the type of interaction that is expected begins to shape or predetermine our responses in this situation. This is the power and influence of interpersonal interactional patterns.

The fact that interactional patterns themselves are powerful determiners of behavior does not minimize, limit, nor exclude the role played by other important influencing variables such as temperament, will-power, intentions, etc. But it is also important to count among these important variables the established pattern itself. If the pattern under consideration is a positive, constructive one, then we enjoy the power of its positive influence on interaction. However, if the pattern is a negative or destructive one, then we lament over its adverse power.

Patterns Are Learned

Interpersonal interactional patterns are established by people as they interact with each other. As interaction proceeds, the pattern itself is learned by the participants as they engage in its creation or formation. Likewise, the participants learn their respective roles within the interactional pattern. Because patterns are learned, we must conclude that they can be unlearned or, more precisely, modified or changed to patterns more to our preference. The fact that patterns of interaction are learned and subject to modification makes possible the great potential for improving upon undesirable interactional patterns and converting counterproductive ones to productive patterns.

INTERACTIONAL ROLES

Interactional Roles Are Learned

Similarly, the interactional roles we play or assume are also learned and modified within the context of interpersonal interaction. The potential for learning many interactional roles exists. This potential exists <u>directly</u> as people actually engage in a particular role. This potential exists <u>indirectly</u> as a person learns of a particular role by interacting with another who assumes the role.

Direct Learning

For example, a person may learn the role of "leader" by being in a leadership role within the interactional pattern. Likewise, one may learn the "follower" role by being a follower. This is learning the role directly because the person is directly engaged in the role.

Indirect Learning

A person may learn a role indirectly, not by engaging in the role itself but rather by interacting with another person who is engaged in that role. Thus, a person who is in the leadership role may learn about the follower role by interacting with a follower. Similarly, a person who is in a follower position, may learn of the leadership role though interaction with a leader.

Some Common Interactional Roles

There are many roles that people engage in as they interact with others. A comprehensive list would be extensive and certainly would include both favorable and unfavorable, preferred and not preferred, productive and counterproductive roles. Identified and described here are sixteen or so very common interactional roles. Their desirability or preferability may be dependent upon who is involved in which role under which conditions. Because of their commoness, most poeople are familiar with these interactional roles and have at least intuitive appreciation and understanding of them. Therefore, descriptions of each will be limited.

Leader Role

A leader is one who typically leads, or guides, or generally directs the movement of or gives direction to the interaction. The leader may use his or her own ideas or feelings in performing the leadership function or choose another's ideas or feelings to give direction or guidance. In either case the leader is at the head and significantly influences the type and content of the interaction. Leaders, of course, need followers.

Follower Role

A follower is one who typically follows. One follows another in regard to his or her ideas or beliefs, discipline or "school of thought," etc. The follower may appear to be a servant or attendant to the leader. The follower follows the leadership, guidance, or movement of another, who is typically the perceived leader but not exclusively. The latter point is dependant upon how strongly the follower tendency has been established in the person who follows. Followers are also viewed as adherents, partisans, or admirers who demonstrate allegiances to the leader. Some followers are followers by choice or by occasion. Others will be followers by acquiescence, while some will be followers by default, etc.

Bystander Role

The bystander is a person who is present but typically not involved. Sometimes they are chance lookers-on and sometimes they are on-lookers by choice or preference. The bystander may be involved in the interaction intellectually or emotionally but is <u>not actively</u> involved in the actual interaction which the bystander is viewing.

The bystander may be internally taking sides or in possession of an opinion but it is not expressed and therefore not part of the interaction. A bystander may even enjoy vicarious pleasure, success, etc. or may even suffer from a reprimand not directed at him. The bystander may demonstrate how he is indirectly affected by the interaction he has viewed through his demeanor, affect, or other behavior change.

Neutral Role

A neutral person refrains from participating in interaction be it benign, controversial, or otherwise. The distinction here is that the neutral person as compared to the bystander is deliberately and intentionally non-committal, uninvolved, or non-participatory. The neutral person typically shows no particular intellectual or emotional kind, color, or characteristic. This person is interactionally gray, without hue, neither for nor against. He remains neutral or disengaged: "It's not my job!" "It's not my problem!" "Don't involve me." "I don't want to take sides."

Challenger Role

A challenger is one who calls others to engage in a contest of skill, strength, knowledge, etc. The challenger's position may be to call to fight as in a "battle of the wit" or physically.

The challenger may simply demand an explanation: "Show me that you know what you are talking about." "Why do I have to do that?" "What is the purpose of this anyway?" "Prove it to me (I'm from Missouri.)."

The challenger is one who may object to the qualifications of others: "Who died and made you boss?" or the legality of a situation: "I don't think you can get away with that." The challenger is the person who will typically make an assertion about the impropriety of an act, take exception to an issue, policy, etc. or even lay claim to something: "You can't do that! It's my job." Challengers often keep others "on their toes" or force greater clarity of thought and reason in others by the demand for proof, explanation, justification, etc.

Interferer Role

Note the difference between the challenger and the interferer. The interferer is one who typically clashes, comes in collision with or opposes the claims, desires, or intent of others. The interferer does this in such a way as to <u>hamper</u> interaction, action, procedures, etc. The interferer may interpose or intervene for a particular purpose which often runs contrary to what is going on or with what another or the majority wants. The net result of this interference is that interaction or progress, etc. becomes "bogged down."

The interferer may take part in the affairs of others or meddle or interfere with the disputes of others. Such interference or meddling may often cause others to strike against each other or against another so as to hamper or hinder interpersonal interaction. This interference is sometimes intentional and sometimes unintentional.

Resister Role

A resister is a person who will withstand interaction or strive against or oppose it or its effects. There is also a tendency to refrain or abstain from interaction, behavior, etc. The resister will often take a stand or make efforts in opposition or act in opposition or offer resistance of a general or specific nature. Interaction with a resister "feels" like moving against the grain, swimming upstream, climbing mountains, etc. Some resisters are powerfully so and can be emotionally very exhausting to our efforts to engage them.

Martyr Role

Some are willing to suffer, even die, rather than renounce their position, belief, etc. This is the martyr. This is the person who will go to all extremes on behalf of any belief, principle, or cause regardless of the suffering or sacrifice involved. This willingness to undergo severe or constant suffering is often by choice and sometimes seems to be the martyr's pleasure. Martyrs are easily tormented and occasionally torment others. Martyrdom is the condition of suffering or death of the martyr. Martyrdom is typically prized by the martyr.

Victim Role

The victim is the one who suffers from any destructive, injurious, or adverse action or lack of action of another person or persons. A victim may also be one who is duped, swindled or "coned." Some people are victimized unintentionally; they suffer from the "fall out" or consequences of the actions around them. Others are intentionally victimized by the actions or inactions of others. Some are innocent victims while others are victims of their own actions or inactions. In the latter case, it is common for victims to not appreciate or be aware of their own role in their victimization.

Scapegoat Role

The scapegoat is the person who is made to bear the blame for others or to suffer in their place. An ancient Jewish ritual was to send a goat into the wilderness after the chief priest on the day of Atonement had symbolically laid the the sins of the people upon it. People do this to other people to escape blame, guilt, or otherwise avoid the consequences of their own actions.

The modern day versions of this ancient practice are the political "spin-doctor" and political scapegoat. The scapegoat may or may not be partially at fault but typically is given the lion's share of the blame.

Helpless Role

The helpless person is one who is unable to help himself. He may be pretending to be or simply may be weak, dependent, incapable, inefficient or shiftless. Helplessness of this sort is learned. Independence, self-sufficiency, competence, proactiveness are normal, positive outcomes of healthy growth and development. Their opposites are often the result of mismanagement by significant caretakers and significant others.

Of course the physically handicapped or otherwise impaired person may have to learn to live with certain limitations and learn to rely on others for help. However, the drive to be independent, self-sufficient, etc. is very strong even among emotionally healthy individuals who happen to have some physical impairment.

The helpless sometime learn to use their helplessness - real or imagined - to their advantage or to get what they want. The wise parent or teacher will want to minimize strengthening this behavioral tendency.

"Everything happens to me!" Role

For some, life happens to them, things happen to them, circumstances seem to fall in their lap. We all know at least one person like this. If a meteor were to enter the atmosphere nearby, it would land on that person's house. Of the few trees that are uprooted by a high wind storm, one falls on this person's car. Bad or unwanted things seem to happen often to this person. A dark cloud follows him. What is it about these people? Are they simply innocent victims or does their own behavior or lack thereof make them more vulnerable or set them up for unpleasant consequences.

Consider the person who is often late paying the auto insurance premium. On one consequential occasion of being late one more time, our player is involved in an automobile accident. The insurance company denies coverage. An innocent victim? This person typically appears to be an innocent victim; however, his own behavior or lack thereof may often contribute to the events that seem to happen to him.

Mediator Role

The mediator is the one who brings about an agreement, peace, etc. between people. The tendency is for the mediator to settle disputes by mediation, to reconcile, to effect a result or act as an intermediary. Agreement, compromise, or reconciliation is the goal the mediator strives to accomplish through his actions and interactions with others.

Arbitrator Role

A slight variation on this theme is the arbitrator. The arbitrator has goals that are similar to those of the mediator but the distinction is that the arbitrator will often settle the dispute himself or decide between opposing parties or sides. The mediator is more of a conduit or facilitator whereas the arbitrator will actually render an arbitrator's decision.

Problem-solver Role

Problem-solvers are people who work toward a solution to a problem. It is done by attempting to clear up or explain matters or situations, to work out the answer or solution through active involvement and participation. The problem-solver's goal is to solve the problem, hopefully with permanency.

Peace-maker Role

Peace-makers want freedom from war or hostilities. The peace-maker attempts to obtain an agreement between contending parties to abstain from further hostilities. A truce or armistice is preferred in place of open hostility or discord. Peace-makers strive for freedom from strife, civil commotion, mental disturbance, and hostile interactions. They prefer public order, security, harmony, amity, calm, and quiet. Sometimes this preference may supersede a concern for justice, fairness, or seeking a resolution of the underlying causes for the hostility. What price do we pay for peace? For some, the cost of peace-making has certain limits. For others, it is peace at all costs.

Dysfunctional Roles and Patterns

There are many types of interactional patterns and roles that are dysfunctional. These may be so prevalent that they seriously

debilitate the person and family. This debilitation may be so significant that some health professionals may refer to a person or family as dysfunctional. This characterization is often used in reference to alcohol and drug troubled individuals and families. The helping professions have amassed a large body of descriptive data and knowledge about a wide array of personal, interactional, and familial dysfunction.

If is not my intent to focus on these per sé but certainly these types of interactional roles and relationships must be acknowledged. I encourage the reader to look to other sources to cover my intentional omission. However, child abuse shall be addressed minimally herein. Furthermore, some additional descriptive information and resources pertaining to this topic have been included in Appendix B and Appendix C.

Child Abuse

Since physical, psychological and sexual abuse or exploitation of children is agonizingly prevalent in this culture, helping professionals must equip themselves with the knowledge and skill needed to recognize symptoms of such abuse and must know what their personal and professional responsibilities and limitations are in this area. Each of us must pursue this education on our own and make whatever provisions are needed if it is not a part of our formal training so we will be well informed and helpful in these matters. That is why I have included in the Appendix some materials that I hope will get you started in this endeavor.

There is one particular book which was written by a friend and colleague which I regard as a profound book in terms of its content and novel approach. *You Will Plant Your Vineyards Once More* by Georgia Bradley Houle is a book about incest and child molestation. It was written for the adult victim and for others who need and desire to understand the victim. In recognizing the spiritual nature of man, Part One uses the Scriptures, which are augmented with drawings to move the reader from the agony of victimization to resolution. Part Two is for counselors, parents, chaplains and others concerned about the victim. The book teaches the counselor and other practitioners about issues, concerns, and recommended practices.

In this book, Georgia Houle describes five common roles assumed by perpetrators to control their victims. These are offered in part to help the victim understand how he/she is being controlled by the perpetrator with the ultimate goal of ending this destructive pattern of interaction. The five perpetrator roles are the *game player*, the *instructor about sexual issues*, the *power person*, the *briber*, and the *manipulator*.

Some who read this book will themselves be victims. Some are aware of this and have acknowledged this to themselves at least. Others are not consciously aware of their victimization, because the memories have been repressed so deeply or abuse took place at such an early age that memories seem not to exist. What we know is that these memories do exist but they are embedded in the psyche and must be acknowledged and reconciled under the guidance and assistance of a qualified helping professional. Whatever the reasons for your interest in this topic, do yourself and others a service and read Georgia Bradley Houle's book *You Will Plant Your Vineyards Once More.*

VARIABLES TO CONSIDER ABOUT INTERACTIONAL ROLES

There are many questions to consider or ponder in relation to interactional roles. Among the more salient are concerns about central tendency, frequency, variety, choice, and opportunity. What influence do parents, parenting partners, children and sibling have? Role learning and the desirability of certain roles are also major concerns.

Central Tendency

When considering these various roles, we must consider a number of questions or related concerns. The matter of "central tendency" emerges. A particular role may not represent totally a given person's interpersonal interactions. However, a particular role may represent substantially how one interacts with others. When this is so, this particular role represents a person's central tendency. That is, more often than not a particular person may be found engaging in a particular role when involved in interpersonal interaction.

Role Variety

Of course people may be found assuming various roles as they interact with others. Greater facility here or the ability to assume and function well in a variety of healthy interactional roles serves the person well. Therefore healthy families will encourage family members to assume and practice and help them gain facility in many healthy interaction roles. Conversely, healthy families will try to minimize the acquisition of unhealthy interactional roles among family members.

Choice

Are these roles by choice or not? People may freely choose a given interactional role. However, at times we are forced to assume a particular role, or manipulated, or cajoled, etc. Sometimes circumstance mitigates our assumption of a particular role. Sometimes we assume a role by default. Certain situations precipitate certain behavior that is demonstrative of a particular role. These and others factors influence the roles we engage in and present opportunities for learning these roles to our advantage or disadvantage.

Frequency

What is the frequency of certain people assuming particular interactional roles? The same or similar factors mentioned earlier are operative here also. The more frequently a person assumes a given interactional role the greater the potential for learning and assimilation into the personality structure and accommodation therein. Likewise, limited or no exposure to certain roles tends to lessen opportunities for learning and assimilation and accommodation. Once again, healthy families strive to provide many opportunities for family members to assume often other healthy interactional roles and patterns. Minimizing the assumption of unhealthy roles serves to lessen the chances that they will become integrated into the personality structure.

Role Opportunities

Does the family offer family members opportunities to experiment with, practice, and develop different roles? This is a crucial question! The extent to which families provide these opportunities to family members is an indication of family emotional health and happiness. Success in life and living requires a broad knowledge base and skill repertoire. The family unit is the first setting where we come face to face with life and living in a social context.

The functional roles of the family as described in an earlier chapter were intended to assist the reader to develop a broader perspective concerning parental and familial roles. The individual interactional roles described in this chapter are offered for the same purpose. Healthy families provide family members with many opportunities to experiment with, practice, and develop healthy interactional roles.

Parental Influence

How do parents influence the roles children assume? Children are initially dependent upon the good will of their parents. If the parent responds to the very young child's dependency appropriately, the child's needs are met or satisfied. Very soon, however, the child's striving for autonomy will emerge. If the parent responds appropriately to these changes, the child's growth and development is supported and he emerges with greater independence, self-sufficiency, decision making ability, will power, and less dependence upon the parent.

However, if the parent does not respond appropriately, the child's autonomy striving may be stifled. The outcome will be negative: shame, doubt, and stronger dependency. This may or may not be what the parent wants. The outcome may or may not be by parental design. Nonetheless, the parent's interactions with the child will surely influence in large measure the interactional roles assumed by the child and these roles may or will become integrated into the personality structure of the child.

Parenting Partner Influence

How do parents influence the roles their parenting partners play? Parenting partners influence the quality and frequency of interaction each has with the child. Recall the discussion pertaining to the step-parent and child relationship in Chapter 1 as one example of this influence.

For purposes of this discussion, consider the father who desires to participate more fully in the care and nurturing of his infant child. He wants to diaper, bathe, feed, entertain, etc. his infant child. A partner who looks upon this participation favorably and is not threatened by her partner's level of involvement with the infant will allow, encourage, and supports the father's efforts. In fact, she may reinforce his behaviors in a variety of ways by assuring him of the excellent job he does and letting him know how fortunate she believes she is that he is so involved in parenting their child.

She may even boast or brag to others of his outstanding involvement with the care and nurturing of their child. These reinforcements shall certainly strengthen the nature of his involvements with his child. Furthermore, these interactions will help to establish a pattern of high quality involvement between father and child. This good beginning will have far reaching effects upon future interactions between parent and child. This good beginning will also influence the quality of the relationship parenting and marital partners share.

In contrast, a wife who looks upon such involvement by the father as an infringement of her domain, may be somewhat threatened. Rather than allowing, encouraging, and supporting the father's preferred involvement, she may not allow, or limit, or discourage, and not support any offering by the father to participate more fully in the care and nurturing of their child. Such negative reinforcements may lessen the father's efforts to be involved. His relationship with his child and his partner will be diminished as a consequence.

Parental Self-influence

How do parents influence the role they themselves play in their interactions with their children? How parents view their parenting role and the skill and knowledge they bring to the parenting situation is important. One's desire or level of motivation to parent in certain ways shall influence the nature of interpersonal interaction and the patterns that are established and perpetuated.

Attitude is critical in this regard. Consider the father previously identified as wanting to be very much involved in the care and nurturing of his child. He has a predetermined notion of the type of relationship he prefers and the degree of involvement he wishes to have with his child. His images of what constitutes a good parent are strong and motivate him to be directly involved in parenting. Furthermore, his images of the good and helpful partner may also be operative. Thus this parent will play a substantial role in the kind of interactions he shall have with his child and the patterns that are established and perpetuated.

In contrast, the father who regards child rearing as "women's work" not only has a counterproductive attitude but also has determined for himself that he will be minimally involved in the care and nurturing of his infant child. This predetermined position will limit the quality and frequency of his interactions with his child and may even establish a pattern of limited involvement with the child. Such a pattern shall have far reaching implications for future interactions with the child. This position shall also have a measure of influence on the relationship these parenting partners share.

Child Influence

How do children influence the roles parents assume? This is another fortuitous question. Let's pick up where we left off in the preceding paragraph. Let us assume that as the child enters the stage of autonomy that very strong autonomy strivings emerge. The parent who gets the message and interprets the child's needs correctly will cooperate with the child and help manage the child and structure the home environment in such a way that the child moves forward smoothly in his development.

But this is not to say that the child has been the passive recipient of the parent's sensibilities. In fact, because this child's autonomy strivings were so strong, the child put the parent on notice, so to speak. The messages from the child to the parent were: This is important to me! Please help me become independent and self-sufficient. This is something I must do in order to grow and develop well. Fortunately the parent did not resist or demand dependent behavior for that would have surely produced different results.

Sibling Influence

How do children influence the roles their siblings assume? Brothers and sisters exert considerable influence on the roles their siblings assume. Consider the older brother who has a younger sister. He has taken a protective posture and these protective behaviors have been reinforced by the parent who praises him for the good care he provides and his vigilant behavior and protective attitude. The parent assures him that both his sister and his parent are very fortunate to have someone who is so kind, helpful, watchful, etc. These reinforcements strengthen his inclination to be protective of his younger sister.

But how does the sister influence his behavior? How does his behavior influence the sister's behavior? The sister is very accepting of the services he provides. She has made it easy for him to assume this protective role. She further reinforces his inclination to interact with her in this fashion by actually soliciting his help and protection. She will go to him when she needs a jacket zippered. She asks that he intervene on her behalf when another playmate has taken a toy from her. She looks to him for physical and psychological comfort when she has fallen and hurt herself. Her actions reinforce his inclinations. His responses to her reinforce her behavior toward him. The pattern is established and perpetuated by both siblings.

211

Role Learning

How are these various roles learned? Interactional roles are learned within the context of interaction. The brother cited above is learning to be protective. The interactions he has with his sister and parents reinforce the learning or assimilation of this role and the behaviors that support it. His sister is learning to be dependant upon others and to rely on the protection of others. The parent may be learning to rely somewhat disproportionately on the assistance the son provides in the child rearing of the daughter.

Role Influence

How are people influenced by these roles? Regarding the above example with respect to the present, the answer is already apparent. With respect to the future, consider the following assertions. These interactions have importance for what each is learning about other future relationships yet to be established. In future relationships with females and children, this brother may come to expect that his role is one of protector.

In future relationships with males and her children, this sister may come to expect protection of herself and her children. In future relationships with other children, this parent may come to expect the same degree of assistance from her first born son.

These expectations may or may not be reasonable or realistic but they exist nonetheless and shall influence future interpersonal interactions and the patterns that evolve from these.

VARIABLES TO CONSIDER ABOUT INTERACTIONAL PATTERNS

Similar kinds of questions about roles also emerge regarding the patterns that have been established. Some of the more salient questions concern pattern valence, strength and influence, the influence of people on these patterns, the form and structure of patterns, and the direction they give to interpersonal interaction.

As we begin to ponder the strength of influence of interpersonal interactional patterns, many questions begin to emerge. Asking these questions is essential to our understanding of these patterns and their influence and crucial to our effort to change them to patterns that are more to our preference.

How are people affected or influenced by certain interactional patterns? Certainly people are affected in a variety of ways depending on the individuals involved and the circumstances and situations that influence their interaction. Certain patterns have a favorable impact upon the individuals involved. Some patterns have an unfavorable effect. Some patterns are growth enhancing while others may be growth limiting or even stifling. Some patterns we wish to preserve. Others we wish to change or eliminate.

Valence of Patterns and Roles

An interactional pattern or role may be positive, negative or neutral. It may be constructive or destructive, productive or unproductive, helpful or unhelpful. A pattern of interaction or role may be perceived as good or bad, desirable or undesirable, and so forth.

How an interactional pattern or role is perceived or regarded varies as to who the perceiver is and his frame of reference. That is to say that one's value system, expectations, etc. will significantly influence one's perception of interaction and how it shall come to be regarded. For example, most people might regard extreme forms of discipline as abusive; yet, some might regard them as necessary in order to "break the will" and make children compliant.

Player Influence

What influence do people have on their patterns of interpersonal interaction? How do people influence the formation, perpetuation or change of certain patterns? Obviously, some people shall have a constructive influence upon the type of interactional patterns that they help create, perpetuate or change. In contrast, some people will have a counterproductive or even destructive influence on their interpersonal interactional patterns. Some people are more capable of change than others. Some are proponents of constructive change while others may be resistive to changing a pattern.

Pattern Form and Structure

What "form" or "structure" characterizes a particular interactional pattern? Does it usually consist of two people, three people, etc.? Is interaction dominated by one person or is there equality in the interaction of participants? Is the dominant person dictatorial, a benevolent despot, democratic, etc.? Is authority or influence shared equally or monopolized by one or are they more individualized? Do participants interact as individuals or are there alliances or even estrangements?

Pattern Strength

What is the force, power or strength of influence of certain patterns with regard to family life and living? Does a particular interactional pattern contribute positively to family life and living or does it have a negative influence? Do certain patterns make the home a comfortable and nurturing setting or a very unpleasant place? The home environment may have an abundance of positive patterns which contribute positively to family life. However, there might be one or two or a few patterns that are so powerfully negative in their influence that these significantly undermine the influence of the more positive patterns. They may in effect establish a "tone" or "climate" in the family.

Directional Influence

What direction do certain patterns give to family life and living? Certain patterns take family life in a positive, healthy direction while other patterns may take it in a negative and unhealthy direction. Certain patterns by their unique nature and conscious intent of the participants are directed toward positive interaction within the home environment. However, some patterns lead the family members in negative or counterproductive directions. This negative direction may be the consequence of the pattern itself or the conscious or unconscious influence of one or more of the participants. Of course,

conceivably there are patterns that are more or less directionless. They neither lead the family in positive or negative directions. Their influence on family life and living is neutral, directionless, neither good nor bad.

Personal and Familial Factors

Similar concerns emerge once interactional patterns and roles have been established between family members. How do these influence family life and living? What influence do they have on the kind of interactional patterns that become established in the future? How are people affected by these patterns? What form or structure do these patterns assume? How is their influence, power or strength on family life and living measured? What direction do these patterns give to family life and living?

There are numerous variables that influence these considerations or questions. Some of the variables that are especially important in their influence on interaction and the patterns that evolve from that interaction are part of the person's psyche. These variables are termed "intrapersonal" factors. Still other influential factors are found outside the people involved or are external to the interactional participants. These are termed "extrapersonal" factors. However since they take place between people and influence their interaction they are also "interpersonal" variables.

Additionally, some factors are within the family unit or are a function of the family unit. These are termed "familial" or "intrafamilial." Also there are influences that are outside the family unit. These are termed "extrafamilial." Although extrafamilial variables are separate and apart from the family, they exert their influence nonetheless.

Intrapersonal and Interpersonal Factors

Intrapersonal factors are also important to our consideration and understanding of the establishment and perpetuation of certain interactional patterns and their influence on the parent and child relationship. Some of the more common intrapersonal factors that influence interactional pattern formation and perpetuation are as follows:

213

Conscious, Subconscious, and Unconscious Motives and Needs

People have many needs which influence their motives and motivation regarding the way they go about satisfying those needs. Level of awareness varies pertaining to these needs and motives. Some people are keenly aware of what they need to live a satisfying life and go about meeting those needs in a most direct or straightforward manner. Others take a more circuitous route to need satisfaction even when they are fully aware of what they want and why.

Unfortunately, people are not always fully aware of their needs and need satisfying strategies. We can be made aware of these with relatively little effort because some are not deeply contained in our psyche. They are harbored at the subconscious level. A little introspection, probing, and help from our friends or loved ones can make us more aware of these. In effect, they can be made part of our conscious level of awareness. When our consciousness level has been changed in this manner, we are in a better position to proceed.

However, some of our needs, wants, and desires are much more deeply contained in our unconscious level of awareness. Much more introspection and sometimes psychotherapeutic intervention or assistance is required to bring these needs and motives to the foreground of our consciousness. People actually resist this process because often our unconscious contains issues and concerns that we have not been able to adequately manage previously. Some memories may in fact be psychologically painful. Our psyches try to be kind to us and protect us from this discomfort by burying these memories deeply and often covering them with distracting matters or very effective camouflage.

Consider one parent who has generally grown well and has developed many positive attitudes, has knowledge, has skills and other attributes. Among these is a strong sense of independence and self-sufficiency. This parent wants her child to know the benefits of independence and self-sufficiency also. Consequently she encourages the child's efforts to assert his independence and to do things for himself. She provides encouragement when he seems to be so inclined. His efforts are praised generously.

She provides support and guidance when needed. No wonder he seems well on his way to establishing a strong sense of autonomy.

In contrast, consider another parent whose role as caregiver is among the very few roles that have brought her satisfaction and meaning in her life. Someone finally needs her and loves her unconditionally. She feels good when she can identify what her young child needs and then bring satisfaction to him. She feels purpose and success in her life. Her child's dependency has brought new meaning and good feelings about herself.

What happens when her child begins to assert his need to be independent and self-sufficient? Will she feel her purpose and feelings of success are threatened? Will she encourage her child's efforts or try to maintain his dependence upon her? She may need to keep him dependent in order to give purpose or meaning to her life and role as parent. She may or may not be aware of her need in this regard. Therefore her efforts to discourage his independence and self-sufficiency may go unnoticed by her. She explains: "He is still too young to do that by himself. I still have to help him." No wonder he shows many dependent behaviors and seems to be less skilled than many of his agemates.

Certain Obsessions or Compulsions

Certain behaviors beset or dominate our actions or influence a certain persistence of feeling, idea or action. Sometimes we seem unable to escape these. The feeling, idea or action dominates. These are obsessions. Some are healthy; some are not. Some receive disproportionate attention, while some are managed more sensibly. On occasion these feelings, ideas, or behaviors are compelling. That is, there is a strong irrational impulse to carry out a given act. The feeling, idea or behavior seems to take over. We seem to lose our ability to manage it appropriately. This is a compulsion.

These show themselves in subtle ways and in profound ways. They are sometimes overt and at other times they are covert. Sometimes they are innocuous. Sometimes they are of considerable consequence. But they always have an influence on interpersonal interaction when others are involved. Recall the song's

214

lyrics: "I want a girl just like the girl that married dear old dad." Some professionals suggest that people often seek qualities in a mate that approximate a parent's qualities. In effect, we marry our mothers and fathers to some degree. This certainly would support to some extent the psychoanalytic notion of the "Oedipus Complex" and the "Electra Complex."

Occasionally our present behaviors are efforts to create a previous comfort. Consider the infant who is playing on the floor at a distance from his parent. He occasionally looks up to reaffirm her presence. He does this periodically throughout his occupation with his toys. However, every so often he must leave his toys behind. He crawls to his mother and then sits upon her lap. They exchange niceties. He crawls down from her lap and back to his toys and resumes his play with them. He repeats these actions several times during this play period. His periodic return to the comfort of his mother's lap and the interaction that ensues is called "psychological refueling."

As this child grows older, he plays at an increasing distance from his mother. Nevertheless, he shows the same pattern of maintaining regular eye contact and occasionally returning to her lap for an acknowledgement, caress, hug, etc. and then he returns to his play.

When he enters kindergarten, he is able to work independently at a learning center. He can be observed to periodically look up to see where the teacher is and what she is doing. And occasionally he leaves his work station to talk with the teacher face to face at close proximity. Sometimes he will bring his work to her for her approval, which she generously bestows upon him. He smiles profusely and returns to his toys or task.

Once again he has been refueled. He is not aware of this phenomenon and its origin; nor is the teacher. However, if the teacher generally understands young children, she is aware that he has a need to engage her periodically throughout the day and she accommodates his need with appropriate interaction.

The Repetition Compulsion

These phenomena (especially the repetition compulsion) partially explain why children from alcohol troubled families often choose alcohol troubled mates. Some of this choice making is imbedded in the comfort of the known or familiar pattern. The child knows well the patterns of interaction. The adult child may not be equipped to manage interaction with a non-alcohol troubled significant other. And so the choice to some measure is predetermined.

Some of this choice is influenced by hope. That is, the child was unable to help the parent with the problem. The child simply was too inexperienced to help with this adult problem. However, as an adult, this child may believe that he or she can provide help to the alcohol troubled mate. After all, the adult has greater experience, knowledge and skill. Helping the mate solve this problem not only helps the mate but also symbolically helps the parent. The adult child of an alcoholic parent hopes to be able to do now in adulthood what could not be done during childhood. Sometimes this works. Usually it does not without professional assistance.

A similar phenomenon occurs with children that have been abused. They sometimes choose abusive mates. The same principles apply. Some of this choice making is the influence of the power of the pattern and/or the lack of alternate patterns of interaction to replace the former. There is also the promise of new beginnings, the potential to be helpful this time - hope. Success is possible but often it is limited without adequate professional intervention.

Personal Interpretation or Perception

We try to place our interactions with others into perspective. Sometimes this is easy to do and at other times it is more challenging. Whichever it turns out to be often depends upon what we each bring to the interaction. Our level of development, experience, etc. are factors as we attempt to interpret accurately what we experience. An individual person's interpretation or perception of what is going on may be accurate or inaccurate.

Consider the child who walks into his parents' bedroom at night to find them "making love." The sounds, the movement, the relative position of their bodies is confusing to the child. The child becomes upset and cries out, "Don't do that daddy! You're hurting my mommy!" as he attempts to separate the two. The young child interprets what he saw as an act of aggression perpetrated upon the mother by the father.

As adults, we know this not to be the case, because we bring a different level of knowledge and experience to this situation. And this knowledge and experience influences our interpretation. However, the child is lacking in these insights and understandings and so his interpretation is dominated by the sight, sound and moment, which to him means something very different than they actually mean.

Understanding the Intent or Meaning of Interaction

As the antagonist in the movie, *Cool Hand Luke* said to the star protagonist, Paul Newman, "What we have here is a failure to communicate." It is apparent and invariable that failed communication, or faulty communication, or inability to attend adequately to what is being said, often contributes to misunderstandings about what is actually being said, or what is the underlying meaning or intent, etc.

Communication is not simply talking to or with another person. *Communication is creating understanding between people.* There are many things that can interfere with effective communication or prevent us from communicating effectively with others. Effective communication requires skill as a listener and as a speaker. Being specific is essential when communicating with children. Telling them what we expect rather than what they are not doing correctly is better. Parents should understand that children often hear what they want to hear or attend to just part of what they hear. Their needs and needs systems influence what they attend to and how they interact with their parents.

Consider the parent who relies regularly on an older child to baby-sit a younger sibling. A regular pattern is established where the youngest child is cared for by the older sibling so the parent may attend to chores, keep appointments, etc. The older child is not always thrilled with this responsibility but generally cooperates and does a good job. Being excused from this responsibility is always received with great joy, as spending time with playmates is now possible and of course preferred.

On this particular occasion, the parent states to the elder child, "I will not need you to baby-sit today until 4:30." The child responds with an excited, "Great!" and darts out of the house to join playmates elsewhere. The 4:30 time approaches, and the baby-sitter has not arrived. Fifteen minutes pass, then one-half hour, then an hour. No sign of the baby-sitter. At 6:30 the elder child strolls in and is unprepared for the verbal assault the parent thrusts upon her for causing the parent to miss her appointment with the physician. The daughter is dumbfounded and attempts to explain: "You said that you did not need me to baby-sit today!"

In this case the child heard the first part of the parent's statement but not the latter crucial part. This child heard what was most desired, not having to baby-sit today. The "until 4:30" part went unnoticed or was not processed. The child's desire to be excused modified her ability to process all that was communicated. The parent did not confirm the child's understanding as to what time she was needed. It was a straightforward message and the parent assumed there was no need to clarify, or confirm their understanding of the situation.

Beliefs About the Interaction and People's Intentions

Generally speaking, people have a reservoir of beliefs which reflect how we think, feel, and behave. A belief is something we accept fully as true even though it may not be true or proven. A belief functions as a firm persuasion of the truth and we often put our faith in what we believe.

We hold certain beliefs about people, their intentions, and the nature and quality of our interactions with them. These beliefs have some degree of influence on the interactions we engage in with particular people. Children and parents have beliefs about one another's basic personality, motives, etc. Likewise they have beliefs pertaining to themselves, their own personality, intentions, etc. Some of these beliefs are justified, others are not. Some beliefs are based on past concrete experience, while others are one's imaginings or even "projections" of what one actually believes about others.

Consider a parent and child engaged in a discussion of the child's future career options. Having had similar discussions before and reviewing those discussions to some extent on this occasion, the child responds with apparent frustration. "I believe you really don't want me to go into human services. You prefer I get a job in the computer science field. You don't care about what I want! Money is the only thing that is important to you." The parent is dumbfounded and replies, "Of course I care about what you want to do. But I don't want to see you struggle financially as I have had to do, because I chose a poor paying career."

From this brief exchange, we can speculate that there are many issues and concerns driving this interaction in addition to what each believes about the other and one's underlying motives, intentions, etc. If we believe that a person is on our side, we behave very differently than if we believe that a person is against us. If we believe we are well understood, we don't experience the frustration of being misunderstood and the consequences that it has for interpersonal interaction.

Expectations Associated With Interaction

Expectations strongly influence our interactions with people and potentially even shape behavior. Recall the discussion of teacher expectations on student behavior in a previous chapter. There are many concerns or questions pertaining to expectations. Are expectations realistic or unrealistic, reasonable or unreasonable, too high or too low, etc.? Do these expectations take into consideration a person's capabilities, interest, motivation, and other important variables?

Consider the following examples of people's interactions and their expectations:

Example 1: Child to parent:
"You expect me to get all A's."

Example 2: Parent to child:
"I am not your slave. I expect you to help me out by picking up your toys, putting your dirty clothes in the clothes hamper, and washing some dishes occasionally."

Example 3: Parenting partner to partner:
"You expect me to put up with your stuff! You are driving me and the children crazy with your never-ending demands. Don't you have anything better to do but complain?"

Assumptions Made About Interaction

Assumptions may be accurate or inaccurate. They are often a function of the quality of communication. The more effectively people communicate about their relationships and interactions, the more likely assumptions are going to be accurate and mutually agreed upon and shared.

Speculate about the frustration both parent and child feel when plans are in jeopardy because of an erroneous assumption: "I assumed that you did not need me to baby-sit so I made plans to go out tonight. Do you really expect me to cancel them at the last minute?" Consider: Is this an inaccurate assumption or a manipulative ploy to get out of baby-sitting? Is this a well-established pattern or something novel?

As parents and children communicate, parents can minimize the need for assumptions and the problems associated by being specific and concrete with their children. Children are very literal in their interpretations and they often apply their highly egocentric interpretation when comments, instructions, guidelines, etc. are too general.

Consider the following two comments made to a young child. The first is very general. The second is more specific and concrete. "Do you remember what happened yesterday?" vs. "Remember to stay in the yard. If you leave the yard, you will have to come indoors. That was our agreement. Do you remember?" Which one has the greatest potential for an erroneous assumption to be made or for misinterpretation?

217

Values

The values the participants have are power influencers of interaction. Are values in agreement or in conflict? When participants have similar values, interaction is likely to proceed more smoothly. When values are in conflict, interaction is often problematic or potentially troublesome.

Consider the following exchange between parenting partners:

Initiator: "Honey, I think it is important for Billy to decide for himself. Don't coerce him to do what you prefer him to do. He will only resent that and you. Besides, remember how you felt and behaved when your father coerced you into working with him in the family business."

Respondent: "I know. I know. But I want him to be successful and have a good life. I want..."

Initiator: The partner interrupts, "You want him to be happy too? "

Respondent: "Yeah."

Initiator: The partner continues, "Well, were you happy when you were coerced to work in your dad's business?"

Respondent: "No!"

Temperament

Some temperaments mesh well and others clash. Some people are calm, relaxed, irritable, easily distracted, etc. Some people are active, energetic, inactive, lethargic, etc. When both parent and child are more or less evenly matched as to temperament and activity level their interaction is more likely to proceed smoothly. However, when there are large discrepancies, the interaction is more likely to be rough.

A parent who is energetic and likes doing many varied things will enjoy more favorable interactions if the child is similarly interested in a variety of activities. The child will not have to be encouraged to any great degree or prodded to try new things. The parent will experience good feelings about herself, the child and the activities they share. The child will most likely have similar positive feelings.

Both add to their reservoir of positive shared experiences and feelings.

In contrast, if a child seems to be disinterested, the parent may have to expend greater effort in motivating the child and maintaining his interest in the chosen activities. There is a greater likelihood that the parent in this case will experience fewer positive feelings and more negative feelings as both interact. The child may also feel a greater share of negative feelings if his sense is that he is being coerced to do things he does not want to do. Both are adding negative feelings and thoughts to their reservoir of shared experiences.

Participant Age and Developmental Level

Variations in maturity, intelligence, self-sufficiency, etc. are often a function of age and developmental level. Hence, the type of interaction we have with others is influenced in large measure by each participants age and developmental level. Parenting a child of three years is one matter. Parenting the same child of thirteen years is yet another matter.

Parents are occasionally heard advising their children to act their age. What then is age appropriate? What can be reasonably expected from a three-year-old, a thirteen-year-old? A family counselor may have to advise a parent that what the child needs at this time in his development is a parent and not a playmate; therefore, you must ...

Our needs are a function of our developmental level and how growth and development has proceeded. If needs have been met adequately and appropriately, growth is promoted. If needs have not been met adequately and appropriately, growth may be impaired. These principles apply to both parents and children.

The parent who has grown well and has had his or her needs substantially satisfied, will be able to focus on what the child needs for healthy growth and development. The parent who has suffered deprivation in certain areas of development may be handicapped in her parenting efforts to satisfy the child's needs.

The parent who is secure in her various roles as parent, partner, lover, worker, etc.,

218

will be less threatened by the child's increasing autonomy strivings to be independent of her than the parent who is considerably less secure in these areas.

Physiological State or Condition

Health or lack of health of a parent, child or spouse can greatly influence the type and quality of interaction with others. If one is rested, interaction is likely to be different than if one is significantly fatigued.

The following example is from a self-study made by a former student of mine. She is typically a very healthy and energetic person. It poignantly illustrates how physical and psychological health influence parent and child interactions. Her preface explains why she willingly granted permission to me to share it with you.

Case Study Example:
Preface:
I thought that since I had been sick so long that I would write down my honest feelings and thoughts in hopes that it will be of some help to us later when we are dealing with a parent who is ill or in some kind of difficult situation. Of course this is only one way of feeling and not everyone reacts the same way but I hope it will remind me when I am well of the surprising feelings that come through and that it will give me some idea of how other parents may feel whether they are ill or under some kind of stress.

Episodes:
At first everything went along as usual except I couldn't understand why I felt so lazy and I forced myself to do things. I did notice that when the kids argued I couldn't breathe and was too tired to listen to them. I also started to make excuses for not doing things.

When the doctor called me a week later and said I had pneumonia and I should continue to rest, I was agitated that I was going to have to stay in the house more. How was I going to rest with the kids around? Also I was relieved to know why I was so lazy.

The next week went by with odd things happening. I got very tired of listening to my ten-year-old son's conversations. Michael was really beginning to get on my nerves. At this time also, he stopped playing with his friends and would sit in the house. Every word he said, every noise he made irritated me more. I couldn't stand to look at him because he looked dirty and I didn't have the strength to get him clean.

My three-year-old (Maria) would bring me a book to read and push it in my face. Most times I'd say, " Don't you understand Mama is sick? I don't want to read. Please find a toy to play with."

That week Maria penciled the wall behind the chair, colored the floor in the kitchen and tried to get something off a tall bureau by using the drawers as steps and pulled the bureau over on herself.

This was the incident that made me realize I couldn't cope with the kids as well as I usually could. By the time I lifted the bureau and carried Maria in the other room, I had used all my strength and wanted to vomit. I thought her ankle was broken and felt so helpless I called my husband home from work. She hadn't broken anything but I knew I wasn't taking care of the kids very well. My husband was working to 7:30 every night so my mother started coming to help.

I felt sorry for the kids and really wanted someone to give them some attention. The next time the doctor called and said to come in again in another week after I rested more, it depressed me more than I can say.

I had gotten to the point that when Maria insisted that I read to her, I just said "Get that damn book out of my face and get out of here!" I started to really swear more and I didn't feel so sorry for the kids anymore. Maria was whining much more and self-preservation was overtaking me. More and more I felt that nobody cared that I was sick. The kids did their worst.

Right after that Michael pushed a four-year-old friend of Maria and the little girl was crying. I went after him, but I didn't have the strength to hit him as hard as I wanted. This was the final act. I felt "To hell with you all. I don't care what you do." I made arrangements for my relatives to take care of the kids. I just had to get myself better and if no one was going to help me, then I would help myself and tough stuff to my kids and my husband.

I said to Michael, "If you had acted better then you could have stayed but its your own fault. I just can't take care of you so you can stay at thea (aunt) Mary's house for a few days. None of you care if I ever get better." When my husband called, he got the same tune. So he took some days off and took care of the kids. For the first two days, I stayed in bed and pretended I couldn't hear the kids or anything else. I did not lift a finger and did not care how my husband managed to get things done.

The past week I cried more, felt sorry for myself more than I ever did before. I also was very weak and sick and discouraged.

Postscript:
A week has passed since I wrote my feelings down. As I re-read my words I am shocked at the way I

felt and it's hard for me to remember feeling so upset and discouraged. Now that I am starting to feel stronger, it's hard for me to remember what it was like at all to be sick. So now when I see someone ill or under pressure I hope I have this on hand to read and remember what I felt like.

Meaning of Interaction

Interaction has certain existential features. Certain kinds of interaction take on or acquire certain meaning for those involved. A given interactional pattern may or may not have the same meaning to all involved. A parent providing care to the child may represent different meaning to the parent. One parent may perceive this as an important functional role and appreciate the positive influence on both parent and child. It is a meaningful and worthwhile endeavor. In contrast another parent may perceive this largely as custodial. "I am nothing but a servant or handmaiden." Thus it may not be perceived as meaningful and worthwhile.

The child may have a differing perception as well. One child may perceive the caregiving as an indication that he is loved and cared for. It is meaningful and worthwhile from his perspective. Another child may perceive it as an attempt on the parent's part to prevent the child from doing for himself and he may perceive it as an assault on his sense of self-sufficiency and independence. The parent's behavior has very different meaning to this child.

Communication is a factor here. Sometimes people share a similar sense of the intent and meaning of interaction. Sometimes they do not. For example a parent and child may have very different interpretations of their interaction and consequently their interaction takes on a very different meaning for each.

Consider when parent and child are discussing career options for the child:

Child: "What you really mean is that you think I am too young and too inexperienced to make this decision on my own."
Parent: "No, not at all. What I mean is that I would like you to think about some other options before you decide."

Child: "You don't trust my judgement and ability to decide for myself. You just want me to come to you so you can get me to change my mind."

How did such different perceptions come about? How is it that this interaction has such different meaning for each person involved?

External Factors: Familial and Extrafamilial

Not all the factors which influence interpersonal interaction are within and between the people involved in the interaction. Some of these influences are outside or external to the people involved. Other people, separate and apart from the interaction may also have an influence on the interaction two or more people share. Likewise, there are certain situations or circumstances that are not directly a part of the interaction but that influence what happens nonetheless. These crucial people, situations, circumstances may be within the family unit (familial) or outside of the family unit (extrafamilial).

There are six main categories of external factors that will be identified and described herein. Included for discussion herein are the following:

1.) sanctions,
2.) models of interaction,
3.) what the environment teaches,
4.) the communications or messages from others,
5.) the structure of the family unit, and
6.) outside institutions, events, situations and circumstances.

Sanctions

Sanctions exist inside and outside of the family unit. Sanctions are the approvals and disapprovals we receive or that are communicated to us in a variety of ways. These influence our interactions with others and the patterns of interpersonal interactions that evolve.

Consider the adages or "old sayings" we have heard throughout our lives: "Honor thy

220

father and mother." "Children are to be seen and not heard." "Spare the rod and spoil the child."

Consider what is said directly to the child in the following examples.

A parent to the child: "You take such good care of your little sister. You are going to be a very good parent someday."

An outside observer to the same child: "You are so helpful to your parents. I wish I had a child like you."

Sanctions are not always directly and verbally communicated. A smile, a wink, an affirmative nod of the head may serve to positively sanction certain behavior. In contrast, a raised eyebrow, a sneer, a clenched fist followed by a pointing finger in our direction serve as negative sanctions. There are many overt and covert ways to express approval or disapproval in non-verbal ways. Individuals external to the family unit may also send a variety of messages that actually influence interaction within the family unit.

Models of Interaction

Examples of interpersonal interaction modeled by parents, siblings, and other people within the family unit show us how to interact with each other. Relatives, friends, acquaintances, television characters, and other people, real and fictitious, show or teach us how to interact with others also. These models of interaction provide us with a pattern or model to mimic, imitate, emulate, identify with or reject. We respond to these models consciously or unconsciously, intentionally or unintentionally.

Of course these models of interactions are always subject to individual interpretation and creative assimilation and accommodation into the personality structure. For example, a parent who is conciliatory and willing to compromise in order to facilitate family life may have a child who becomes conciliatory and capable of compromise. In contrast, another child may perceive the parent to be "spineless" or a "whimp" and may reject the parent's example. This child may in fact develop a non-conciliatory, non-compromising personality. What has each child learned from the interactions he has observed and been a participant of?

What do these models of interaction show us or teach us? They may teach patience or impatience, tolerance or intolerance, assertion or submission. These models may teach aggression or nonaggression, expression or repression, to fight back or submit. In the case of the two children above, one learns conciliation and compromise. The other learns you get more of what you want by being non-conciliatory and non-compromising, because others are weak and will give in to your demands rather than fight with you. Wow, such a difference!

The Environment Teaches
We Learn

We certainly learn what we live. Significant others, the immediate environment, and the culture at large shall influence what we learn and how we learn it. If we live with tolerance, we will learn tolerance. If we live with love, we will learn to give and receive love. The impact of our role models and the influence of our interactions with these role models is poetically expressed by Dorothy Law Nolte in the following:

CHILDREN LEARN WHAT THEY LIVE

If a child lives with criticism,
He learns to condemn.
If a child lives with hostility,
He learns to fight.
If a child lives with ridicule,
He learns to be shy.
If a child lives with shame,
He learns to feel guilty.
If a child lives with tolerance,
He learns to be patient.
If a child lives with encouragement,
He learns confidence.
If a child lives with praise,
He learns to appreciate.
If a child lives with firmness,
He learns justice.
If a child lives with security,
He learns to have faith.
If a child lives with approval,
He learns to like himself.
If a child lives with acceptance and friendship,
He learns to find love in the world.

221

Messages Given and Received

What others inside and outside of the family unit communicate or fail to communicate about interaction may influence current and subsequent interactions within the home. These communications may be overt or covert. They may be verbal or non-verbal. These messages may be intentional or unintentional. Once again, a raised eyebrow, a gasp, a disapproving look can influence our interactions. A smile, an approving nod, a statement such as "Go for it!" can impart a positive sanction or approval of behavior or intention.

What messages do we give our children? What messages are they receiving from us? What messages do our children give to us? What messages do we receive? The messages that are given may not be the same as those received. What some parents regard as an effort to motivate may be actually discouraging to the child? For example: The parent attempts to encourage the child by saying, "You can do better than that." However, the child interprets this as meaning that what he has done is not good enough. He thinks to himself, "Nothing I do satisfies her. Oh, why bother!" The child gives up; he does not try or persist. So much for motivation!

The Structure of the Family Unit

The structure of the family unit is represented by different features or characteristics. The stage of the family unit or where the family is developmentally shall significantly influence interaction. The family unit's needs and characteristics are also important determiners of family interaction. Family size and composition are important variables as well. Recall an earlier discussion about stages of family development in a previous chapter.

How the family as a developmental entity interacts with each family member and helps meet or fails to meet individual needs is important to interaction within the family unit.

Case study example:

I vividly recall an eighteen-year-old female child who expressed the view that her mother spent almost all her free time with the eight-year-old son. The daughter further expressed that she often felt she was in competition with her brother for her mother's attention, whenever she attempted to engage her mother in conversation in her brother's presence.

Seven years later this pattern is still very apparent; yet slight improvement is acknowledged. Such improvement is most likely the consequence of greater maturity on the part of both children. Notwithstanding these improvements, the basic pattern still persists. The children still seem to be in competition for the mother's attention and the mother continues to admonish the daughter because she is "older and ought to know better."

Single-parenting has advantages and disadvantages for both parent and child. The single parent does not have to consult with the other parent or make adjustments in her position because the other parenting partner has a somewhat different view concerning the matter. However, the single parent does not have the helpful input of another parenting partner, nor the support of one who is in agreement.

For the child, interaction may be easier because there is only one mindset to adjust to. Unfortunately, there is no other parent to make an appeal if the child feels he has been managed unfairly. There is no other parent to advocate for the child if the parent has gone too far or overboard in managing the child. There are certainly many other advantages and disadvantages for both parent and child in a single-parent situation.

Outside Institutions, Events, Situations and Circumstances

Certain institutions, events, situations, or circumstances outside the immediate family unit can and may affect family interaction. Some of these are greatly removed from or very distant from the family unit while others are in close proximity.

Institutions

Certain institutions like school, church, club, and the work place may affect or influence what kind of interactions take place within the home. Both parents and children have had to contend with school homework. Is the teacher being reasonable in her expectations? Is the child task-oriented and self-directed or does the child need a task-master to direct and monitor his school homework? Is the parent willing or not willing to assist? Does the parent perceive this as a normal part of growing and developing as a student or is it perceived as an invasion of the peace and tranquility of the family environment? And who actually assumes responsibility for seeing that the school homework is done correctly and completed on time?

Every parent with a school aged child will have to contend with the matter of school homework. Those that have, know the effect this outside institutional requirement has upon parent and child interaction. Many could write a book on this topic.

Circumstances and Situations

Certain circumstances or situations, which often originate outside of the home can have a significant influence on what goes on within the home. Loss of job, accident, job promotion, job-related relocation, Armed Service duty, reactivation of a Reserve or National Guard unit are such circumstances.

For a period of my career I worked with unemployed parents who were receiving Aid to Families with Dependent Children (AFDC). Unemployment caused the family to apply for public assistance. It was my job to work with the unemployed parent toward re-employment or job training in preparation for another kind of work. What impressed me the most was how much a person's self-concept and self-esteem is tied to being gainfully employed, and how rapidly self-esteem and self-worth is diminished and depression sets in following unemployment.

But even more significant was the rapid disintegration or break down of family interaction. As the time of unemployment increased, so did the incidence of negative family interaction. I saw proud, productive men resort to drinking and consider suicide. I saw supportive and loving wives become critical, nagging mates. I saw children totally confused by these rapid and profound changes in family relationships. All suffered but the young children suffered most because they did not understand and no one was taking the time to explain to them what was happening in their

lives. My eyes water as I relive the suffering they shared with me. And I feel the frustration of my often futile efforts to help.

Much of what is "out there" comes into the home and has its influence subtly or profoundly. Even those things that do not affect us directly, shape nonetheless our attitudes, beliefs and expectations. We sometimes shake our heads. Occasionally we cry out, "Someone ought to do something about that!" We conclude that our culture is going to "hell in a hand basket." We feel the pride in our nation's assistance to another country in the form of disaster assistance. We resent the exportation of foreign aid money, when so many of our own are needy and receive little or no assistance from our government. We joke that the economy has become so bad that organized crime has had to lay off eighteen judges. To think that family life and living is not affected by all that is around us is to be a fool.

Sociological Events or Movements

Large more encompassing events and other sociological movements or phenomena may also exert their influence on our interpersonal interactions. War, the pacifist movement, drugs, the war on drugs are to be counted here. Mass unemployment, the "Job Corps," the War on Poverty are such matters. The "ERA", the Civil Rights Movement, Roe vs. Wade have had profound effects upon family life and living. The music we and our children listen to influences our interpersonal interactions: rock 'n' roll, punk rock, hidden or subliminal messages, etc.

Other phenomena include such religious sects like the Moonies, the Jonesville gang, White Supremacists, and other political and/or religious indoctrinations. There are certain wholesale notions like "You can't trust anyone over thirty" that are among these also. In some degree, we have seen the institutionalization of certain interpersonal interactional problems like the "generation gap," or "Men (or women), you can't live with them, you can't live without them."

In some instances, men are pitted against women; the young against the old, parents vs. children, white against black, the haves vs. the have nots, etc. Certainly there are events and

223

people who bring us together. "Make love not war." America is a wonderful salad bowl. When we add to it, we add variety. Variety is the spice of life. We are joined in a "Rainbow Coalition" and strive to make the ideal real. Each of us, to some degree, for the better or for the worse has been affected. Our lives are different as a consequence. Our families are different because of how each of us has been changed by these events or movements.

References

Houle, G. *You Will Plant Your Vineyards Once More* (West Greenwich, RI: Consortium Publishing, 1986).

QUESTIONNAIRE KEYS

In order to fully appreciate the significance of the choices made on the questionnaires, it is strongly recommended that you read Chapter 9: Child Rearing Approaches - Philosophy and Practices. This chapter in particular and the other chapters concerning child rearing approaches will help you develop a more comprehensive appreciation of the significances of the questionnaire choices. Furthermore, such a review will help you make the necessary descriminations concerning the "c" choices.

Questionnaire 1: Ideologies Concerning Family Structure and Roles

The "a" choices represent a more traditional view of the family in terms of its structure and roles. This is especially European in mindset and origin and represents what many people originally residing in Europe brought with them when they immigrated to the USA.

The "b" choices represent a more democratic or egalitarian view of family structure and roles. It also represents an effort by Americans to put into effect within the family unit the same guiding principles of the American democratic form of government.

Questionnaire 2: Basic Child Rearing Approache In Terms of Parent's Viewpoint

The "a" choices in this questionnaire represent an autocratic or autocratic like approach to parenting. This choice correlates highly with the "a" choice of Questionnaire 1, which represents a traditional mindset.

The "b" choices are indicative of a democratic philosophy concerning parenting. It is very highly correlated with the "b" choices of Questionnaire 1.

The "c" choices are representative of either an indulgent or protective attitude about parenting. In order to make a distinction between them, it will be important for you to familiarize yourself with the content of the chapters addressing child rearing philosophy and practices, especially Chapter 9.

Questionnaire 3: Parental Response to Specific Child Behavior

The "a" choices in this questionnaire are indicative of autocratic or autocratic like practices in response to specific child behavior. The "a" choice correlates highly with the "a" choice of Questionnaires 1 and 2.

The "b" choices represent democratic practices and responses to specific child behavior. This choice is very highly correlated with the "b" choice in Questionnaires 1 and 2.

The "c" choices are representative of either an indulgent or protective attitude about parenting. In order to make a distinction between them, it will be important for you to familiarize yourself with the content of the chapters addressing child rearing philosophy and practices, especially Chapter 9. The "c" choice is very highly correlated with the "c" choice in Questionnaire 2.

Choice Profile

You may wish to develop a profile of the choices you and others made on these questionnaires. There are a variety of ways of doing this. To me the most simple and expedient approach is to develop a percentile profile for each category of choices (a, b, c) for each questionnaire (1, 2, 3). To do this you will need to count the "a", "b", and "c" choices for each questionnaire and then compute what percentage of the total number of choices this represents. In order to make this computation you need to know that there are a total of 10 choices for Questionnaire 1, 15 choices for Questionnaire 2, and 35 choices for Questionnaire 3.

Example: I shall provide an example to illustrate the process for developing a percentile profile for these questionnaires.

Questionnaire 1

Seven "a" choices = 70%
   Computation: 7 divided by 10 = .70, then move the decimal point two places to the right to express as a percentage.
Three "b" choices = 30%
   Computation: 3 divided by 10 = .30, then move the decimal point two places to the right to express as a percentage.

Questionnaire 2

Ten "a" choices = 67%
   Computation: 10 divided by 15 = .67, then move the decimal point two places to the right to express as a percentage.
Three "b" choices = 20%
   Computation: 3 divided by 15 = .20, then move the decimal point two places to the right to express as a percentage.
Two "b" choices = 13%
   Computation: 2 divided by 15 = .13, then move the decimal point two places to the right to express as a percentage.

Questionnaire 3

Twenty-five "a" choices = 71%
   Computation: 25 divided by 35 = .71, then move the decimal point two places to the right to express as a percentage.
Seven "b" choices = 20%
   Computation: 7 divided by 35 = .20, then move the decimal point two places to the right to express as a percentage.
Three "c" choices = 9%
   Computation: 3 divided by 35 = .9, then move the decimal point two places to the right to express as a percentage.

If we place these percent profiles side by side we can more easily compare and contrast the choices made in each category on each questionnaire. This example was chosen to show a fairly strong and reasonable correlation between the choices on the three questionnaires.

Questionnaire 1	Questionnaire 2	Questionnaire 3
a = 70%	a = 67%	a = 71%
b = 30%	b = 20%	b = 13%
	c = 13%	c = 9%

RECOGNIZING ABUSE *

Do you think a child you've met might be abused? Only an expert can verify abuse, but there are many signs a lay person can recognize. Any one of them may not mean a problem, but if there are several and they occur frequently, it's likely that the child needs help.

PHYSICAL ABUSE

Child's Appearance:

- unusual bruises, welts, burns or fractures
- bite marks
- frequent injuries, always explained as "accidental"

Child's Behavior

- reports injury by parent
- frequently late or absent or often comes to school much too early; hangs around after school is dismissed
- avoids physical contact with adults
- wears long sleeves or other concealing clothing to hide injuries
- unpleasant, difficult to get along with; demanding; often doesn't obey; frequently breaks or damages things; is unusually shy, avoids other people including children; seems too anxious to please; seems too ready to let other people say or do things to him/her without protest
- child's story of how an injury occurred is not believable; it doesn't seem to fit the type or seriousness of the injury
- seems frightened of parents
- shows little or no distress at being separated from parents
- apt to seek affection from any adult

NEGLECT

Child's Appearance

- often not clean, tired, no energy
- comes to school without breakfast; often does not have lunch or lunch money
- clothes are dirty or wrong for the weather
- seems to be alone, often for long periods of time
- needs eye glasses, dental care or medical attention

Child's Behavior

- frequently absent
- begs for or steals food
- causes trouble in school, often hasn't done homework; uses alcohol or drugs; engages in vandalism or sexual misconduct

RED FLAGS

Behavioral Indicators of Child Sexual Abuse: [1]

- overly compliant behavior
- acting out, aggressive behavior
- pseudomature behavior
- hints about sexual activity
- persistent and inappropriate sexual play with peers or with self
- sexually aggressive behavior with others
- detailed and age inappropriate understanding of sexual behavior, especially in young children
- arriving early at school and leaving late with few, if any, absences
- poor peer relationships or inability to make friends
- lack of trust, particularly with significant others
- nonparticipation in school and social activities
- inability to concentrate in school
- sudden drop in school performance
- extraordinary fear of males (in case of male perpetrator and female victim)
- seductive behavior with males (in case of male perpetrator and female victim)
- running away from home
- regressive behavior
- clinical depression
- poor self-image
- sleep disturbances
- withdrawal
- suicidal feelings
- secretive

Cues in Father-Daughter Incest: [2]

- blurring of generational lines and role reversals between parent and child
- father acts as suitor to daughter
- mother acts as rival to daughter
- father jealous of daughter being with peers and dating
- father over-possessive of daughter
- father often alone with daughter
- favoritism by father toward daughter over other siblings
- siblings jealous of daughter chosen by father

Physical Cues: [2]

- stress related illnesses
- venereal diseases
- painful discharge of urine
- pregnancy
- stomach aches
- genital infection, lacerations, abrasions, bleeding, discharge

Cues in Younger Children: [2]

- bedwetting
- altered sleep patterns
- overly compulsive behavior
- compulsive masterbation
- separation anxiety
- hyperactivity
- fears or phobias
- learning problems
- excess curiosity about sex

Cues in Brother-Sister Incest: [2]

- brother and sister like boy-friend and girl-friend
- sister being fearful of being alone with brother
- brother and sister embarrassed when found alone together
- sister antagonizing to brother; brother does not retaliate

Dynamics of the Family of Sexually Abused Child: [1]

- poor supervision
- poor choice of surrogate caretakers and baby-sitters
- inappropriate sleeping arrangements
- blurred role boundaries
- sexual abuse by a family member
- failure to protect
- abuse of power
- fear of authority
- isolation
- denial
- secretive
- lack of empathy
- poor communication patterns
- inadequate controls and limit setting
- extreme emotional deprivation and neediness
- magical expectations

REFERENCES

1. Handbook of Clinical Intervention in Child Sexual Abuse by Suzane Sgroi (Massachusetts: D.C. Heath and Company, 1982).

2. The Broken Taboo by Blair Justice and Rita Justice (New York: Human Sciences Press, 1979).

* This information on recognizing abuse was compiled by the Child & Family Agency of Southeastern Connecticut, Incorporated, 255 Hempstead Street, New London, Connecticut 06320, Telephone: 203-443-2896

INCEST AFTEREFFECTS CHECKLIST
FOR ADULT CHILDREN OF ALCOHOLICS

Do you find yourself on this list?
Could incest have happened to you?

Incest is such a traumatic violation of trust that people often forget that it ever occurred. But the emotional scars live on, confused in their seeming meaninglessness. The ongoing problem with trust, touch, compulsive behaviors, paralyzing depression, guilt, sex and relationships can, when the cause is unknown, feel crazy and out of control. This checklist can be used as a guide to help survivors identify themselves and know that there are real reasons for these underlying difficulties.

If you find yourself on this list, you could be a survivor of incest. "Incest" does not require overt sexual interaction. It can mean simply being touched in a way you did not want to be. It could even occur through an emotionally suffocating, confusing relationship where obvious sexual touch did not take place. Incest is the use of a minor child to meet sexual or emotional/sexual needs of an adult in a position of trust or authority with that child (adults such as parent, mother's boy-friend, baby-sitter, teacher). It is the abuse of the power relationship, not the blood relationship, that determines the damaging effects of the experience.

Incest is especially common in alcoholic families. This is due to the alcoholic's damaged judgement, distorted sexuality, and weakened moral system. Often the alcoholic doesn't remember the experience; or applying the same defenses as he does to his drinking and other alcoholic behaviors, he denies, minimizes, projects blame. Furthermore, not all alcohol-related incest is attributed to the disease of alcoholism. As you will see from this list, adult children of alcoholics and incest survivors share many common experiences and characteristics.

Could this have happened to you? If so, there is help available through self-help groups and therapists who understand both incest and alcoholism and who will help you understand that <u>you are not to blame.</u>

THE LIST

01. Fear of being alone in the dark, of sleeping alone
02. Nightmares, nightterrors (especially pursuit, threat)
03. Alienation from body, not at home in own body
04. Splitting
05. Failure to heed signals of body or take care of it
06. Eating disorders, alcoholism, drug/alcohol abuse, or total abstinence
07. Phobias (including car phobias, agoraphobia)
08. Need to be invisible, perfect, or perfectly bad
09. Skin carving, self-mutilation (physical pain is manageable)
10. Self destructiveness, self-abuse
11. Depression (sometimes paralyzing); seemingless baseless crying
12. Guilt/shame, feeling marked, low self-esteem, feeling worthless, high appreciation
13. Going into shock (shutdown) in stress or crisis (stress often = crisis)
14. Feeling crazy, feeling different
15. Hysterical symptoms
16. Compulsive behavior
17. Blocking out some periods of early years (especially 1 - 12 years)
18. Childhood hiding, hanging on, cowering in corners (security seeking); adult nervousness over being watched
19. High risk taking (daring behaviors) or no risk taking
20. Trust issues (can't trust, total trust, trusting non-discriminantly)

21. Pattern of being a victim (victimizing self after being victimized, especially sexually; no sense of own power or right to set limits, or to say no)
22. Rigid control of thought process
23. Fear of losing control
24. Anger issues (fear of actual or imagined rage; constant anger; inability to own anger or express it)
25. Intense hostility for gender of race of perpetrator
26. Power, control, territoriality issues (the victim lost control)
27. Feeling demand to "produce and be loved" (love was not giving); relationships mean big trade-offs; abandonment issues
28. Sexual issues: sex feels dirty; aversion to be touched (especially by surprise, also during GYN examination); trouble integrating sexual and emotional, confusing and overlapping of affection, sex, dominance, violence, aggression; sexual fantasies include dominance and rape (results in guilt); feeling betrayed by body; must be aggressor or cannot be; strong aversion to a particular sexual act; impersonal, promiscuous sex with strangers concurrent with inability to have sex in relationships; sexual acting out with strangers to meet power or revenge needs; shutdown; crying after orgasm; all pursuit feels like violation; fear/avoidance of sex; sexualizing of all meaningful relationships (also avoidance); conflict between sex and caring; homosexuality is not an aftereffect
29. Choosing ambivalent relationships (in true intimacy, issues are more likely to surface; in problem relationships, blame can be placed elsewhere. Note issue with lover ("pro-survivor").
30. Poor body image
31. GYN problems
32. Denial, no awareness at all, pretending or minimizing; having dreams or memories and claiming "maybe it's my imagination" (These are actually flashbacks, which is how remembering begins.); strong, deep negative reactions to a person, place or event which seems inappropriate thus feeling the self to be unreal and everything else real or vice versa; image flashbacks (a light, a physical feeling, a place) without any sense of their meaning
33. The "secret", "telling the story"
34. Swallowing and gaging sensitivity
35. Wearing a lot of clothing, even in summer; baggy clothing

This list was compiled by E. Due Blume, C.S.W., a Long Island psychotherapist, with the help of survivors who shared their experiences.

Index

234

Nolte, Dorothy Law 221
non-custodial parent 117
non-intervention 57
nuclear family 99

obsessions 214
obsessive 85
Oedipus Complex 215
optimism 186
optimistic 186

parental effectiveness 33, 106
parental responsiveness 50
parental role 43
parenthood 190, 192, 193, 195
parenting partners 210
passive acceptance 178
passive control 178
passive manipulation 178
pattern 203
peace-makers 208
perception 20, 21, 104, 140, 216, 220
perceptions 72
permanence 4
personality 48, 72
personhood 48, 71
physical handicaps 74
physiological state 140
Piaget's stages 36, 79
poverty 110
power 169
power structure 103
prerequisite 34, 39
pride 183
primary psychological parent 23
privileges 184
proactive 69, 109
problem-solvers 208
protective 146, 150, 151, 152, 155, 156, 157, 170, 173
pseudo-love 47
pseudo-loving mechanisms 47
psychological condition 140
psychological connectedness 21, 24
psychological parent 22
psychological parent and child relationship 15, 19, 20
psychological refueling 215
punishment 58, 114, 154, 168

quality 21
quality defined 20
quality of interaction 20

reactive 69, 109
readiness 39, 50, 154
recipient parent 10
recipient parenting 49
recipient parents 11
reciprocity 26
reinforcements 58
repetition compulsion 215
research concerning child rearing 196
resister 206

responsibility 30, 185
responsiveness 26
rewards 58
right to know 10
right to privacy 9
rights 80, 184
risk-taking 173
ritualistic behavior 85
rituals 85
Rogers,Carl 21
role models 47, 58, 169, 221
roles 146, 147, 151, 205, 212

sanctions 220
scapegoat 207
Schickendanz, Schickendanz and Forsyth 23
secondary psychological parent 23
self-absorption 182
self-actualization 77
self-centered 176, 182
self-concept 123, 174, 180
self-concept development, 165
self-confidence 165, 179, 185, 186
self-esteem 123, 165, 174, 180
self-spoiling 84
self-sufficiency 180, 185
self-worth 123, 165, 174, 180, 181
sense of entitlement 177, 181
sensory impairments 74
separation 116, 118, 119
sexual abuse 208
sexual lifestyle 105
sexual preference 105
shame 104, 166
sharing 178, 194
shyness 178
siblings 192, 195, 211
significant others 221
single-parent families 102
single-parenting 222
situational modification 59
situations 223
skill 48
skill development, 174, 180
skills training function 44
social interaction skills 186
sociological movements 223
special need 140
Spock, Benjamin 14
spoiled brat 177
spoiling 83
stage descriptions 79
stagnation 182
step-families 7
step-parent 7, 14
step-parent and child relationship 7, 13, 14
step-parent families 92, 104
stereotype 147
submissiveness 178
substance abuse 112
substitution 83, 84
Surgeon General 112

235